FDC
1-
6/19

The Weaker Vessel
Woman's Lot in Seventeenth-century England

~

ANTONIA FRASER

Volume Two

PHOENIX

This edition produced for The Book People Ltd,
Hall Wood Avenue, Haydock, St Helens WA11 9UL

First published in Great Britain in 1984
by William Heinemann
First published in paperback in 1993
by Mandarin Paperbacks

Paperback edition published in 2002
by Phoenix,
an imprint of Orion Books Ltd,
Orion House, 5 Upper St Martin's Lane,
London WC2H 9EA

Copyright © Antonia Fraser 1984

The right of Antonia Fraser to be identified as the author of this work has been
asserted by her in accordance with the Copyright, Designs and Patents Act 1988.

All rights reserved. No part of this publication may be reproduced, stored in a
retrieval system, or transmitted, in any form or by any means, electronic, mechanical,
photocopying, recording or otherwise, without the prior permission of the copyright
owner.

A CIP catalogue record for this book is available from the British Library.

ISBN 978 1 4072 1612 6

Printed and bound in Great Britain by
Clays Ltd, St Ives plc

The Orion Publishing Group's policy is to use papers that are natural, renewable
and recyclable products and made from wood grown in sustainable forests. The
logging and manufacturing processed are expected to conform to the environmental
regulations of the country of origin.

www.orionbooks.co.uk

Contents

PART THREE

Afterwards – A Continual Labour

∽⦥∾

'Believe me, child, life is a continual labour, checkered with
care and pleasure, therefore rejoice in your position, take
the world as you find it, and you will I trust find heaviness
may endure for a night, but joy comes in the morning.'

ADVICE OF RACHEL LADY RUSSELL TO HER DAUGHTER, 1695

CHAPTER FOURTEEN
Worldly Goods

~

'He is not a pleasant man – very few are; neither is [he]
the very next sort for entertainment. One thing pleased:
when he said "With all my worldly goods I thee
endow", he put a purse upon the book with two
hundred guineas.'

DOROTHY DOWAGER COUNTESS OF SUNDERLAND
ON HER NIECE'S BRIDEGROOM, 1680

O n the eve of the Restoration, Pen, Sir Ralph Verney's
second sister, wrote: 'I pray God send we may live to
see peace in our times and that friends may live to enjoy
each other.' Pen had been one of that melancholy galaxy of
unmarried Verney girls who remained at Claydon while Ralph
went into exile, their portions caught up in the legal tangles
caused by their father's death in the King's cause. For such dowerless young ladies, there were no brilliant matches available: it
was more a case of 'thank heaven, fasting, for a good man's love'[1]
– or any man's hand in marriage.

Sue Verney, for example, made do with a debt-ridden and
drunken widower, spending her early married life at his side in
the Fleet prison. Despite this, Sue loved her designated spouse
most sincerely during their few years together, before she died in
childbirth. Peg Verney was married off to Thomas Elmes –
described as 'a very humoursome cross boy' who was soon to
make her cry 'night and day'. Peg's own temper was not of the
sweetest, and ultimately this cross-grained couple separated. Pen
Verney, she who had quarrelled with Peg when asked to share a
personal maid as an economy, drew her cousin John Denton; the
best that could be said of him was that he *had* stopped drinking

... But Pen was in no position to be critical. 'Sir, she was sensible her portion lay in a desperate condition,' wrote her brother Henry to Sir Ralph, 'besides, she grew in years and was not to all men's likings'.[2]

That left Moll and Betty. Moll was said to be 'the plainest of them all', but blessed – or cursed – with 'a great deal of wit'; in addition she was 'wild as a buck' and thus 'too indiscreet to get a discreet man'. Moll, refusing the offer of an elderly bridegroom, ultimately made a disastrous match with one Robert Lloyd. (She was probably pregnant beforehand, for there was talk of shipping her to Ireland or even Barbados to avoid disgrace.) As for Betty, she was variously described as 'of a cross proud lazy disposition' and 'so strangely in love with her own will' that she loathed all efforts made on her behalf.[3] She was undeniably too cross and wilful for anyone who knew her to be willing to take her.

In 1662 cross-patch Betty bestowed herself privately upon a poverty-stricken curate named Charles Adams out of sheer despair. She had met him when he was preaching at church; none of her relations were asked to the marriage. Betty angrily rebutted charges that she had thrown herself away: 'I am not so much lost, as some think I am, because I have married one as has the reputation of an honest man, and one as in time I may live comfortably with.' All the same it was Betty's family which was faced with the problem of the Adamses' livelihood; meanwhile Betty managed to blame them not only for her present poverty but for almost everything that had happened to her since childhood. Her sister Peg Elmes wrote: 'Sometimes I am weary of hearing it, how she was cast off and forsaken and left to herself ... sent to a person's house to a school, like a baby.' Dr Denton referred to Charles Adams and Betty as 'Adam and Eve' in search of a living; it was not intended as a compliment. Only Betty's most charitable sister Cary Gardiner reflected that there were other examples of ladies marrying clergymen ... Lady Mary Bertie for example.[4]

The mingled sulks and despair of Betty Verney on the subject of marriage highlighted one problem of post-Restoration society: it was even more difficult for an ill-endowed girl to find a husband than it had been before the Civil War. And in cases where the possibility of a good dowry did exist, more not less money was required from the father in return for an adequate widow's jointure. It has been pointed out that the average ratio of dowry (given by the father) to jointure (settled on the girl by the bridegroom's family) rose from 4 or 5 to 1 in the middle of the sixteenth century to between 8 and 10 to 1 by the end of the seventeenth.[5]

The troubles of a gently-raised female at this period might be twofold. On the one hand her own portion was liable to have suffered from the effects of sequestration, confiscation and so forth like that of the Verney girls. Many different kinds of ruin had been brought upon families during the recent conflicts which made it difficult to provide a dowry for an unmarried daughter. At the same time these same families, or their equivalents, might well hope to remedy their fortunes by the time-honoured manoeuvre of capturing an heiress. But in this respect the daughters of the aristocracy and gentry were now meeting with what might be described as unfair competition from those richly-cargoed vessels, daughters of the City merchants.

Such brides could bring their husbands large and welcome amounts of cash. Few gentlemen's daughters could compete with this. 'Ours are commodities lying on our hands,' wrote Sir William Morrice of his daughters shortly after the Restoration, while 'merchants' daughters that weigh so many thousands' were sought out in marriage in their place. Sir William Temple blamed the first noble families 'that married into the City for downright money' for introducing 'this public grievance' by which the level of portions was raised all round, and landowners with many daughters were ruined. By the end of the century the agreeable whiff of good City money was to be detected in the grandest homes: the Widow Wheeler, she of the goldsmith's shop at the sign of the Marygold who married her husband's apprentice Robert Blanchard, would number the Earls of Jersey and Westmoreland among her descendants; in 1682 the prudent marriage of the Marquess of Worcester with a Miss Rebecca Child, aged sixteen, daughter of the East India merchant Sir Josiah Child, secured at least £25,000 for the future ducal house of Beaufort.[6]

But if the young gentlemen were prepared to sacrifice birth for the sake of wealth – and the evidence shows that such marriages across classes were on the increase – their impoverished sisters were by tradition inhibited from making the same social leap. Although Lady Sandwich, wife of Pepys's patron, declared herself happy to settle for 'a good Merchant' for her daughter Jemima in October 1660, Lord Sandwich retorted that he would rather see her 'with a pedlar's pack on her back' so long as she married a gentleman rather than 'a citizen'. So the numbers of such girls' potential bridegrooms diminished, and the number of unmarried females of this class rose with the century.[7]

There was a further dismal element in the growing excess of women over men in the population as a whole. At the end of the seventeenth century Gregory King stated that women outnumbered men by a ratio of 28 to 27 (on his figures there were 100,000 more females than males in England and Wales as a whole). In 1662 John Graunt, in 'Natural and Political Observations ... made upon the bills of mortality', had noted that more males were born than females every year, and as a result 'every woman may have an Husband, without the allowance of Polygamy', notwithstanding the fact that men lived more dangerously than women, travelled more and adopted professions which demanded celibacy (such as Fellows of university colleges).[8]

Graunt was too optimistic. As Gregory King expressed it, the excess of males born annually – 7,000 – was 'not much more than equal to the males carried off extraordinary by wars, the sea and the Plantations in which articles the females are very little concerned'; while females in general enjoyed a greater life expectancy. A pamphlet of 1690, *Marriage Promoted in a Discourse of its Ancient and Modern Practice*, thought the neglect of marriage threatened the destruction of 'these Nations'. Nearly half the people of England were dying single and a third of the others marrying far too late: men should be *obliged* to marry at twenty-one.[9]

All this put a further premium on an heiress. Marriages were no more constructed on a basis of pure affection after the

Restoration than they had been before the Civil War. During that wild period of the Commonwealth the Digger Gerrard Winstanley had actually declared that every man and woman should be free to marry whom they loved, with 'the Common Storehouses' as their portion:[10] such sentiments expressed exactly that kind of frightening radicalism which the post-Restoration world was anxious to eliminate from its memory. Nobody now believed – if anybody ever had – in 'the Common Storehouses' or in free liberty to marry for love.

In 1664 King Charles II wrote one of his racy, chatty letters about the scene at the English court to his sister in France: 'I find the passion Love is very much out of fashion in this country, and that a handsome face without money has but few gallants, upon the score of marriage.' At about the same date the Comte de Gramont, according to Anthony Hamilton, author of his *Memoirs*, was given a lecture on his arrival in England. 'Young women here expect serious intentions and a husband with landed property,' the exiled French writer Saint-Evremond told him sternly. 'You have neither.' He also warned Gramont that it would be a 'miracle' if any gallant proposition he made (other than that of matrimony itself) was considered.[11]

In the 1630s a cruel rhyme had celebrated the marriage of the rich but plain daughter of a Lord Chief Justice to John Lisle:

> Neither well-proportioned, fair nor wise
> All these defects four thousand pounds supplies.

Half a century later, Anne Killigrew, that sensitive observer of a materialist court, bewailed exactly the same situation in her *Invective against Gold*:

> Again, I see the Heavenly Fair despis'd,
> A Hag like Hell, with Gold, more highly priz'd …[12]

The difference was the rise of a weariness, a cynicism on the subject; that too perhaps a legacy of the Civil War and Commonwealth period when some kind of liberty had been enjoyed simply through lack of parental supervision. As a result, the state of marriage was mocked as though by universal agreement, especially in literature. (The English young ladies, married off according to wordly principles, also proved very much more susceptible to illicit offers of 'gallantry' than Saint-Evremond had predicted to the Comte de Gramont, the Comte himself experiencing quite a few of these delightful 'miracles'.)

'I rather fear you wou'd debauch me into that dull slave call'd a Wife,' observed Cornelia to Galliard in Aphra Behn's *The Feign'd Curtezans.* Another of Aphra Behn's spirited heroines, Hellena in *The Rover,* was equally forthright on the tedium of matrimony: 'What shall I get? A Cradle full of Noise and Mischief, with a Pack of Repentance at my Back.' Nor was a more romantic attitude to be expected from the other party to the contract. Willmore, Hellena's lover, responded for his own sex that marriage was as certain 'a Bane to Love' as lending money was to friendship. Keepwell, in Sir Charles Sedley's *Bellamira,* about to be married to the eponymous heroine, resolved to avoid 'the odious names of Man and Wife, In chains of Love alone we will be tied.'[13]

Yet few women looked to another fate. When Mrs Hobart, the oldest of the Maids of Honour to the Duchess of York, told a younger colleague, Anne Temple, that 'compared to the inconveniences of marriage, its pleasures are so trifling that I don't know how anybody can make up their minds to it', she was aware that her views were not commonly held. It might be 'the stupidest condition for a sensible woman which you can possibly conceive of', but Mrs Hobart was the first to admit that all the Maids of Honour were in fact desperately keen to get married. Besides, Mrs Hobart was in the words of Anthony Hamilton 'susceptible only to the charms of her own sex'. It was all very well for such a plain and sharp-tongued woman to die unmarried in 1696 at the age of sixty-three (the title of 'Mrs' being honorific); Anne Temple on the other hand fulfilled a more normal feminine ambition for all Mrs Hobart's warnings, by marrying the middle-aged widower Sir Charles Lyttelton in 1666 and giving birth to thirteen children thereafter.[14]

It was, however, no coincidence that the two Verney girls who ended their lives most happily did so as wealthy widows – as we have seen, an enviable position throughout the century. Cary lived at court cheerful and well provided-for, following her happy second marriage to John Stewkeley of Hampshire. Thus were memories of her early humiliation at the hands of her first husband's family expunged by a life of good-natured and worldly ease in middle age. What troubles she had were caused by her passion for gambling, something which possessed many court ladies at the time.[15]

As for Pen, married life with John Denton scarcely seemed to justify the argument that any husband was better than none when one was growing older and 'not to all men's likings'. He too, like Sue's husband, was debt-ridden and imprisoned for it. He also had a vicious streak: Dr Denton referred to him as Pen's 'brute of a husband' who was apt to 'lay her at his feet' with his blows. After John Denton's death, however, Pen made a far more satisfactory match to the elderly Sir John Osborn, finding to her surprise that by her settlement she was now worth £6,000. 'I fear her good fortune will make all old women marry!' exclaimed Cary. When Sir John died in his turn, Pen was able to enjoy twenty good years at Whitehall, housekeeping for her brother and gossiping and playing cards with a series of aristocratic female cronies. She also used her position to boss about her Stewkeley nieces, Cary's daughters, in a way which added to her general enjoyment, if not to theirs.

In old age Pen boasted that she had lived her 'Laborious life' entirely to 'make a fine show to the world,' never wasting one shilling to give herself pleasure. She died in 1695 at the age of seventy-three. Her will certainly made a fine show, for she left a series of bequests to those grand ladies whose company she had so much appreciated, so that it reads like some roll-call of the peerage: 'The Countess of Lindsay to have a silver scallop cup and grater, the Countess of Plymouth a serpentine cup with a silver cover, the Countess of Carnarvon a Silver Toaster to toast bread on' and so forth, and so on.[16]

In one sense the climate of the times had changed after the Restoration: parents in general no longer believed in exercising absolute authority over their children in the making of a match, however unwelcome. The ideal union was now one arranged by the parents to which the young couple concerned were consenting. Such an attitude was however very far from representing a new endorsement of that tender passion of love, generally condemned before the Civil War. It was quite simply practical: most sensible people had come to the conclusion that marriages forged on the anvil of agreement caused far less trouble to society in the long run; as Margaret Duchess of Newcastle put it, no one should marry 'against their own liking' because it led directly to adultery.[17]

The pre-war Puritan handbooks of domestic conduct had first pointed out this fact (so obvious to us now, so revolutionary then). As the years passed, the aristocratic fathers too softened: in 1650 Algernon, tenth Earl of Northumberland wrote of the projected marriage of his daughter to the son of Lord Grey of Wark that he would never use 'the authority of a father' to press his children 'to anything of this kind'; however 'if she likes the man', the parents on both sides were in agreement.[18] (Lord Northumberland's enlightened attitude proved a boon to his daughter, for this was the melancholy youth whose mind was distracted, as witness the fact that he had fallen in love with his mother's chambermaid.) Twenty years earlier his father, the ninth Earl, had flashed fiery words when Algernon, then Lord Percy, had defied him to marry Lady Anne Cecil (see p.32).

In 1673 the most influential book on domestic conduct published after the Restoration – *The Ladies Calling*, the work of a divine named Richard Allestree – summed up the prevailing view as follows: 'As a daughter is neither to anticipate, nor to contradict the will of her Parent, so (to hang the balance even) I must say she is not obliged to force her own, by marrying where she cannot love; for a negative voice in the case is sure as much the Child's right, as the Parents'. 'Allestree even went so far as to say that it would be sacrilege for a maiden to make a vow of marriage where she hated. This was the principle to which Mary Countess of Warwick adhered, when arranging a match for her husband's orphaned niece Lady Essex Rich: having rejected certain suitors in advance for not being sufficiently 'viceless', Lady Warwick then allowed Lady Essex 'her free choice or not, to do as she liked or disliked' out of those she had already vetted. (The consequent match with Daniel Finch was, as we have seen on p.64 extremely happy, but was cut short by Lady Essex's premature death.)[19]

In the 1670s it was the dearest wish of the childless Sir John Brownlow of Belton that his nephew and heir should marry his wife's niece Alice Sherard, a girl who was trained by her in household matters and whom she had virtually adopted.[20] Nevertheless in the codicil to his will Sir John was careful to make it clear that this pet plan should only be carried out if the young couple 'shall affect one the other' – there was to be no duress. In the event, eight months after this will was written, the couple *did* marry. Although Alice was only sixteen and her bridegroom was dispatched probably on the same day, to his studies at Cambridge, the foundations had been laid for a stable dynastic union, to the satisfaction of all parties, old and young.

What would have happened to Alice Sherard if she had declined the honour of being chatelaine of Belton, for which she had been carefully groomed by her aunt? Nothing drastic certainly; but Sir John Brownlow's codicil also stated: 'if the said Alice Sherard shall dislike the said Match and by any refusal on her part the said Match shall not take place then this legacy to be void' – the legacy in question being 1,000 pieces of gold in a special box marked with the initials A.S.

That was the point. In the language of Hannah Woolley in *The Gentlewomans Companion*, published the same year as Sir John Brownlow's will was made, nothing, not 'affluence of estate, potency of friends, nor highness of descent' could make up for 'the insufferable grief of a loathéd bed'.[21] That might be so; but money, connections and birth were still the values which prevailed in the marriage market. While many parents had come to agree with Hannah Woolley both in principle and in practice about the need for consent, nobody seriously thought of substituting different values where the initial selection of partners was concerned.

Over children too, the theoretical authority of the parent remained intact in the second half of the century even if custom asked that it should be exercised more kindly. There was a pretty to-do in May 1667 when the eligible young Viscount Maidstone, heir to the third Earl of Winchilsea, was secretly married off at the age of fourteen to one Elizabeth Windham, without his father's knowledge, let alone his permission.[22] The whole affair sounded extremely dubious – at least to the ears of the outraged Earl of Winchilsea, then absent on a diplomatic mission in Belgrade. The boy had lived in the same house as his bride for some time while at Cambridge, and was encouraged by her relations to make advances to her. Still, the young Lord kept his head sufficiently not to consummate the marriage after the ceremony (or else was too frightened of his father to confess it). Writing back to King Charles II in a state of righteous indignation on the subject, Lord Winchilsea passed on his boy's account of the fateful afternoon: how he had been made drunk 'by their putting of wine into his beer' at the time of the marriage, but that as soon as the bride's mother left the chamber 'he ran out of the room'. Lord Winchilsea concluded triumphantly 'Nor doth he know whether she [the bride] be a man or a woman.'

To the Earl of Clarendon, Lord Winchilsea summed the matter up: this 'foulest piece of fraud and abuse' would shock all parents who claimed a title in 'the happy disposal of their children'. Still, a year later Lord Winchilsea had not succeeded in getting the marriage annulled. At some point the marriage was evidently consummated: Lord Maidstone died young, but left a posthumous son Charles behind him, the child of his Cambridge bride, who in time inherited his grandfather's title to become the fourth Earl of Winchilsea. When the time came for this boy to be married in the 1690s his widowed mother, Elizabeth Viscountess Maidstone, wrote a careful letter to his guardian Lord Nottingham about the possible choices: 'He has seen both these ladies and thinks them very beautiful, but if we were permitted to make choice, your Lordship knows our first desire...' Lord Nottingham's eventual choice of Sarah Nourse, an heiress worth £30,000 in money and land, as the bride was acceptable to Lady Maidstone not only for financial reasons but also because 'My son has seen the lady and likes her very well.' Unlike the earlier Maidstone match, therefore, which had flouted the conventions, this projected union had everything to be said for it by the standards of the time.

In 1701 *The Athenian Oracle*, one of the early magazines for answering young ladies' queries, came down firmly on the side of parental authority. The questioner had vowed to leave her father and mother as soon as possible because they treated her so unkindly, and an opportunity presenting itself, wondered which obligation came first, her vow or her duty to her parents. The answer came back: 'Your Vow does not oblige you, for your Body is the Goods of your Father, and you can't lawfully dispose of your self without his knowledge and consent, so that you ought to beg God Almighty's Pardon for your Rashness' (in making the vow in the first place).[23]

Similarly the wife's legal position remained humble, as it had been at the beginning of the century. In the categorical words of John Evelyn to Margaret Godolphin on the subject: 'marriage entitles [the husband] to your person, and to all you bring with it of worldly goods, and he can do with it what he pleases without your consent'.[24] (The exception to this, already noted, was the development of the concept of the trust in Chancery, which if held for an heiress could not be swallowed up in the husband's property – see p.14; but this of course only applied to a tiny percentage of women.)

The wedding of Lucy Pelham and Gervase Pierrepont at East Hoathly in Sussex in March 1680 celebrated a match made very much in this world; as a result it was not a very cheerful affair. The choice of Halland, the ancient seat of the Pelhams, was dictated by a mixture of economy and family pride. The bride's mother would have preferred the fun of a jaunt to London, but Sir John Pelham 'thought it would be more expense, and not handsome because of his great relations'.[25]

Gervase Pierrepont himself represented no maiden's dream. The bride's aunt was the former Dorothy Sidney, now styled Dowager Countess of Sunderland (her second marriage to Sir Robert Smythe was conveniently swallowed up in the senior title). Lady Sunderland wrote tartly: 'He is not a pleasant man – very few are; neither is [he] the very next sort for entertainment.' The high point of the ceremony was that moment when the groom, by tradition, placed a purse upon the prayer book to accompany his vow: 'With all my worldly goods I thee endow.' A few years earlier at court the young William of Orange had deposited his own little heap of symbolic gold when wedding his cousin Princess Mary of York. King Charles II, the bride's uncle, had been in a merry mood and had commanded the fifteen-year-old Mary: 'Take it up, take it up. It's all clear gain to you.' In this case the congregation at East Hoathly was enchanted to see that Mr Pierrepont put down a purse containing 200 guineas! As Lady Sunderland commented: 'Everybody puts somewhat, but this is the most I have heard.'[26]

Whether this large sum was all clear gain to the new Mrs Pierrepont depends on one's attitude to that other sort of price she had to pay for it. At the time, commented Dorothy, she seemed pleased enough by events: 'but she loves more compliments and mirth than she will ever find. I prepared her, as well as I could, not to expect it . . .'[27]

Lucy Pelham, one of the two daughters of Lady Lucy Sidney by her marriage to Sir John Pelham, a Member of many successive Parliaments, was born beneath that glittering net of aristocratic family relationships which spangled English society after the Restoration and onwards. When the time came for Lucy herself to be woven into this net by means of marriage the negotiations were entrusted to her mother's sister Dorothy – since both Pelhams were kept in the country, the one by inclination and gout, and the other by illness alone.

Dorothy Sunderland's life had changed. Gone was the delicious magic of her youth which had led the poet Waller to make her his Sacharissa. Robert Earl of Sunderland, the ambitious rising politician, and his clever wife Anne, reigned at Althorp.

Dorothy Sunderland was now in her sixties, living as she put it 'in twilight' in a little house in Whitehall. Gone too were the days when her own daughter Dorothy Spencer had reigned at Rufford in Lancashire as wife of Lord Halifax. Dorothy Spencer had died in 1670 and two years later Lord Halifax took Gertrude Pierrepont as his second wife. (Betty, for whom he wrote the famous *Advice to a Daughter*, was the fruit of this second union.) There is a story that Dorothy in these latter days asked Waller when he would write some more poetry for her. The poet is said to have replied: 'When you are as young again, Madam, and as handsome as you were then.' If true, the sourness was all on Waller's side – his poetry had gone sadly out of fashion. Dorothy, who described herself lightly as 'the poor old dolt in the corner' can hardly have been much put out by the rebuff; her correspondence shows that her humour and common sense remained pristine, with her Halifax grandchildren, Nan Savile in particular, close to her, and her friendship with their father uninterrupted despite his second marriage.[28] Indeed, far from living 'in twilight' Dorothy the Dowager Countess acted as the secret matriarch of this golden world, reconciling in herself the political differences which existed between its various members.

Romantic figure as she may have been in the past, Dorothy in old age displayed a brisk attitude to the whole subject of marriage. The selected bridegroom was a grandson of the Earl of Kingston and a first cousin of Halifax's second wife. Even more to the point was the fact that Gervase Pierrepont was rich. Apart from that, frankly there does not seem to have been much to say for him; and it is significant that Dorothy did not try to say it.

She wrote approvingly of Pierrepont's 'good fortune' – £200 a year and £5,000 more in 'money' – besides which there was an aunt of seventy in the offing, from whom more was expected, one who was conveniently suffering from a quartan ague. As to the rest: 'One finds that he does not talk ... another finds fault with his person who have little reason, God knows, to meddle with that.' In Dorothy's own opinion 'the worst of him is his complexion, and the small-pox is not out of his face yet; he had them but eight months ago.' His person was certainly not 'taking'. On another occasion she wrote even more straight-forwardly that it was 'ugly'. Nor was this wealthy pock-marked Beast endowed with the kind of sparkling wit which would make up to Beauty for his appearance. He was 'well enough dressed and behaved', said Dorothy, but 'of few words', otherwise 'very bashful', certainly too bashful to speak to strangers. Nevertheless Dorothy was optimistic about the success of the match. After all Mr Pierrepont was no more ill-favoured than Edward Montagu, Lucy Pelham's sister's bridegroom; 'and his wife kisses him all day, and calls him her pretty dear'.[29]

What was Lucy Pelham's reaction to all this? Dorothy, who had a special fondness for her Pelham nieces, made it clear that she had no wish to ruin Lucy's life for the sake of a good fortune: 'I desired her to tell me if she had any distaste to him, and I would order it so it should not go on, and her father should not be angry with her. But,' Dorothy added, 'she is wiser than to refuse it.'

Nor did Lucy refuse the match negotiated by her clever aunt – which included a splendid jointure for the widow after her husband's death: 'I demanded a thousand a year and his London house and I have got it', wrote Dorothy triumphantly. The girl's father would never have thought of asking for the house as well: 'but a very pretty house so furnished as that will be very consider-able to a woman'. Then there were six coach-horses to be bought, with Lady Halifax, Mr Pierrepont's cousin, to choose the coach. Lucy was to have her own page as well. In return the bride's father engaged to give a dowry in a ratio of 7 to 1 to the jointure: £7,000 pounds, £1,000 of which was payable on his death. Even Lucy's brother Tom, who disapproved of some of the financial clauses, admitted that his sister needed 'no persua-sion' to marry Mr Pierrepont; although it should perhaps be mentioned, as an example of Dorothy Sunderland's famous wisdom, that she did not allow the pock-marked Mr Pierrepont to call on his future bride until her father had come to town to complete the arrangements.[30]

The only hitch which occurred concerned high politics, not the humble affections. It was unfortunate that the marriage negotiations, in early 1680, were taking place at a time of mounting tension over the possible 'Exclusion' of the Catholic Duke of York from the royal succession. In a complicated situation, Robert Earl of Sunderland and Lord Halifax represented roughly speaking, rival political views. Sunderland naturally raised his eyebrows at the thought of his kinswoman marrying into the Halifax set. From the other point of view, Lucy's brother Tom Pelham, who had ranged himself far more violently against the King than the moderate Halifax, found the marriage equally unwelcome.

However, Dorothy Sunderland's granddaughter Nan Savile was said to be 'very comical' about the whole business, dangling invitations to Rufford before Mr Pierrepont's eyes.[31] Somehow all this was smoothed over, perhaps because Dorothy Sunderland's own political sympathies lay with her erstwhile son-in-law Halifax. Finally the wedding was allowed to take place.

At first Lucy seems to have been most contented with her new life. She was a giddy young woman wrote her aunt, and 'delighted with liberty and money'. Of Mr Pierrepont she said that he was as kind as she could desire, allowing her to have everything 'to the uttermost of his fortune', and begging her to buy whatever plate or furniture she wanted, and he would pay for it. Dorothy was not quite as happy about all this extravagance as her earlier matchmaking might have indicated. She intended to advise her niece not to abuse her husband's generosity, for his grand relations would not think well of her if she proved herself too 'expensive'. She was also surprised – 'Pierrepont blood' not being famous for its open-handedness. Altogether it was a worrying situation, with Lucy 'a little too free and too merry in appearance', and Mr Pierrepont in contrast very grave and lacking altogether in self-confidence; he had 'an ill opinion of his own opinion', wrote Dorothy.[32]

Alas, poor Lucy. Mr Pierrepont, for all his wealth, was but a gilded sepulchre. By June, only a few months after the marriage, Dorothy feared that he would not prove a good husband. He was fond enough of his wife, but 'so unquiet in the house': that is to say he meddled with everything in the kitchen, and interfered with the servants, abusing them to such an extent that they had wearied of their positions and were all leaving. For his part, Mr Pierrepont was threatening to sack Lucy's personal maid, who had been overheard saying: 'God bless her mistress, she would be glad never to see her master again.' Above all, his Pierrepont blood had asserted itself and he was now very mean in everything that was not for show – so much for the visible splendours of the plate and furniture which Lucy had been encouraged to buy.

Lucy herself, according to Dorothy, was very depressed by this turn of events; still, she showed no signs of revolting against her fate. No great natural housekeeper, somewhat bewildered by that side of life, she was generally felt to have 'a hard task' coping with the demands of Mr Pierrepont. Yet she neither complained to nor confided in her aunt on the subject – rather to the latter's annoyance. On the contrary: 'she does observe him [Mr Pierrepont] as much as possible'. Dorothy added: 'Severity not well understood has no bounds.'[33]

Dorothy had originally been waspishly worried that this new 'fond' couple might take to kissing each other in public, and calling each other 'pretty dear' in the manner of Lucy's sister Elizabeth and her unprepossessing husband Edward Montagu. If so, she had intended to exercise her authority over her niece to put an end to such tasteless public exhibitions. In fact, the Pierreponts' married life was more reminiscent of the sad disgruntled marriages of late Restoration drama, that of Squire Sullen and Mrs Sullen in *The Beaux' Stratagem* perhaps ('O matrimony!' cries Mrs Sullen, 'Oh the pleasure of counting the melancholy clock by a snoring husband');[34] except that the Pierreponts' union was less colourful – no scandal smirched Lucy's name. Her earlier giddiness and love of liberty was presumably extinguished by the strain of housekeeping for Mr Pierrepont. Her husband was created an Irish peer – Lord Pierrepont of Ardglass – in 1703, and Lord Pierrepont of Hanslope in Buckinghamshire, in 1714. But Lucy Pierrepont never had any children, so the titles died out on his death.

The story of Elizabeth Percy, that child known as 'my lady Ogle', if its dénouement was less tragic than that of Frances Coke, Lady Purbeck (see p.15ff), showed that the notion of the heiress had lost none of its power to lure in the intervening half-century. This was after all a venturesome – and mercenary – age in which the rumour of a girl's fortune was enough to incite some coarse spirits to extraordinary acts of boldness.

There was that Cornet Wroth who, dining with Sir Robert Vyner at his country house, took the opportunity to carry off an heiress named Miss Hyde in a coach after dinner. When a wheel broke, the egregious Cornet was still not checked: he put the girl across his horse and got as far as the Putney ferry, where another coach-and-six awaited, before his pursuers finally caught up with him. The girl, speechless after her ordeal, was recovered; but Cornet Wroth escaped. In February 1680 the mere rumour that one of Lady Tirrell's daughters possessed a considerable fortune was enough to encourage certain 'robbers' to break into her house in Buckinghamshire. The motive, it was explained afterwards, was not robbery at all, but the desire to lay hands on Miss Tirrell. One of the housebreakers, fearing not to be able to accomplish his design by ordinary means, 'did endeavour to have carried her away under some crafty pretence and to have married her'.[35] Matters had not really progressed very far since the presumptuous Roger Fulwood abducted the schoolgirl Sara Cox from Newington Common in the reign of Charles I (see p.27).

The matrimonial affairs of 'my lady Ogle' were on an even more sensational level, owing to the particular combination of enormous wealth and high position in society. John Evelyn quoted a contemporary opinion: she was 'one that both by birth and fortune might have pretended to the greatest prince in Christendom'. This child's father was Joceline Percy, eleventh and last Earl of Northumberland of the ancient Percy creation. Her mother, Elizabeth Wriothesley, Countess of Northumberland – 'a beautiful lady indeed,' wrote Pepys goggling at her in court in 1667 – was seldom mentioned without some allusion to her celebrated looks.[36] Certainly Lely's portrait of her among the Hampton Court beauties shows an angelic blonde docility; an impression borne out by the blameless quality of her personal life. A daughter of the Earl of Southampton by his second marriage, Lady Northumberland was one of the co-heiresses of the Southampton fortune with her step-sisters Rachel Lady Russell and Lady Noel. But through her mother, a Leigh, who had been the sole heiress of *her* father, the Earl of Chichester, Lady Northumberland was also extremely rich in her own right. Elizabeth Percy was her only surviving child.

At the death of the Earl of Northumberland in 1670, it was possible to see in Elizabeth Percy merely a little red-headed girl of three years old. More romantically, one could see in her 'the last of the Percies' (she inherited all those ancient resonant Percy baronies which could pass through the female line). It was also possible to envisage this small child as a prize to be captured. On the whole society took the latter view.

Still in her early twenties and quite apart from her beauty said to be worth £6,000 a year, Lady Northumberland was also now herself a natural target for a stream of suitors. In September 1671 bold Harry Savile found himself staying at Althorp at the same time as the lovely widow. Finding her door open, he entered in his nightgown, went right up to her bedside, and started to call 'Madam! Madam!' until Lady Northumberland awoke. He then acquainted her with the passion he had long nourished for her but had somehow been unable to confess in the hours of daylight. Lady Northumberland, in a fright, called her women, and Harry Savile was advised to leave Althorp as soon as possible. He did so, and subsequently went abroad rather than fight the duel which would have been proposed to avenge Lady Northumberland's honour.[37]

Thereafter the young Lady Northumberland resided chiefly in Paris, her valuable affections having been secured by Ralph Montagu, Charles II's Ambassador to the French court, who married her three years after her first husband's death. In 1696 Francis Viscount Shannon would dedicate the second edition of his *Discourses and Essays*, in which he strongly advocated against marrying for 'mere love', to Lady Northumberland, then keeping herself 'in a kind of religious retirement'; but there seems to have been something of love implicit in the widow's selection, for the unprincipled but fascinating Ralph Montagu had the knack of attracting the opposite sex. Ralph Montagu's motives were more cynical and the marriage was not a very happy one, any more than Lady Northumberland enjoyed her sojourn in France. Here the tart wit of Madame de Sévigné found an ideal target in the appearance of this famous English beauty – her features were not good, she looked surprisingly old and careworn and in case her dress might be supposed to atone for these defects: '*elle est avec cela mal habillée, point de grâce*'.[38] One of Lady Northumberland's problems abroad was not understanding the French language; one hopes that as a result she was at least spared knowledge of Madame de Sévigné's chauvinist criticism.

Meanwhile at home the child Elizabeth Percy fell into the care of her strong-minded paternal grandmother, widow of Algernon, tenth Earl of Northumberland. (She was his second wife; Lady Anne Cecil, that bride he had insisted on marrying for love, had died in 1637). Indeed, old Lady Northumberland seized the opportunity of her daughter-in-law's second marriage to insist that the marrying off of Elizabeth Percy was to be her, grandmother's, sole concern.[39] The younger woman, being of a far gentler character, made no exaggerated counter-claim but protested that it was very hard that her own child 'should be disposed of without her consent' – especially since Elizabeth Percy 'if she had no other children must be her heir'. In the end some kind of accommodation was reached between the two Countesses of Northumberland on this important subject, by which the ladies both agreed not to marry off the girl without each other's consent – and without her consent as well. (It was also incidentally agreed that Elizabeth Percy should not be married below the age of legal consent.)

Nevertheless it was the old Countess, a redoubtable and scheming character, who in effect won out, since she retained control of the girl in England. The first match she arranged, in 1679, when Elizabeth Percy was only twelve, had at least the merit of dynastic suitability: this was with the thirteen-year-old Lord Ogle, heir to the Duke of Newcastle. Immediately on marriage, he assumed the surname of Percy. Dorothy Countess of Sunderland, however, thought him 'as ugly as anything young can be'.[40] Either for this or some more worldly reason connected with old Lady Northumberland's intrigues and Elizabeth Percy's tender age, her mother did not approve of the match. This led to a quarrel between young Lady Northumberland and the new Lady Ogle.

Rachel Lady Russell, Lady Northumberland's wise step-sister, tried to effect a reconciliation between the two in a letter to her niece on the subject of her marriage: 'You have my prayers and wishes, dear Lady Ogle, that it may prove as fortunate to you as ever it did to any and that you may know happiness to a good old age; but, Madam, I cannot think you can be completely so, with a misunderstanding between so near a relation as a mother...' Lady Russell begged Lady Ogle to seek her mother's pardon. After all Lady Northumberland's advice had had but 'one aim and end ... your being happy'.[41]

But Lady Ogle did not enjoy happiness to a good old age, at least not just yet, and not with this bridegroom.

A few months later Lord Ogle died. What was to happen to 'my Lady Ogle' now? Rumours abounded, correspondence of the period avidly reported the latest supposed developments in her situation as though the fate of 'my lady Ogle' was some major matter of State. Everyone was talking 'about Lord Ogle's death and Lady Ogle's position'.[42]

The person soon selected for Lady Ogle by old Lady Northumberland was Thomas Thynne Esquire of Longleat Hall in Wiltshire, and some kind of contract between the two was signed. This produced consternation in more than one quarter. The match was not considered worthy of Lady Ogle by the world at large, she whose name had been coupled with a bridegroom as august as the Prince of Hanover. Nor was Mr Thynne himself a specially savoury character, having seduced another girl under promise of marriage, before abandoning her for the lure of Lady Ogle. Lord Essex, Lady Ogle's uncle by marriage, believed that her grandmother had 'betrayed' her 'for money'; the Earl of Kingston or Lord Cranborne (Lord Salisbury's heir) would have been far more suitable.[43] Another unsavoury participant in the whole affair was the financier Richard Brett, who was rewarded by Thynne with valuable property for helping to bring about the 'sale' of Lady Ogle; Brett's wife being a connection of the heiress.[44]

As for Lady Ogle herself, it was said that 'the contract she lately signed rises in her stomach'. It may be that Lady Ogle had encountered a powerful counter-attraction in the shape of the handsome Count Königsmarck, who had been paying her court. At this point the drama increased when Lady Ogle herself vanished from her grandmother's house. On 10 November 1681, as Sir Charles Hatton wrote excitedly, no one yet knew with whom or to where she had fled. But it was generally believed that 'she went away to avoid Mr Thynne, whom she sometimes [that is, previously] married'. This marriage, which took place in the summer, had not been consummated before Lady Ogle's flight. There was now a rumour that it would be made void and that Lady Ogle would be wedded to George Fitzroy, one of Barbara Duchess of Cleveland's sons by Charles II, who had recently been granted that Northumberland title which had become extinct at Lady Ogle's father's death.[45]

The next stage of the drama took place when Mr Thomas Thynne, the unsuccessful husband – or suitor – of Lady Ogle was shot by a posse of Count Königsmarck's men; with five bullets in his belly he died next morning. Now the furore reached new heights. Had there been a duel? Duelling was against the law, and the King did all he could to enforce the prohibition but it was at the same time a recognized social procedure where honour was concerned. Murder hardly came into the same category. Count Königsmarck's men tried to maintain that one of them – a Pole – had challenged Mr Thynne to a duel, but unfortunately this man was known to have asked the Swedish Ambassador the night before 'whether if Mr Thynne was removed, his master might not marry the Lady Ogle according to the law of England'. The girl Thynne had betrayed was said to have played some part in the conspiracy, hence the satirical epitaph:

Here lies Tom Thynne of Longleat Hall
Who never would have miscarried,
Had he married the woman he lay withal;
Or laid with the woman he married.[46]

The responsibility of the Count himself – who had fled – was another much debated point.

In fact the Count only got as far as Gravesend where he was found in a boat 'disguised in a poor habit'. He was taken to Newgate and subsequently put on trial. However, his men loyally stuck to the story that there had been a challenge to a duel. It had actually been refused but one of their number, 'the Polander', had failed to appreciate this fact and thus fired the fatal shot.[47] So the Count was acquitted. (His men were hanged.)

None of this of course had improved the Count's chances of marrying Lady Ogle although, imperviously, he did renew his suit. In any case on 30 May 1682, the exciting chase was ended. Steps had been taken earlier in the year to render the Thynne marriage contract void at the Court of the King's Bench. In May Lady Ogle was married to the nineteen-year-old Charles Seymour, sixth Duke of Somerset. No one could deny that that was a splendid match: the latest bridegroom was dark and handsome, generous and cultivated. His only defect – an overweening arrogance on the subject of his ancestry, which led to his being termed 'the Proud Duke of Somerset' – was perhaps not such a defect after all for one who was herself 'the last of the Percies'. It showed tact on the part of the new Duchess that she did not finally hold the 'Proud Duke' to that promise which was part of the marriage contract, to change his surname from Seymour to Percy.

So the former Elizabeth Percy, Lady Ogle, lived in splendour for forty years as Duchess of Somerset, bearing her husband thirteen children, and ornamenting the court of William and Mary. Later her political influence was feared by the Tories under Queen Anne, when she became First Lady of the Bedchamber following the fall of Sarah Duchess of Marlborough. This incurred for her the enmity of Swift and thus was her red hair (and her dramatic past) angrily mocked:

Beware of carrots from Northumberland;
Carrots sown Thynne a deep root may get,
If so be they are in Somer set.[48]

For all the *Sturm und Drang* which had surrounded the early years of 'my lady Ogle', it is appropriate to note that her aunt Rachel Lady Russell, the tragic much admired heroine of the same period, was herself an heiress and as such made a supremely happy marriage. It was possible in the second half of the seventeenth century, as it had been in the first, for love to flourish under rich bedcovers. The sorrows which came to Lady Russell, came from her husband's political convictions and his defeat at the hands of the established order. Her pleasures were on the contrary produced by her acceptance of the rules of society, within which framework she brought her own remarkable character and intelligence to play.

Rachel Wriothesley was born in 1636, the daughter of the Earl of Southampton by his first wife, a French Protestant noblewoman named Rachel de Ruvigny. Where her education was concerned, like her future sisters-in-law the Ladies Diana and Margaret Russell, she benefited from a domestic chaplain, Dr Fitzwilliam; at the age of seventeen she was married to Lord Vaughan, heir to the Earl of Carbery, a match later referred to as 'acceptance without choosing on either side'. In later years Lady Russell would describe herself as having been at this period fond of 'a great dinner and worldly talk', following a sermon which was not too long.[49] The only child of this marriage was born and died in 1665, in which year died also Lord Vaughan.

In a financial sense, however, the important event in the life of Rachel Lady Vaughan was the death of Lord Southampton two years later without a male heir. The three daughters who were his co-heiresses – 'my sister Noel, my sister Northumberland and myself' as Rachel described them – now cast lots for the valuable properties which formed part of his fortune. It was in this historic manner that Rachel acquired Southampton House and that area known then as 'the manors of Bloomsbury and St Giles' which was to provide the foundations of the great London property holdings of the Russell family. Rachel Lady Vaughan was now in the vastly desirable situation of being a wealthy and childless widow in her early thirties who had complete control over her fortune – and thus over her future. Although her fortune could not perhaps be compared with that of her step-niece 'my lady Ogle', certainly her immediate fate was likely to be preferable. And so it proved.

William Russell was in fact the second son of the Earl of Bedford, one of his immense brood of children by Anne Carr, the good Countess sprung from the bad mother, but his eldest brother was sickly and it was tacitly assumed that William was the heir; this brother died in 1678 and William then succeeded to the courtesy title of Lord Russell. Otherwise he was intelligent and charming if also, as time would show, of that steely stuff of which political martyrs are made. He was, however, a few years younger than Rachel Lady Vaughan. Still, a fortune glossed over such matters wonderfully. Although the wooing took some two years to complete, in view of the vested interests on both sides, it was finally successful. Rachel Lady Vaughan and William Russell were married on 31 July 1669. From his family accounts we know that William Russell spent lavishly on his own clothes for the occasion: £250 on cherry-coloured silk, scarlet and silver brocade and gold and silver lace.[10] (We do not know what the bride wore.)

William Russell now happily acquired control of Rachel's Bloomsbury properties, according to the laws of the time, just as her father's residence of Southampton House became their family home in London. In personal terms an equally blissful union was inaugurated. Two daughters – Rachel and Katherine – were born in 1674 and 1676; the Russells' joy was completed when a son, named Wriothesley in compliment to his mother's family, was born in 1680. Since Rachel Lady Russell was by now forty-four, there must have been some anxiety about the prospect of a male heir. Certainly the old Earl of Bedford at Woburn Abbey gave the messenger who brought him the news a present of sixteen guineas, nearly twice as much as had greeted the news of the arrival of the girls.[11]

The Russells were seldom apart, except when William went to

visit the family estates at Woburn, and even then, as Rachel quaintly expressed it in 1675, she did not like to let 'this first post-night pass without giving my dear man a little talk', in the shape of a letter. Both were particularly fond of their own house (part of Rachel's inheritance) at Stratton in Hampshire. Rachel painted a placid domestic picture to William away at Woburn: the little boy asleep as she wrote, the girls singing in bed, with little Rachel telling herself a long story, 'She says, Papa has sent for her to Wobee, and then she gallops and says she has been there, and a great deal more.' Lady Russell ended her letter on a cheerful gourmet note: 'but', she wrote, 'boiled oysters call'. In June 1680 she told her husband more spiritually: 'My dearest heart, flesh and blood cannot have a truer and greater sense of their own happiness than your poor but honest wife has. I am glad you find Stratton so sweet; may you live to do so one fifty years more'. On another occasion she was writing with 'thy pillow at my back; where thy dear head shall lie, I hope, tomorrow night'.[52]

'I know, as certainly as I live, that I have been, for twelve years, as passionate a lover as ever woman was, and hope to be so one twelve years more.' Thus Rachel Lady Russell in September 1682. Less than one year after this declaration of an ideally happy wife, William Lord Russell was on trial for conspiring to kill the King and the Duke of York in what was known as the Rye House Plot. His specific guilt remains doubtful although with the other extreme Whig, Algernon Sidney, William Russell admitted he had declared it was lawful to resist the King on occasion. Significantly, when reasons were given to Charles II for leniency towards Lord Russell, the monarch tersely replied: 'All that is true, but it is as true that if I do not take his life he will soon have mine.'[53] In a test of strength between the King and the Whigs therefore, William Lord Russell was cast in the role of the Whig martyr, a role he was not unwilling to fulfil.

During the period between Lord Russell's arrest on 26 June 1683 and his trial which began on 3 July it was Rachel who beavered away, seeking support. And at the trial itself she caused a thrill of anguish by her appearance at her husband's side in the courtroom. Officially, the defendant in a treason trial at this date was not allowed a legal adviser; the Attorney-General, to antici-pate Lord Russell's protests, declared that he could have a servant to take notes for him. A sensation of a different sort was caused when Lord Russell announced: 'My wife is here to do it', or in another version: 'I require no other assistance than that which the lady can give me who sits by my side.'[54]

'If my lady will give herself that trouble', was the embarrassed reply of the Chief Justice. The Attorney-General then offered two persons to write for Lord Russell if he so wished; the aston-ishment caused by Lord Russell's announcement being a striking commentary on the low level of female literacy at the time.

The predictable verdict was guilty and the sentence execution. Rachel's frantic efforts to bring about a reprieve, her own desper-ate pleas for mercy, the pleas of her relations and those of Lord Russell were all unavailing. The date was set for Friday 21 July. On the Thursday, Lord Russell told Gilbert (later Bishop) Burnet he wished for his own sake that his wife would cease 'beating every bush', and 'running about so' in the useless task of trying to save him; and yet when he considered that 'it would be some mit-igation [to her afterwards] that she had tried everything he had to let her continue'. And there was a tear in his eye as he turned away. But he received his beloved children for the last time, according to Bishop Burnet, 'with his ordinary serenity' and Rachel herself managed to leave without a single sob.[55]†

Late that night the husband and wife said goodbye for the last time. Lord Russell expressed 'great joy' at that 'magnanimity of spirit' which he found in Rachel to the last; parting from her was of all things the hardest one he had to do. As for her, he feared that after he was gone and she no longer had the task of his reprieve to buoy her up 'the quickness of her spirits would work all within her'. They kissed four or five times and still both managed a stoical restraint.

After Rachel's departure, William mused aloud on his great

---

†This touching family scene, together with 'The Parting of Lord and Lady Russell' and Lady Russell pleading for mercy from King Charles II, was to become a favourite subject among Victorian painters, figuring in exhibitions at the Royal Academy throughout the nineteenth century.[56]

blessing in having had such a wife, one who had never begged him to turn informer and thus save his own life. How terribly this last week would have passed, he told Bishop Burnet, if she had been 'still crying at me'! God had showed him a 'signal providence' in granting him a wife of 'birth, fortune, great understanding, great religion, and a great kindness to him' – note the order even at the last in which these benefits were listed – 'but her carriage in this extremity went beyond all'.

After Lord Russell's death, Rachel Lady Russell's conduct in her bereavement justified her husband's fears for her. Through the intercession of Lord Halifax, she was allowed to place a public escutcheon of mourning over the door of Southampton House; this permission indicated that the King did not intend to profit from the forfeiture of Lord Russell's personal estate (a penalty which was generally exacted after the death of a traitor). In other ways Lady Russell withdrew into a more private world of lamentation. No visitors were ever allowed to call at Southampton House on Fridays – the fatal day – and in addition 26 June, 3 July and 21 July were kept sacred to commemorate his arrest, trial and execution.

A few months after Lord Russell's death, Rachel's old mentor Dr Fitzwilliam advocated a recourse to the Scriptures for comfort. In reply, Lady Russell burst out that nothing could comfort her because of her lack of *him*. 'I want him to talk with, to walk with, to eat, and sleep with. All these things are irksome to me. The day unwelcome, and the night so too…'[57] Even her children made her heart 'shrink' because she remembered the pleasure their father had taken in them. Two years later she was still torturing herself with thoughts that she could have done more to save him.

At the death of Anne Countess of Bedford (an event probably brought forward by the shock of her son's execution) Rachel took the opportunity to visit the family vault at Chenies in Buckinghamshire where her husband's body was entombed. She defended her decision to Dr Fitzwilliam. 'I had considered. I went not to seek the living among the dead. I knew I should not see him anymore, wherever I went, and had made a covenant with myself, not to break out in unreasonable fruitless passion.' She went deliberately to 'quicken my contemplation' as to 'whither the nobler part was fled, to a country far off, where no earthly power bears any sway, nor can put an end to a happy society.'[58]

When Lady Russell went to London for the sake of her little boy's future, she determined to be brave about visiting Southampton House: 'I think (by God's assistance) the shadows will not sink me.' Yet every anniversary destroyed her resolution by 'breaking off that bandage, time would lay over my wound'. In 1695, suffering in fact from cataract of the left eye, she was said to have wept herself blind. In extreme old age, listing her sins in shaky handwriting, Rachel included the fact that she had been inconsolable for the death of him who had been 'my dear Mr Russell, seeking help from man but finding none'.[59]

It was natural that this tragic widow should resolve never to marry again; instead she resolved to see 'none but lawyers and accountants' in the interests of her children. Both decisions were much applauded by a society which admired Lady Russell's heroism in adopting such a stern and secluded way of life. So by degrees Lady Russell fulfilled the highest expectations of her time for a great lady.†

Her future efforts were entirely for her family. She succeeded in getting the attainder on her husband's title reversed so that her son Wriothesley could bear it. She carefully arranged, as we shall see in the next chapter, important worldly matches for her daughters. As for Wriothesley, he was not yet thirteen when old Sir Josiah Child, the magnate of the East India Company, described by John Evelyn as 'sordidly avaricious', but doubtless with compensating qualities, proposed the boy a bride in the shape of his granddaughter; this was Lady Henrietta Somerset, offspring of Lord Worcester and Miss Rebecca Child. Although

---

†This admiration for Lady Russell's thoroughly feminine withdrawal did not fade. In 1815 Mary Berry, Walpole's friend, editing her letters, referred to Lady Russell with approval as having spent the rest of her existence, unlike most heroines, 'within the pale of private life and female duties'; an example which should be more widely followed.[60]

Sir Josiah used a clergyman as his envoy, he found Lady Russell's reply disappointingly cold. As for the tactful response that the young lord was still being educated, that made Sir Josiah indignant: he wrote back that that had never been 'a bar to parents discoursing of the matching of their children, which are born to extraordinary fortunes'. City money was evidently not the problem, nor necessarily youth: for only two years later the young lord was duly married off to another Child granddaughter. Elizabeth Howland. This granddaughter was even richer, which may have been the point. The sum of the young couple's ages came to twenty-eight years, wrote a contemporary; the bride alone, however, was worth a total of £100,000, a new Howland title being created for the Russell family as a compliment to her possessions.[61]

Rachel was clearly determined to show herself a sympathetic mother-in-law to the girl, only just in her teens; a year after the marriage she approved the news that Mr Huck the dressmaker had taken her in hand. While Lady Russell herself believed fashion to be 'but dross', she prayed constantly that her daughter-in-law might be 'a perfect creature both in mind and body; that is, in the manner we can reach perfection in this world'. In this perfection, Lady Russell was wise enough to see that Mr Huck the dressmaker had his place.[62]

As for Wriothesley, Marquess of Tavistock after the elevation of his grandfather to the dukedom of Bedford, when he turned out to be weak and an inveterate gambler – with a dead hero for a father and a doting mother did he ever have a chance? – Rachel Lady Russell was there to act as an intermediary in confessing his gambling debts to his dreaded grandfather

At the death of the old Duke in 1700, Rachel only waited a few days before writing to King William and asking for the Garter 'his grandfather so long enjoyed' on behalf of her twenty-year-old son. 'Sir, I presume on your goodness to forgive a woman's troubling you,' she wrote: not only the new Duke 'but I know the whole family would always look upon it as a mark of your grace and favour to them'.[63] Even in her sixties with problems of eyesight Rachel could be relentless where the advancement of her family was at stake.

'Grandmamma Russell', as Rachel was ultimately known, lived to be nearly ninety, still keeping Fridays as a day of recollection. She died in 1722. The *Weekly Journal* commemorated one who had been the heroine of her age, as well as being married to a hero, as follows:

> Russell, the chaste, has left this earthly stage,
> A bright example to a brittle age ...
> No arts her soul to second vows inclin'd
> No storm could frighten his unshaken mind ...

She was in short, like her husband, 'Proof against all, inseparably good.'[64]

CHAPTER FIFTEEN

Divorce from Bed and Board

~~⌐

> 'A Divorce is from Bed and Board; and is not void in
> respect of the Marriage so as that the Injured [Party]
> may marry again.'
>
> *The Athenian Oracle*, 1701

There was no such thing as divorce in the seventeenth
century, at least not in the sense the term is understood
today. This does not necessarily imply a starry-eyed view of
human nature, still less a higher level of marital happiness: the
pragmatic need for the separation of miserable or discordant
couples was well appreciated, as it had always been, and such
separations took place on a number of different levels of society.

In 1670 the Earl of Lauderdale, later created a Duke, Charles
II's viceroy in Scotland and a member of the acronymic Cabal,
was conducting a flagrant liaison with Bess Countess of Dysart.
His wife separated from him and went to live in Paris; but
Lauderdale paid for her and she was allowed to take with her not
only her own jewels but also – to Bess's disgust – the Lauderdale
family heirlooms.[1] After her death, Lauderdale and the flame-
haired Bess were able to marry; as Duke and Duchess of
Lauderdale they held proud court in Scotland.

A less grandiose form of separation occurred when one
spouse absented herself or himself without formality from the
other spouse's side. In the 1650s Tom Oxinden had married a
fourteen-year-old heiress whom he brought home under proper
supervision. As he wrote to his step-mother: 'I hope she carries

herself civilly and dutifully towards you and lovingly towards my sisters, as I have often desired her to do.' A few years later the bond was not sufficient to prevent Tom falling in love with Mrs Zutphenia Ower, wife of Robert Ower of Sydal. The pair went off and lived together. In 1662 Elizabeth Oxinden, the deserted wife, heard to her satisfaction that 'the Lady' and her husband were not happy together, Tom looking lean and pale. It must have given her less satisfaction when the ne'er-do-well Tom took to being a highwayman, was apprehended and died in prison in 1668. At this point Elizabeth Oxinden was free to marry again, did so, and bore four children by her second husband.[2]

The Oxindens belonged, roughly speaking, to the middle class and there was no question of Elizabeth Oxinden remarrying before Tom's death since details of his unfortunate existence filtered through to her. It was however quite possible in a ramified country like England for an errant husband (or wife) of a lower class to disappear altogether. Under such circumstances a second – bigamous – marriage might take place in the lifetime of the previous partner. Before the Hardwicke Act of 1753 which not only necessitated parental consent for minors but also made void those marriages performed without publication of the banns or a licence, such ceremonies were not too difficult to accomplish. In this manner it could be said that the propertyless classes enjoyed a kind of *de facto* liberty denied to their wealthier contemporaries. (Evidence of this popular 'divorce' in defiance of the rules is provided by the case-books of Richard Napier.)[3]

The sort of marriage which had been preceded by a financial settlement, with negotiations for a dowry then and a jointure to come, presented more of a problem when its component parts began to fall apart. Money was a powerful shackle, particularly for the woman. A wife was unlikely to secure any kind of maintenance if she separated from her husband, and legally had of course no money of her own, all of this having been handed over to her spouse on marriage. When Lady Hatton, mother of Frances Coke, separated from her second husband Sir Edward Coke, part of their violent quarrel over money concerned her wish to preserve that property she had inherited from her first husband, Sir William Hatton.[4]

Influential relations were a help. Lady Isabella Rich, the daughter of the Earl of Holland and the heiress Isabel Cope of Kensington, married Sir James Thynne of Longleat. When Charles I was at Oxford, she acted the part of Egeria to the court (it was her knowledge of statecraft which had prompted Ann Lady Fanshawe's unfortunate intrusion into her husband's political affairs – see pp. 68–9). Lodged at Balliol College, Lady Isabella and Ann Fanshawe could cause 'a flutter' appearing in Trinity College Chapel 'half-dressed like Angels'. Dorothy Osborne described Lady Isabella as 'the loveliest thing that could be looked on'. And her talent for music, combined with her air of nonchalance, inspired Waller to a poem, 'Of my Lady Isabella playing on the Lute', beginning:

> Such moving sounds from such a careless touch!
> So unconcerned herself, and we so much!

Aubrey however put his finger on her disadvantage as a wife: 'most beautiful, most humble, most charitable etc.,' as she was, Lady Isabella 'could not subdue one thing'.[5]

She became the mistress of the Royalist leader, the Marquess of Ormonde, finding him 'too agreeable', and bore him an illegitimate son (her marriage to Sir James Thynne was childless). Later she became involved in Royalist plotting, her father the Earl of Holland having been executed for his part in the second Civil War. Lady Isabella left England in 1650, finding refuge with Ormonde's charitable and sensible wife Elizabeth Desmond.[6]

It was hardly surprising under the circumstances that a formal separation was arranged between Sir James Thynne and his wife, the deed being dated 1 November 1653.[7] The real point of this extremely long and detailed document was not however that husband and wife should 'freely and voluntarily for ever hereafter permit and suffer each other to live separate and apart the one from the other'; nor even that Lady Isabella should be accounted, so far as her husband was concerned, as 'feme sole', that is he should exercise no control over her; since both these states of affairs obtained already. Both sides were actually concerned to establish proper financial arrangements: Lady Isabella abandoned her claim on 'all her Jointures and title of Dower' settled on her at her marriage in 1640, in return for proper provision and maintenance.

Yet it was seldom that a woman, even supported by influential relations, secured more than the partial return of what had once been theoretically her own; Lady Isabella's allowance being a small part of what she had brought with her on marriage.

Not all the matches arranged by Mary Countess of Warwick for her Rich nieces were as happy as that of Lady Essex and Daniel Finch. Lady Essex's sister, Lady Anne Barrington, was made of flimsier stuff. Like many late seventeenth-century ladies Lady Anne heartily disliked living in the country. In 1658 wilful Betty Verney had written yearningly from the bedside of her sick sister of her London memories: 'Hyde Park and the cherries there is very pleasant to me.' It was also taken for granted that more estimable characters would share these sentiments: that admirable woman Lucy Countess of Huntingdon 'naturally loved London very well', wrote one of her children in 1664. But as time wore on, the connection between London and adultery (at least for wives) and the country and boredom (at least for wives) did not only exist in the plots of Restoration plays. Husbands punished their wives or alternatively secured the sanctity of their marriage beds in advance by dispatching their wives away from temptation. 'To send a man's wife to the Peak' was a phrase coined when the second Earl of Chesterfield sent his Countess back to his Derbyshire estates in a fit of jealousy.[8]

In 1679 Lady Anne's husband, Tom Barrington, made a stand after a lengthy period of unhappiness. 'But for you living in London', he told her, 'I shall not, nor ever will consent thereto…' For fifteen years he had conformed to her humour, and now she must conform to his and live 'a soberer life in the country'. Furthermore she must settle all her estates on their children. The negotiations were left to Lady Anne's brother-in-law Daniel Finch. He proceeded carefully: while not defending Lady

Anne's rash conduct in London, he pointed out that she must receive some allowance in return for her estates; otherwise it was 'as if my Lady had committed so great a fault as that she must pay a thousand pounds a year per annum to repair it'. Lady Anne might have been a bad wife, but she had been a good mother, rising in the middle of the night to care for her child and visiting it while at nurse daily. Fortunately for Lady Anne the situation was resolved when Tom Barrington died; three years later she was able to marry again without hindrance.[9]

Unofficial separations brought their own problems, also financial. Peg Verney never really got on with her husband Sir Thomas Elmes – neither of them was sufficiently even-natured to make a go of it – and after a few years what amounted to a separation was tried. Sir Thomas believed that 'to part in Love', that is, amicably, might increase the affection they felt for each other; but he was concerned that it should be 'done in a way that nobody may know, certainly *guess* they will, but *know* they need not'. There was an attempt at a *rapprochement* which did not really work; for the rest of her life Peg was involved in arguments with Sir Thomas over the kind of money due to her, if any. At her death Sir Thomas angrily took the line that Peg had had no right to make a will leaving away money from him (because she was legally still his wife).[10]

When it came to an official arrangement it was possible to secure a form of divorce – *divortium a mensa et thoro*, divorce from bed and board as it was known – in the ecclesiastical courts. This was the kind of process threatened by the father of Mary Joyce in January 1661, as reported by Pepys, because she and her husband Will led 'a strange life together, nothing but fighting, etc.'.[11]

The word 'divorce' was generally applied to such cases, but we should in fact find the term judicial separation more accurate, since it was an important aspect of the process in the ecclesiastical courts that the parties concerned, including the injured party, were not free to marry again. This was in accordance with Canon Law. Although at the start of the century some preachers had been suggesting that remarriage might be possible for the innocent, this prohibition was strongly restated at the ecclesiastical conference of 1604.

Occasionally people did remarry, thus forfeiting the money which they had deposited as a security against doing so. In November 1605 the beautiful Penelope Rich, inspiration of Sir Philip Sidney and long-time mistress of Sir Charles Blount (by whom she had borne several children), obtained this type of divorce *a mensa et thoro* from Lord Rich in the ecclesiastical courts. It was specifically laid down that neither should remarry in the lifetime of the other. Despite this, six weeks later Penelope Rich was married to Sir Charles Blount. However, since this was a clear violation of Canon Law, her children by Blount were not made legitimate; and ironically enough Penelope Lady Blount, who had been happily received at court throughout her long adulterous liaison, was now debarred from it.[12]

William Whateley was a country vicar in the early seventeenth century, known as the Roaring Boy of Banbury for the power and vitriol of his sermons. In 1619, in a tract called *A Bride-Bush*, he stated that adultery and desertion annulled the marriage contract and thus permitted remarriage. He was promptly called before the Court of High Commission and obliged to recant; he withdrew the assertion in print in a second tract of 1624, *A Care-Cloth*. Only the Commonwealth Marriage Act of 1653 brought in a brief period of greater latitude; the notion of marriage as a purely civil ceremony denied the iron grip of Canon Law. The Act stated that the innocent party should be allowed to marry again according to the recommendations of the Westminster Assembly of Divines. (Milton's famous proposals on the subject of divorce were obviously framed with the idea of remarriage in mind.)[13] But although reformers continued to press for this possibility, with the Restoration this sophisticated Puritan interlude came to an end.

If the parties were anxious to remarry, the simplest method was for them to secure a decree of nullity which established that the marriage had been void *ab initio*, from the beginning. *The Ladies Dictionary* of 1694, a comprehensive work, referred to divorce 'in our Courts' as *only* being through nullity; grounds including Consanguinity and Affinity (of blood) as well as Precontract and Impotency. To be cynical, a decree of nullity was expensive but not impossible to secure. Of the various grounds, non-consummation, if applicable, was the obvious one to choose; it was a subject however which might produce some strange assertions. When Frances, later Countess of Somerset, had been determined to get rid of her first husband, the Earl of Essex, she did so on the remarkable grounds that, although not impotent towards women in general, Essex was impotent towards her in particular. With the support of King James, Frances secured her decree of nullity and was able to wed Robert Carr, Earl of Somerset, the royal favourite. On the other hand when Lady Desmond sued Lord Desmond in 1635 it was on the more straightforward grounds that her husband had 'insufficiency to please a reasonable woman'.[14]

A marriage was also held to be void from the beginning if a previous contract existed. Since a pledge to marry in front of witnesses – spousals *de praesenti* as it was known – could be held to be a valid contract, this technicality might be brought into use. Aphra Behn for example used it to round off her play of 1676, *The Town-Fop, or Sir Timothy Tawdrey*, with a happy ending. Lady Diana's uncle Lord Plotwell promised 'to untie the Knot', and successfully did so on grounds of a precontract (it was helpful that Lady Diana's own marriage had not yet been consummated). In real life, it was not so easy. The familiar economic question remained: How was the woman to be supported in the future? At the end of another of Aphra Behn's plays, *Sir Patient Fancy*, a young woman who had chosen an old man out of financial necessity ("'Twas to that end I married you, good Alderman') succeeded in getting a separation from him, without having to return the money.[15] But this ideal – from the female point of view – was seldom realized in real life.

What if no possible grounds for nullity could exist? What, for example, if children had been born of the marriage so that consummation had demonstrably taken place? There was one further expedient which developed in the late seventeenth century, and that was *divortium a vinculo matrimonii*, literally a divorce from the bond of matrimony. This could only be obtained by a private Act of Parliament. A petition and Bill had to be presented to the House of Lords, which would be debated during its various readings, according to customary parliamentary procedure. It was nearly always preceded by a separation *a mensa et thoro* in the ecclesiastical court; or an action at common law against the co-respondent for 'criminal conversation' with the plaintiff's spouse, or for assault and battery.[16]

The expense and difficulty of such proceedings were prodigious. The prolonged tribulations experienced by Henry, seventh Duke of Norfolk in ridding himself of his adulterous wife Lady Mary Mordaunt demonstrate that even the 'first Duke in England, installed Knight of the Garter, lord high Marshal of England, and one of the lords of his Majesty's Privy Council' was not immune from this general rule.[17] Only a little over 200 cases were heard before the Matrimonial Causes Act of 1857 made it possible to obtain a divorce in England other than by Act of Parliament; and only six of these were at the suit of the wife. In any case the wife was handicapped because adultery alone was not sufficient grounds for her to get her Bill through (whereas it was for the husband).† For the vast majority of the population other than the wealthy and privileged few, only the ecclesiastical form of 'divorce' was open to them, with no prospect of a happier second union. As *The Athenian Oracle* wrote in answer to a query in 1701, laying down the established practice of the time: 'A Divorce is from Bed and Board; and is not void in respect of the Marriage so as that the Injured [Party] may marry again.'[18]

The property laws made it difficult for women caught in an unhappy marriage to struggle free because there was no guarantee they would not end up poverty-stricken. But where divorce was concerned, men had their burden too. Because a valid marriage was indissoluble except by such an expensive protracted process as an Act of Parliament – which might be condemned by society for a variety of reasons unconnected with the marriage

---

†It was not until 1857 that divorce was made generally available in England – to men on grounds of their wives' adultery alone, and to wives on grounds of their husbands' adultery, accompanied by cruelty or desertion.

itself – it was not so easy for a man to dispose of a wanton wife. Ironically, the wanton wife had a peculiar advantage at this period which the legalization of divorce in 1857 took from her.

In particular, the offspring of her liaison with another man, if technically born within wedlock, were not so easily denied the inheritance of their legal father. As in the case of Frances Lady Purbeck and her child, unless the husband had been indisputably absent 'beyond the seas' for an agreed length of time, the burden of proof remained upon him to establish that the child could not possibly be his. In 1635 the Earl of Essex, prejudiced against womankind in general from the conduct of his first wife Frances, later Countess of Somerset, became convinced by spiteful gossip (in the manner of Othello) that the child his second wife was bearing was not his. He announced that he would not own it unless the baby was born by 5 November. When the baby was in fact born on that very date, neither suspicious husband nor innocent – and insulted – wife were any happier and the marriage collapsed. A deed of separation was arranged; even then Lord Essex tried to insert a clause in the deed saying that his wife would forfeit her jointure if she gave birth to any further children because 'whosoever got them, yet my Lord must father them by the law', until the Countess of Essex indignantly refused to countenance it.[19]

In about 1632 Edward Scott of Scot's Hall married Catherine, the daughter of the first Baron Goring, but the couple only lived together for about two years. While her husband was serving at the front, Catherine Scott gave birth to children at Oxford and elsewhere. Her husband disowned them and brought an action in the ecclesiastical courts for separation, while she brought an action for alimony in Chancery. Then the husband brought a petition to Parliament in 1656. But a divorce was never obtained. Thomas Scott was thus perforce acknowledged by his 'father' as his heir, and succeeded to Scot's Hall at Edward Scott's death in 1663.[20]

The most notorious matrimonial case of the seventeenth century was however that of Lord and Lady Roos.

It could not be said that the title of Lord Roos was a lucky one. John Manners, who bore the courtesy title of Lord Roos, was the third and surviving son of John, eighth Earl of Rutland, who had succeeded to the title on the death of his cousin without male heirs in 1641. The two sons of Francis, sixth Earl of Rutland, who had earlier borne the courtesy title of Lord Roos, died in youth: as we have seen (on p.128 ff.), these deaths were ascribed to the malevolent influence of the Flower family, the so-called Belvoir witches, who died themselves as a result.

Even the Roos title had a miasma of doubt attached to it. The ancient barony of Roos or de Ros, the premier barony of England, was, unlike the earldom of Rutland, able to pass through the female line. The sixth Earl's remaining child, his daughter Catherine, had married James I's favourite, the first Duke of Buckingham; her only surviving child, George, second Duke of Buckingham, was a prominent if maverick figure at the court of Charles II. The Duke of Buckingham claimed – as a matter of fact perfectly correctly – the ancient Roos barony through his mother. When pressed, the male line of the Rutland family based their use of the Roos title on another creation, that of Roos of Hamlake in 1616. But this new creation had been made specially for Francis the sixth Earl until such time as he should inherit the ancient barony on the death of a female cousin (which occurred in 1618). This new barony of Roos of Hamlake, which could pass to sons of the sixth Earl, had in fact become extinct at his death in 1632.[21]

This complicated and confusing squabble did not stop John Manners, heir to the eighth Earl of Rutland, bearing the courtesy title of Lord Roos at the time of his marriage to Lady Anne Pierrepont on 21 July 1658; but it was to have some bearing on his matrimonial affairs later.

In advance, the match had the air of being an ideal one. The bride was the daughter and heiress of Henry Pierrepont, Earl of Kingston and later Marquess of Dorchester, a highly eccentric figure as it happened but that was considered less important in 1658 than the fact that the marriage united two families 'very noble in themselves, and of great fortunes, and allied to all the great families of the kingdom'. Anne Pierrepont was seventeen and brought with her a dowry of £10,000, £6,500 of it paid by Lord Dorchester on 21 July.[22] John Lord Roos was twenty and, as the last male heir of the ancient Rutland family, someone on whose future progeny many family hopes were pinned.

Around the time of the wedding lavish and traditional disbursements were made: £93 was spent on two pearl necklaces for the new Lady Roos, and £50 on crimson velvet for a coach. The famous miniaturist John Hoskins, described in the family accounts as the 'picture-drawer', was commissioned. A dozen pairs of 'gesiment' (jasmine, i.e. yellow) coloured gloves were ordered for distribution among the guests according to custom, and two dozen gloves for Lady Roos. Five shillings were 'given the poor at the gates the wedding-day' and six shillings went to the trumpeters.[23]

In spite of all this, the marriage was a disaster, virtually from the start. A daughter, born early in 1659, must have been conceived very close to the wedding (she did not live). Beyond that, there were few signs that Lord Roos and Lady Anne enjoyed any kind of marital happiness together. The Earl of Clarendon summed up the sexual problem between them with his usual magisterial concision: Lady Anne 'not finding the satisfaction she expected where she ought to have received it, looked for it abroad where she ought not to find it'. As for Lord Roos, he was indulgent enough, as men 'conscious of any notable defect' were wont to be, wrote Clarendon, 'not strictly inquiring how she behaved herself'. The picture was completed by the fact that Lady Anne was, at any rate in the opinion of Clarendon, 'of a humour not very agreeable' and made little effort to dissemble or conceal the contempt she felt for her husband.[24]

Not all Lady Anne's contempt was necessarily based on Lord Roos's sexual inadequacy. For Lord Roos had another interest – drink; he also gambled and led a life generally felt to be unsatisfactory by his contemporaries. When he related how Lady Anne accused her husband of 'debauchery' and 'being always in drink', Clarendon added: 'which was true'. At some point there was a tacit separation and at some point after that, after various 'acts of passion' (that is, anger) which gave both 'mirth and scandal' to the world at large, what purported to be a reconciliation but was in effect very much on Lady Anne's terms: 'the lady having the ascendant over the lord who was very desirous to live quietly upon any conditions, that he might enjoy himself though he could not enjoy her'.[25]

Once again Lady Anne slipped away from Belvoir to London. But on this latest occasion she overstayed her leave by several months; what was more she returned clearly pregnant, or as Clarendon phrased it, 'in so gross a manner that it appeared that she had kept company too much'. This at last stung the passive Lord Roos into making some kind of protest. He taxed Lady Anne 'that she was with child' and asked her: 'Who [be]got it?'

To this Lady Anne replied, with more spirit than tact, that 'whoever got it, if it proved a boy as she believed it would, he should be Earl of Rutland'.[26]

Lord Roos's reaction was to confide all to his mother, Frances Countess of Rutland, daughter of the first Lord Montagu of Boughton and 'a lady of very great spirit and most exalted passion' (unlike the Earl of Rutland, a mild-mannered man from whom Lord Roos seemed to have inherited his desire for a quiet life). Already the Countess had noted how little 'kindness' Lady Anne showed to her husband at Belvoir and reproved her for it; either for 'want of wit' or out of some archetypal resentment at her mother-in-law's interference, Lady Anne had ignored the warning. Now the Countess took her revenge; grimly she confined the 'great-bellied lady' to her chamber, removing Lady Anne's own attendants and surrounding her with Manners vigilantes, in case Lady Anne tried to fudge the date of the baby's birth in some way, so as to falsify the date of its probable conception.[27]

Lady Anne although confined was not silenced. She managed to get a message of protest to her father the Marquess of Dorchester, describing how she was held prisoner, and feared for her life since the Countess was at the very least threatening to make her miscarry, if not to kill her. Nevertheless in the course of time Lady Anne did give birth safely to a living child. It was a boy just as she had predicted. That of course increased the complication of the situation, since this boy was now the eventual male heir to the earldom of Rutland. (A girl would have had no such inconvenient rights.) So the baby was rapidly baptized Ignoto, a name which left the whole subject of his paternity in abeyance. He was taken from his mother's side by the Countess of Rutland and placed with a poor woman locally to be nursed. Lady Anne herself, after she had recovered from the ordeal of childbirth, was allowed to travel to her father.[28]

In the Marquess of Dorchester, however, Frances Countess of Rutland had found a worthy adversary; she might be celebrated for her 'most exalted passion' but Lord Dorchester was notorious for his fits of irrational bad temper, sometimes accompanied by actual physical violence. In 1638 he had committed an assault within Westminster Abbey itself, and during a service; in 1641 he had been charged for the extremity of his language in the course of a debate in the House of Lords. A servant to Charles I – he had acted as one of his commissioners at the Treaty of Uxbridge – he had eventually come to terms with the Commonwealth regime; but he was back in the Privy Council of Charles II by August 1660.

Lord Dorchester's other claim to the attention of his contemporaries was that he was an amateur chemist. This brought him more ridicule than respect. When someone observed in 1676 that a man of his age was either a fool or a physician, Lord Dorchester – being one for litigation when physical violence would not serve – promptly brought an action of *scandalum magnatum* against him.

When Lord Dorchester received notification of his daughter's treatment at the hands of her husband and her family, he rushed into action. First he challenged Lord Roos to a duel, and when this was refused, an exchange of letters took place, subsequently published. Their tone was not temperate. Lord Dorchester referred to Lord Roos's 'Sottish and Clownish paper', written no doubt in one of his drunken fits, and charged him with cowardice as well: 'If I may see miracle, you with a Sword in your hand ... but if it was a bottle, none would be more forward.'[29]

Lord Roos for his part excoriated gleefully on the subject of

Lord Dorchester's chemical experiments: 'Sir, sure you were among your gallypots and glisterpipes, when you gave your choler so violent a purge, to the fouling of so much innocent paper, and your own reputation (if you had any, which the wise very much doubt)!' As for his own drunkenness, Lord Roos grandly dismissed it: how harmless were these 'Tertian fits of mine, which are easily cured with a little sleep' compared to Lord Dorchester's evident dottiness. (To this Lord Dorchester replied that they were not Tertian but Quotidian, daily.) In general Lord Roos sneered at his father-in-law for his challenge: 'If by your threatening to ram your sword down my throat you do not mean your pills, the worst is past and I am safe enough.'[30]

Lord Dorchester's next action was to appeal to the King. He wanted to see justice done not only to little Ignoto, still kept from the care of the only parent who was undoubtedly his, but also to his daughter in whose innocence the indignant Lord Dorchester continued to believe. He still believed in it following the hearing in front of Charles II at which some very dubious evidence of Lady Anne's conduct was produced. As well as Lady Anne, the Countess of Rutland and a host of other ladies appeared at the hearing, but there were 'so many indecent and uncleanly particulars' given, that many of the latter had to leave.[31]

A good deal of the evidence came from servants who sometimes contradicted indiscreet statements they were supposed to have made previously. Had Lord Roos ever said that 'although he lay not with his wife [at night], he did in the day? Had Lord Roos ever observed that if only Lady Anne had arrived three weeks sooner or stayed three weeks longer 'then he would have owned the child'? Both these remarks were now denied by the men who were supposed to have passed them on.[32]

Despite all this washing of dirty linen, at the end of the hearings Charles II 'left it as he found it'. He refused to pronounce on the guilt of Lady Roos or the parentage of Ignoto. That is to say, although Lady Roos had clearly made some very rash statements to her husband, the King could not be sure that they had not been made out of a desire to provoke his jealousy (and thus perhaps secure that appropriate affectionate response which

Lord Roos had hitherto been so laggard in making). 'He doth not find ground whereon to make judgement to condemn the lady.' On the other hand Charles II, a worldly man, could see that there was absolutely no question of a further reconciliation. He therefore suggested a separation, and a proper settlement by which the Rooses could live peacefully asunder. As for the child, that 'might be placed in the hands of some third person to be agreed on both sides, to prevent the apprehensions of either parties'. The King's last word on the subject was that if this tactful solution was not accepted, then there would have to be recourse to the law.[33]

Lord Dorchester interpreted this decision as a triumph. He carried Lady Anne home with him, convincing himself that her virtuous life in the future would vindicate her in the eyes of the world, and so that the point should not be missed gave instructions to his steward that the King's document should be read aloud, preferably in churches. As to the child, that should be restored to its mother; or if not to her, at least to someone on whom she could rely. Lady Anne should also be granted an allowance by her husband, and have her portion repaid (although she would relinquish the prospect of a jointure).[34]

Even if Lady Anne had been prepared to conduct herself discreetly as her father hoped, it is difficult to see how the situation could in fact have been resolved as Lord Dorchester and the King desired. There was the question of the boy Ignoto: either he was the legitimate issue of Lord Roos, in which case he stood in line for the earldom of Rutland, or he was not, in which case Lord Roos lacked a male heir, and needed to provide himself with one. Before he could do that, he needed to get rid of his present wife. At first Lord Roos hung on to custody of the boy, saying that 'although the child be not of my begetting, so long as the law reputes it mine, I must and shall keep it'. But this, it is clear, was merely a manoeuvre in order to induce from Lady Anne a confession of the truth. The Earl of Rutland told Lord Dorchester that his son 'knows best that the child is none of his'; once Lady Anne had admitted to the King what she had already confessed to her husband, then she could have the child and do what she liked with it. Money was another matter: the Rutland family certainly did not take the line of Lord Dorchester that Lady Anne's portion should be restored to her father despite her behaviour. As for an allowance, 'I will give none but what the law determines', declared Lord Roos. And then he required the vital confession first.[35]

The first of a long series of legal proceedings to get rid of Lady Anne Roos was instituted in the House of Lords by the Rutland family. Lord Dorchester was said to be quite exasperated by their attitude, which combined the mercenary and the moral: why should he relinquish any part of his estate, i.e. the money that had constituted her dowry, to make up for 'the miscarriages of his daughter'?[36] Implicitly the Rutland family was fining Lord Dorchester for having sold them a bad bargain in the shape of Lady Anne in the first place.

Unfortunately Lord Dorchester's faith in his daughter's virtue was not justified. Lady Anne, growing bored with a discreet but dull existence under her father's roof, fled from his protection. Reverting to her former defiant ways, she led a life which became a public scandal. (Given her situation, one has to admire her courage if not her morals; or perhaps it was sheer miscalculation, based on her original contempt for her husband, which induced her to take such risks.) At some point she secured custody of Ignoto and she also gave birth to another child, also a son. These two boys went through life known as John and Charles Manners respectively, the family name of the man who was still in the early 1660s their legal father.[37]

Lady Anne's behaviour disgusted and infuriated Lord Dorchester. In one of those sudden volte-faces to which this passionate and peppery man was prone, he abandoned her cause altogether. He flung himself urgently on the side of the Rutland family and was henceforth prominent among his daughter's attackers. It was certainly bad luck for Lady Anne that as well as having an inadequate husband, she was also saddled with a half-crazy father. Supposing as we must that she had inherited her own share of instability from Lord Dorchester, it was also bad luck that it manifested itself in her reckless sexuality; so much less socially permissible in a woman than violent arguments and ridiculous chemical experiments in a man.

At this point a divorce from bed and board was secured in the ecclesiastical courts, on the grounds of Lady Anne's adultery, without too much difficulty. The next step was to illegitimate Lady Anne's sons and any other children she might bear. This needed an Act of Parliament and a Bill was duly prepared relating details of Lady Anne's 'foul carriage' in full. This Bill was given its first reading in October 1666.

By this time Lady Anne herself had retreated to Ireland, When the Bill to illegitimate the children came to have its second reading in the House of Lords in November 1666, Lady Anne was summoned 'at the last place of her abode that can be discovered', but failed to appear.[38] The Bill seemed all set to go through when suddenly the ancient quarrel concerning the Roos title blew up again.

The Duke of Buckingham complained that the language of the Bill was prejudicial to his own claim to the Roos title. Lord Dorchester, now a fierce Roos partisan, first insulted Buckingham and then had a physical fight with him in the Painted Chamber (although he was nearly twenty years his senior). In the course of this Lord Dorchester had his periwig pulled off and the Duke had a handful of his hair pulled out. Both the fuming peers were clapped into the Tower to cool off, and only released on petitions of apology. The question of the Roos title was not so easily settled. The committee could not find a way of satisfying both parties, and the Bill as a result got further delayed.[39]

It was not until 8 February 1667 that the Act making the children of Lord Roos illegitimate finally received the royal assent.[40] In the meantime, in late January, the active Rutland family had seen to it that no trouble was experienced with the Bill in the House of Commons: no fewer than forty-six Members were entertained at their expense to a dinner at the Dog Tavern, and although Lord Roos himself had a fit of colic and had to rush away (festivities do not seem to have been his strong point), the Members stayed on. Then, 'as soon as they had dined, we carried them to the House of Commons', where the Bill was passed without amendments.[41]

As for the debated Roos title, that matter was not finally settled for a further 200 years.† The Duke of Buckingham died in 1687 leaving no children of either sex; as a result the ancient barony of Roos or de Ros (which could pass through the female line) fell into abeyance between the descendants of his aunts; to one of these the barony was allowed in 1806. On the other hand the Earls and later Dukes of Rutland were permitted to bear the Roos title by both Parliament and sovereign until the late nineteenth century when it was quietly dropped.[42]

Lord Roos was now once more in the happy position as it seemed to him, of being without a legal heir. He was also separated from Lady Anne in the ecclesiastical courts. But the enormous hurdle of the divorce *a vinculo matrimonii* remained to be cleared. Even assuming that this type of divorce was secured by Act of Parliament, it was still by no means clear at this date that Lord Roos would be able to remarry in such a way that the offspring of such a second marriage would be unquestionably legitimate. And that after all was the whole object of the exercise. What point was there in dragging the family name through Parliament to obtain an expensive and controversial divorce if at the end of the day Lord Roos was simply free from Lady Anne? In most senses he was free from her already and he was certainly free from the presumptuous claims of her cuckoo sons. From the point of view of the Rutland family then, the Roos case in Parliament was entirely about remarriage, not divorce.

It was also in the nature of a test case, in quite a different respect. By the late 1660s hopes that Catherine of Braganza, the Portuguese wife of Charles II, would bear a living child were fading (she had suffered two miscarriages). The King however already had a large brood of illegitimate children, and was clearly capable of begetting a great many more (in fact several of his

---

†Today both titles are still represented in the ranks of the peerage: there is a Baroness de Ros (for the ancient barony is currently held by a woman) and Baron Roos of Belvoir is among the titles held by the Duke of Rutland; this new barony being created in 1896.

bastards were born in the 1670s). One way to solve the problem of the royal succession – his brother James Duke of York, already suspected of Catholic sympathies, was heir presumptive to the throne – would be for the King to divorce Queen Catherine and marry again. There is evidence that Charles II did at least passingly consider this solution; he certainly paid keen attention to the debates over the Roos case in the House of Lords, attending them sedulously, and observing in one of his characteristic asides that the whole thing was as good as a play. Once again, it was the question of the legitimacy of the children of a second marriage which obsessed the monarch: heirs to the throne of dubious legitimacy threatening a national disaster where for the Earls of Rutland it was merely a personal misfortune.

There were other interests at stake. Lords Anglesey and Ashley (the latter soon to be created Earl of Shaftesbury), whose sons had married Lord Roos's two sisters, 'drove in on the bill'; it was not in their sons' best interests that Lord Roos should be allowed to remarry, since if he could not both their wives were potential beneficiaries. Lord Castleton took the opportunity to demand a fourth part of the lands settled on his mother, sister to the Earl of Rutland, but later withdrew the claim.[43]

Remarriage then was the issue for most of the interested parties – most but not all. For Lady Anne Roos the issue was quite different: it was the uncomfortable issue of money, her money, her very livelihood. In February 1668 Lady Anne brought her own petition to the House of Lords stating that she had not received a penny from Lord Roos for four years and was thus destitute, yet she had brought a great fortune to Lord Roos on her marriage. None of this was now allowed to her, and she could not dispose of her own estate during Lord Roos's lifetime. Thus she was daily in danger of being arrested for debts, some of which had been contracted while she still lived with her husband. It was this dire state of poverty, she explained, which had caused her to flee to Ireland 'that her friends and relations might not be eye-witnesses of her misery'. While in Ireland she had been unable to travel to England to vindicate her honour. (Rumour said that Lady Anne had in fact travelled to Ireland with her lover; probably both stories were true.) Lady Anne implored Lord Roos to pay her reasonable debts, to give her yearly maintenance in proportion to the dowry she had brought with her, and enable her to dispose of her own estate so that she could support her children and keep them and her out of gaol.[44]

In the spring of 1670 a Roos Bill – for divorce – was once more before Parliament, and in society provided the main topic of conversation. Much turned on the precise interpretation to be given to various texts in the New Testament. The most favourable were those of St Matthew, in particular that verse where Jesus declared that 'whosoever shall put away his wife, except it be for fornication, and shall marry another, committeth adultery' – for this could be held to justify remarriage when fornication had been the cause of separation. (The versions given by St Mark and St Luke were less susceptible of such a favourable interpretation: 'Whosoever shall put away his wife, and marry another, committeth adultery against her'.) Then the various precedents were discussed, the most often quoted being that of the Marquess of Northampton in the reign of Edward VI. After his first wife had been put away for adultery, he had married 'the good and virtuous' Lady Elizabeth, daughter of Lord Cobham; the children of this marriage had been legitimated.[45]

On the second reading of the Bill, Lady Anne was once more called to the House of Lords. This time she did appear and had her petition for maintenance read. At the same time she was asked what she said to 'the scandals' laid upon her by Frances Countess of Rutland. Lady Anne's answer concerned money not morals: her petition she said was no scandal, as she hoped to prove if she had liberty of appeal. She asked to have counsel to speak for her. Lady Anne then left and the House considered the matter. However when Lady Anne was recalled the answer came back that 'she was gone'.[46] There is no evidence that she ever did get her portion returned – particularly in view of the hostility of her father – while her peripatetic way of life indicates that her debts continued to plague her. So Lady Anne ended by being penalized financially for her immoral behaviour; a development which was not exactly planned, but not disagreeable to society either.

As for the Marquess of Dorchester, he stood up in the House of Lords and publicly gave his assent to the Bill because of the 'foul blemish' done by his daughter to her husband; while the Earl of Rutland spoke eloquently of Lord Roos being the 'sole heir male' to the ancient Manners family, with whom the honour must expire if he was not allowed to marry – and procreate – again. Lord Rutland's appeal fell on receptive ears in the Lords. There was general compassion for his family's plight and general indignation that an 'impudent woman' should have brought it about. Although some peers still queried the important precedent which was being set, and the Duke of Buckingham continued to fuss about the use of his own title in the Bill, finally it passed through Lords and Commons.

On 1 March Lord Roos felt confident enough to spend 1s 10d on 'Fagotts' for a bonfire 'at the good accord of the King and the House of Parliament'. On 11 April 1670 the Bill for a *divortium a vinculo matrimonii* received the royal assent (although the Duke of Buckingham succeeded in getting the actual title of Roos left out of it).[47]

The decision created a sensation and was much discussed, often with a sense of unease. Although public sympathy lay with the injured and innocent Lord Roos, the words of the New Testament, especially those of St Mark and St Luke, had to be explained away. A pamphlet printed afterwards of a discussion between 'a clergyman' and 'a private gentleman' stressed St Matthew's text; of the Early Fathers, St Jerome had supported the view that a man could put away his wife for fornication; certain early councils of the church had allowed remarriage. All of this was less convincing than the robust practical statement at the end of the pamphlet that if a man were not allowed to remarry he were 'to be put into a kind of Matrimonial Purgatory, and be rendered thereby incapable to enjoy, either the advantages of a married one, or the freedom of a single man.'[48]

It was to free Lord Roos from the 'Matrimonial Purgatory' into which the wanton behaviour of Lady Anne had cast him that the whole cumbersome long-drawn-out process of the law, lasting one way and another for nearly ten years, had had to be invoked.

As might have been predicted, it was not long before Lord Roos, freed from his purgatory, essayed again those delights of heaven – would that they might not prove once more the torments of hell – promised by marriage. He had in fact been a target for matchmakers for some years, who laid contingency plans just in case this rich prize became available. In 1671 he married Lady Diana Bruce. The choice, out of all the girls in England, was an unlucky one; the next year she died in childbirth, and the child, a boy, died too. (The payment for embalming the body of the second Lady Roos appears in the family papers shortly after that joyous expenditure of 1s 10d on faggots for a bonfire to celebrate freedom from the first.)[49]

Eighteen months later Lord Roos married again: the new bride was Catherine Noel, daughter of Viscount Campden. A son John was born in 1676, who bore in his turn the controversial title of Lord Roos when his father succeeded to the earldom of Rutland three years later. So the Manners succession was secure; too late however for Lord Roos's mother – Frances Countess of Rutland had lived to see her son's divorce pass through Parliament but died a year later.

John, ninth Earl of Rutland, a prominent supporter of William III, was in his later years also famous for his dislike of the town of London; no doubt his early traumatic experiences with Lady Anne had inculcated this loathing. Mainly at Belvoir, he lived till 1711. As for Lady Anne, she was dead before January 1697. She too married again – a Mr Vaughan, about whom little is known except the fact that he was wounded in a duel by the boorish seventh Earl of Pembroke in 1677. John and Charles Manners were still living in 1699, but beyond that vanish from the pages of history.[50] The end of their lives is Ignoto – unknown – as once John Manners's name had been.

Yet the trail of the Roos scandal was not totally obliterated, even in the next generation. If we return to Rachel Lady Russell, that 'bright example to a brittle age', we find that one of her primary aims in her dutiful widowed years was the splendid mating of her two daughters, another Rachel, and Katherine, as well as the care of her son Wriothesley. Rachel – little Rachel, she who had sung in bed and talked of Papa at 'Wobee' – was just fourteen when she married Lord Cavendish, heir to the Earl of Devonshire. Where Katherine Russell was concerned, the most eligible bridegroom in England in the early 1690s (other than her younger brother Wriothesley) was none other than John Lord Roos, offspring of his father's third and fortunate marriage to Catherine Noel.

Once again, as with the union of that other Lord Roos and Lady Anne Pierrepont nearly forty years earlier, everything seemed set fair for the match. John Earl of Rutland, as a Whig, was likely to look upon the daughter of the martyred Lord Russell with sympathy, and the Russells were likely to regard him with similar benevolence. There was a family connection: Catherine Countess of Rutland, born a Noel, was related by marriage to Rachel Lady Russell's 'sister Noel'. As for Katherine Russell herself, she was said to be 'of a sweet temper', had had a suitable education for her position, would be a good manageress, and 'wanted no wit':[51] in short, the ideal daughter-in-law. Nothing was known to the discredit of the young Lord Roos (he was the same age as his intended bride) and a great deal to his credit, including those vast Midland possessions he must one day inherit.

All the same Rachel Lady Russell hesitated. Twenty years later the memory of that frightful decade of scandal and divorce centred on the name of Roos had not utterly faded; besides there were those awkward Manners sons to be remembered, barred from the honours and the estates, but still in themselves constituting a reminder of those ugly days.

In the end, wise woman that she was, Lady Russell decided that it was wrong to avoid 'the best match in England for an imaginary religious scruple'. In characteristic fashion, she managed to sound a note which was both high-minded and worldly. 'If a divorce is lawful', she wrote, 'as agreeing with the word of God, I take a marriage after it certainly to be so. And as for the estate, as we enjoy that by man's law, and that man can alter, and so may alter again, which is a risk I am willing to run, if there should be enough left.'[52]

So John Lord Roos and Katherine Russell, both still just under seventeen, were married in August 1693. The wedding took place at Woburn Abbey. Afterwards the bridal pair made a triumphal progress to Belvoir Castle, something more like the journey of young sovereigns through their own country, than that of a bride and groom going to his father's house. The High Sheriff paid his respects at Harborough. As they approached Belvoir, thousands of people began huzza-ing. At the gates of the castle were to be found twenty-four fiddlers and twenty-four trumpeters. A magnificent banquet was followed by a visit of the bridal pair to the Great Hall where a vast cistern full of wine had been established. Healths were drunk – first in spoonfuls, then in cupfuls; after an hour the level of the cistern had hardly dropped an inch. After that the healths were drunk in great tankards.[53] The celebrations were in short even more magnificent than those which had heralded the arrival of Lady Anne Pierrepont into the Manners fold in 1658.

Rachel Lady Russell herself had to imagine the spectacle of her daughter's apotheosis since her eyesight was by now very bad; she followed to Belvoir more slowly and in some discomfort. Ultimately however, it was a great source of satisfaction to her that all three titles with which she was associated, Bedford, Devonshire and Rutland, were transformed into dukedoms. Bedford – her father-in-law – and Devonshire – her son-in-law – were created dukes in 1695. Transforming the earldom of Rutland into a dukedom took a little more time in view of John, ninth Earl of Rutland's obstinate dislike of London; despite Rachel's pleas he refused to attend the coronation of Queen Anne, the perfect opportunity for securing such titular advancement. Finally in 1703 John Manners, formerly the unhappy cuckolded Lord Roos, was made the first Duke of Rutland. His story had ended happily after all.

The story ended happily in another way. It had been written into Katherine Russell's marriage contract – oh shades of the past! – that she would forfeit her jointure 'if ever she lived in town without his [her husband's] consent'.[14] So amiable, so diligent and so virtuous did this Lady Roos prove herself that eventually her father-in-law relaxed the prohibition. When in 1711 Katherine died giving birth to her sixth child at the age of thirty-five not only Rachel Lady Russell but all her adopted family were cast into despair. It was appropriate that where woman's reputation was concerned, the ghost of the wanton and 'impudent' Lady Anne Roos should be finally laid by the daughter of the noble Rachel Lady Russell; for the one was the classic villainess, the other the classic heroine of the age in which they lived.

CHAPTER SIXTEEN

Benefiting by Accomplishments

'It is no ambitious design of gaining a Name in print
…that put me on this bold undertaking; but the mere
pity I have entertained for such Ladies, Gentlewomen
and others, as have not received the benefits of the tithe
of the ensuing accomplishments.'

HANNAH WOOLLEY, *The Gentlewomans Companion*, 1675

What other course than marriage was open to the gently bred but dowerless female of post-Restoration society? Hannah Woolley, in a book of domestic conduct, addressed herself to those 'many Gentlewomen forced to serve, whose Parents and Friends have been impoverished by the late Calamities, viz., the late Wars, Plague and Fire' (she was writing in the 1670s). Let them forget their glorious past! 'If your Father hath had large Revenues, and could talk loudly of his Birth, and so [you] may think this servile life beneath you, yet thank God you can do something for an honest livelihood, and be never the less submissive.'[1]

What Hannah Woolley meant was that virtually the only respectable profession open to such a relict was that of 'gentlewoman' or waiting-woman to another more prosperous female. A natural chameleon, such an attendant took on the worldly colouring of her employer: thus her status varied considerably, and was not necessarily debased. At the highest level a gentlewoman, acting as a companion, confidante or what would now be termed personal secretary to a great lady, enjoyed a powerful and protected position which had little of the menial about it; as Mrs Wall, confidential servant to the King's French mistress

Louise de la Kéroualle, Duchess of Portsmouth, exercised her own form of petticoat patronage.[2]

In all cases however, intimacy was the rule not the exception. Sighing over Dorothy Sidney, before the war, Edmund Waller took the trouble to apostrophize her waiting-woman Mrs Brangton:

> You the soft season know when best her mind
> May be to pity, or to love, inclined.

Margaret Duchess of Newcastle dedicated her *CCXI Sociable Letters* to 'her friend and former maid' Mrs Elizabeth Topp. Dorothy Osborne had her 'sweet jewel' Jane Wright, daughter of Sir Peter Osborne's bailiff on the island of Guernsey (her sister Maria seems to have married the local rector at Chicksands, an example of delicate upward mobility).[3]

The female correspondence of the time bears witness to the existence of many such 'sweet jewels'. One who proved not quite so delightfully precious was the gentlewoman named merely as 'B–' by Evelyn, describing the testamentary letter of Margaret Godolphin. 'B–' (presumably Beck, her chief maid) was, it is true, to receive the princely sum of £100 from Sidney Godolphin; but this was merely a charitable endowment to enable her to live without employment at her father's house, since no one else would endure her lack of 'good service' with as much patience as had Margaret Godolphin.[4]

Very often the chosen companion would be some form of family connection, a poor relation perhaps, as in the case of 'Cousin Henderson' the intelligent and resourceful kinswoman of Bess Countess of Dysart, subsequently Duchess of Lauderdale. First Cousin Henderson instructed the young Bess Murray (she was the only child of Charles I's faithful servant William Murray, created Earl of Dysart, from whom Bess eventually inherited the title in her own right). Then Cousin Henderson settled down with Bess on her first marriage to Sir Lionel Tollemache, helping her with her business affairs – Cousin Henderson remaining a great deal more literate than her pupil. Finally when Bess's numerous Tollemache progeny began to create those problems in adolescence and later which multiplicity does nothing to alleviate, Cousin Henderson found herself with fresh responsibilities: when young William Tollemache, for example, got into trouble for killing a man in a duel in Paris, it was Cousin Henderson who went over to France to rescue William from the consequence of his rashness.[5]

The ultimate triumph of the poor relation in the guise of gentlewoman was however that of Abigail Hill, better known to history as Mrs Masham. Abigail Hill was the famous favourite who succeeded in supplanting Sarah Duchess of Marlborough in the affections of Queen Anne with disastrous political consequences for the Whigs. In fact the two women – Sarah Jennings, later Duchess of Marlborough, and Abigail Hill – were first cousins, and the ousted Sarah's furious claim that she had raised Abigail from 'a broom' had a great deal of substance to it.[6] Abigail's first appointment occurred before the Queen's accession, her father having been a merchant who ruined himself with unfortunate speculations. Sarah, hearing that she had a relative living in penury, secured for Abigail the post of Bedchamberwoman to the then Princess Anne; Abigail's sister Alice was subsequently made laundress to the Princess's son, the little Duke of Gloucester.

Even then, Abigail's appointment was not made without some awkwardness, since it was known that Abigail had been working as a domestic servant in the household of Lady Rivers (an awkward example of downward mobility), and this would normally have ruled her out from the position of Bedchamberwoman to a Princess, where the work was, as we shall see, menial enough but the public prestige considerable. In principle a Bedchamberwoman had to display respectable antecedents, even if she was spared the haughty standards of a Lady of the Bedchamber: no one below the rank of an earl's daughter was considered.

Abigail was saved by the fact that none of the other members of the Princess's household were 'gentlewomen' – who might be supposed to be contaminated by the arrival of this former domestic servant – except one Mrs Danvers; but she had sacrificed the advantages of her birth by marrying a tradesman.[7] Once appointed, Abigail's duties as Bedchamberwoman included sleeping on the floor of the royal bedroom at night, and emptying the royal slops in the morning. From this – literally – lowly position, Abigail Hill was able to proceed upwards until she had as Queen's favourite achieved the glorious rank of Baroness Masham – Samuel Masham, her husband, being a Groom of the Bedchamber to Prince George of Denmark. The sympathetic approach by which Abigail as Bedchamberwoman was able to win the Queen's confidence stood in contrast to Sarah's natural loftiness of temperament; the attention paid by Abigail to the personal tribulations of the Queen's daily round, and her attempts to alleviate it, was particularly effective where a sick woman was concerned: Queen Anne was plagued with ill health – the consequence of her numerous pregnancies and other cruel afflictions – throughout her reign. This aspect of Abigail's rise, leaving aside her relationship to the Tory Robert Harley, was underlined when Queen Anne hesitated to create Samuel Masham a peer because it was not seemly for a peeress to lie on her floor 'and do several other offices' as Abigail was wont to do; yet Queen Anne was loath to relinquish Abigail's services. In the end a compromise was reached by which Abigail became Lady Masham but she also continued as Woman of the Bedchamber to the Queen.[8]

Thus the career of Abigail Masham stood not only for the triumph of the poor relation, but also for the possibilities of female advancement in the role of personal companion – one area outside marriage where such advancement was to be secured.

Where Abigail Masham emerges triumphant, Paulina Pepys – 'Pall' – the diarist's plain and rather pathetic younger sister, appears as a victim: both of the husband shortage, and of the use of domestic service to cope with the problem of a poor relation. When Samuel Pepys offered to have Pall come and live with him and his wife in London in November 1660, she received his offer with tears of joy; despite the fact that Pepys told Pall quite plainly that he would receive her 'not as a sister in any respect but as a servant'. This was because she had been living with her father in the country, virtually dowerless and with small prospect of finding a husband. Pall arrived the following January, but Pepys, unlike those great ladies such as Lady Sandwich who were graciously inviting their housekeepers to sit down at table with them, was quick to define her position downwards: 'I do not let her sit down at table with me', he noted in his diary with some complacency. 'Which I do at first, that she may not expect it thereafter from me.'[9]

Despite this cutting treatment, Pall was reported as having grown 'proud and idle' by July, and her brother resolved not to keep her.[10] The trouble was that at the same time as Samuel Pepys was trying to define his sister's position downwards (and thus solve the problem of her keep at the smallest expense to himself), his wife Elizabeth was in the process of defining her own position upwards – and since one of the marks of a lady was that she kept a waiting-woman, a waiting-woman was what Mrs Pepys would have. Poor Pall was not really able to fulfil the expectations of either Pepys. One of those unfortunate people, it is clear, who was rendered increasingly disagreeable by adversity, she scarcely added that note of social grace to the establishment desired by Mrs Pepys. Nor was she able to fit easily into the menial position conceived for her by her somewhat callous brother.

Home to the country went Pall. The next time Pepys saw her in October 1662 – still with no husband in view – he found her 'so ill-natured' that he could not love her, and 'so cruel an Hypocrite' that she could cry when she pleased.[11] (While we may accept the fact that Pall was by now thoroughly ill-natured, her tears at her situation were probably quite sincere.)

In the meantime, Elizabeth Pepys's search for the ideal refined attendant or 'woman' as she sometimes simply described her, went on apace; as with her other search for the perfect cook and perfect maid or some combination of the two, it provides one of the most fascinating and long-running of the great domestic dramas of the diary. Admittedly Pepys's particular sexual nature is one of the component parts of the drama: he could not be long close to any pretty young female, without wishing at very least to touch '*ses mamelles*' but such advances were, as we have seen, a recurring problem where female domestics were concerned; gentlewomen were not excepted.

The rise of the idea of the lady, too genteel or too languid or just too ladylike to do her own housework (as opposed to the robust working housewife, whatever her class, of the pre-war period), is amply demonstrated by the gathering domestic ambitions of Mrs Pepys. From a woman who did her own cooking, with the aid of perhaps one servant, she developed into the mistress of the household; one moreover who needed a gentlewoman at her side to sing with her and accompany her to plays. Pepys accurately drew attention to the fact that 'the increase of man's fortune, by being forced to keep more servants ... brings trouble'. At the same time he criticized his wife for not looking neater now she had two servants; and noted that 'want of work' was one of his wife's problems.[12]

The first 'woman' hired was called Gosnell; Pepys hoped that she would make Elizabeth less lonely, and was himself impressed to find that Gosnell had a good singing voice and was 'pretty handsome' (although he did have a dark suspicion that she might have been bred 'with too much liberty' for his household). Convincing himself, however, that Gosnell would cost nothing but her board and her small wages, as well as saving him a great deal of money by occupying his wife at home, Pepys purchased a book of country dances for her arrival.

Gosnell herself had put a different interpretation upon her post. Her singing did please, and she 'dressed' Mrs Pepys, that is, helped her with her toilette and did her hair. (This was beginning to be considered such an arduous job that Betty Verney at about the same date, angrily maidless, said that her arms ached with doing her own hair, and it would be scarcely less exhausting to go out to the plough.) But Gosnell was very put out to find that the Pepyses did not go to the court every week, nor often enough to plays, and she also claimed for herself the 'liberty of going abroad as often as she pleased'.[13] So Gosnell departed – to join certain other moneyless young ladies in another racier world than that of the respectable gentlewoman. With other actresses, we shall meet Gosnell again in the future.

The next suggestion was that Pall should be got back as Mrs Pepys's 'woman'; the economics of it pleasing Pepys, who did not like, as he put it, to spend money on a stranger when he could spend it on his sister. However, the girl who actually filled the position was called Mary Ashwell, a teacher from one of the fashionable Chelsea girls' schools who had the merit of singing well, dancing charmingly after dinner, and being in all respects 'a merry jade'. Too merry perhaps – she got into trouble with Mrs Pepys over a ribbon which had or had not been stolen, and eventually went back to teaching, finding the duties of a 'woman' insufficiently stimulating and wanting a place 'where she might teach children, because of keeping herself in use of what things she had learned, which she doth not here or will there, but only dressing …'.[14]

Meanwhile the exiled Pall still wept. In the summer of 1664 she pleaded to be allowed to return to London to improve her chance of acquiring a husband; even Pepys had to concede that there was a danger in leaving her in the country to grow steadily older 'till nobody will have her' – then she would be 'flung upon' his hands for good. But now Mrs Pepys had set her heart on another symbol of gentility – a French maid; for along with French fashions, French songs, French dances, French wines and French cooking, French attendants had become the rage, as the returning cavaliers imported the civilized delights of their country of exile. (As a result, the absurd use of French by ladies of fashion was to be much mocked in Restoration plays. 'Affected? *Moi?*', exclaims Lady Fancyfull in Vanbrugh's *The Provok'd Wife*.) When this plan foundered, Mary Mercer was procured: a 'decayed' or ruined merchant's daughter, one of the newly poor, like Abigail Masham. For all Mercer's skill at the viol, however, there was soon trouble when Pepys was seen to pay too much attention to Mercer at table.[15] Mercer departed.

At least Mrs Pepys was beginning to see reason on the subject of Pall's dowry (the alternative of housing Pall was grimmer): in October 1665 she agreed that Pall should have £400, despite the fact that times were hard. As for Pepys, a mere three days after a certain Philip Harman's wife died in childbirth, Pepys was considering him as a bridegroom for Pall. With this in view, Pall was allowed up to London to be 'fashioned'. At the age of twenty-five, Pepys assessed her appearance as follows: even though she was 'full of freckles and not handsome in face, she was at least pretty good-bodied ... and not over thick ...' With the possibility of a portion to back up these charms, Pall also acquired another two suitors, even if one of them was 'drunken, ill-favoured and ill-bred'.[16]

Neither of these problems – Mrs Pepys's desire for a gentlewoman and Pall's desire for a husband – were however destined for immediate solution. It was not until 1668 that Pall, now aged twenty-seven, was finally married off to one John Jackson of Ellington in Huntingdonshire, a man with little to say for himself and of plain appearance, but a husband for all that. Pepys's relief was profound; there had been some desperate moments when he feared he would never find her a husband before she had grown 'old and ugly'. To his diary he confided that he could not love Pall, because she was so 'cunning and ill-natured'. However, her appearance improved on marriage, although she remained 'mighty pert'.[17]

As for Mrs Pepys, she heard of a very fine lady who would replace Mercer for £20 a year, able to sing, dance and play on four or five instruments; but this paragon proved on inspection to be 'tawdry' and was in fact perfectly prepared to come for £8. (The genteel importance of the role of gentlewoman is underlined by the fact that even a 'tawdry' one might command more than twice a maid's annual wage.) Under the circumstances Mrs Pepys preferred a girl called Barker; £7 or £8 was laid out on clothes for her by Pepys himself. Barker was 'very plain' but had good connections and a fine singing voice, two at least of the qualifications of a suitable gentlewoman. Barker duly accompanied Mrs Pepys on visits and learned part songs but proved to be a trouble-maker in the household. Her departure in May 1667 occurred when she was discovered to have been 'abroad' without permission and lied about it, so that Mrs Pepys found herself obliged to strike her.

Barker had one persistent complaint: she 'did always declare to her mistress and others that she had rather be put to drudgery and to wash the house than to live as she did, like a gentlewoman'. Pepys found this strange. Yet Barker's outburst explains what a strain might be imposed upon an employee when her mere presence was expected to bestow social prestige upon a household – 'qualities of honour or pleasure' as Pepys put it, while complaining that Barker had failed to provide them.[18] Like any equivocal role, that of gentlewoman could result in a failure of expectations on both sides.

So the way was cleared for the arrival of Pepys's great love, Deb Willet: a witness to the equivocal nature of the role (as had been in their different ways Pall, Gosnell, Ashwell, Mercer and Barker) but in yet another sense. At the beginning Deb only represented yet another attempt to find a suitable companion for Mrs Pepys; this time a mere child was chosen, the Pepyses hoping, no doubt, to avoid the independence of Gosnell and Barker. Deb had been at 'the school at Bow' for seven or eight years, and was said to be a model of good deportment. Mrs Pepys returned from a visit of inspection, reporting that Deb was 'very handsome'. Pepys regarded this as good news about the prospective companion: 'at least, that if we must have one, she should be handsome'. Alas, the handsomeness of Deb was his – and ultimately her – undoing. In vain she performed such duties as accompanying Mrs Pepys to the theatre, dancing and playing cards with admirable gravity and modesty. Her good looks aroused the passionate jealousy of Mrs Pepys, a jealousy which was certainly not without foundation, since Pepys, finding himself quite unable to resist the perpetual physical proximity of Deb, had embarked on a series of daring amorous explorations.

One night after supper in October 1668 occurred an incident which in Pepys's words' 'occasioned the greatest sorrow to me that ever I knew in the world'. Deb was combing her master's hair – not in itself a proof of intimacy, since this hygienic duty was usually performed by maids. Unfortunately Mrs Pepys, arriving suddenly upon the scene, 'did find me embracing the girl con my hand sub su coats; and endeed, I was with my main in her cunny'. It was impossible even for Pepys to gloss over such a flagrant discovery (although he tried). There was a violent scene; the episode led in the end to Deb's dismissal. Pepys, full of 'love and Pity' for her, accepted her departure with anguish; he also warned Deb solemnly against allowing anyone else to take those same liberties to which he had so freely helped himself.[19]

Hannah Woolley, author of several books on domestic practice and conduct under the name of her first husband, wrote out of her own experience. She was born in 1623 (her maiden name is unknown), learning 'Physick and Chirurgery' from her mother and elder sisters, but was early on left an orphan. However, before she was fifteen, she was entrusted to keep a little school of her own, by dint of her exceptional 'accomplishments'.[20] Hannah Woolley lists these (note the relatively low position of writing and arithmetic):

> Needlework of very different sorts
> Bugle-work
> Framing pictures
> Setting out of Banquets
> Making salves and ornaments
> All manner of Cookery
> Writing and Arithmetic
> Sweet powders for hair, or linen

At the age of seventeen she was enabled by these same accomplishments plus the additional asset of speaking Italian and playing several musical instruments to attract a 'Noble Lady Patron' who took her into her household to act as governess to her daughter. This lady taught her further 'Preserving and Cooking', introduced her to court and kept her for seven years until the children had all grown up.

The original role of governess developed into something more consequential. As Hannah put it: 'Time and my Lady's good opinion of me constituted me afterwards her Woman, her Stewardess, and her Scribe or Secretary. By which means I appear'd as a person of no mean authority in the Family.' Hannah was proud of the fact that she read aloud daily to her employer poems, plays and romances (for which she had to learn French, one accomplishment hitherto lacking); she also took great trouble with the letters which she wrote for her.

At the age of twenty-four, Hannah married the master of a Free School at Newport Pond, Essex, by whom she bore four sons, as well as taking in boarders to her school. The Woolleys then moved to Hackney, the centre of genteel education at the time, where they kept over sixty boarders. Mr Woolley died about the time of the Restoration, but in 1666 Hannah married for the second time, one Francis Challinor, a widower of about forty-five. In 1674 she was to be found living in the house of her son Richard in London near the Old Bailey – as a Master of Arts and Reader at St Martin's, Ludgate, he constituted an advertisement for an intelligent mother – and she was probably still alive ten years later.[21]

Hannah Woolley began writing at the time of her first widow-hood, presumably in order to support herself. Unfortunately she found herself enduring some of the less attractive aspects of an author's career: one rogue publisher had her proofs revised by a different hand and another did not pay her. The book in question was *The Gentlewomans Companion*, and Hannah later issued a supplement to her second book, *The Queen-like Closet*, to correct the record. Her first books were however centred on the purely domestic arts; such as *The Ladies Directory in choice experiments and curiosities of Preserving and Candying both Fruits and Flowers*, printed in 1661. She moved on to issues of social behaviour, and later related details of her own life story, in order to enable other women to survive as she herself had done. Apologizing for the personal details, she explained that she had been prompted to write by 'the mere pity I have entertained for such Ladies, Gentlewomen and others, as have not received the benefits of the tithe of the ensuing accomplishments'.[22] It was to her knowledge of these vital arts and artifices as listed above, as well as to her ability to write and add up, that Hannah Woolley firmly ascribed her own survival.

So that while Hannah Woolley wrote with the traditional and understandable bitterness of the female educationalist about the preference shown to boys – parents cared for the 'barren Noddles of their Sons', sending them to university, while the fertile ground of their daughters' brains was allowed to go fallow – she did not herself ask for university education for women, or indeed anything like it.

Hannah Woolley complained indeed about the decline of standards of education among her own sex: 'Most in this depraved later Age think a Woman Learned and Wife enough if she can distinguish her Husband's bed from another's' was one of her gibes. She criticized the men who looked upon women merely as instruments to propagate their families, and were not interested in their minds. She was also, as we have seen, a strong believer in the 'treasury' to be laid up by education, 'by which they [unmarried women] may live without an Estate'. Education would enable such women to gain 'some honest and creditable Employment', she wrote; as a result 'their position will be so established that nothing almost but sickness and death can make an alteration therein'.[23]

But how far, how very far removed were the requirements of Hannah Woolley – based of course on those of society – from that 'modish' Latin and Greek which had once entranced the great ladies at court at the end of the reign of Elizabeth I, or indeed that 'ebri grek and laten' to which Nancy Denton had aspired in the Commonwealth period, to the disgust of Sir Ralph Verney! (See p.170.)

Hannah Woolley put particular emphasis on the art of carving; she had acquired it herself early in life from her 'Noble Lady Patron', and it did of course enable a gentlewoman to exercise public authority over the rest of the household; Hannah gave elaborate hierarchical instructions on how to distribute the best bits in meat and fish (remember that the cod's head was considered a great delicacy). She reminded her gentlewomen that it would appear 'very comely and decent' to use a fork.[24] Her special plea that a gentlewoman should *not* lick her fingers at a meal not only suggests that many people of the period did, but also that a genteel manner at table was more likely to aid an unprotected woman to get on in the world in the reign of Charles II and his successor than all the knowledge which had once filled the august head of Queen Elizabeth I.

The fact that the developing special nature of female education was in itself a restriction was perceived by very few people of either sex at this time. During that period of Puritan revolution when exciting new ideas concerning universal education were promulgated – if not put into practice – by men such as Hartlib, Dury, Petty and Robinson, girls' education received scant attention. Only John Dury's 'Noble School' was adapted to the requirements of both sexes; although girls were intended to become 'good and careful housewives', those capable of learning 'Tongues and Sciences' were to be given encouragement. (Dury may have been influenced by the stern attitude of his wife Dorothy, who wrote a letter to the pious Lady Ranelagh headed 'Of the Education of Girls', attacking the general frivolity.) Hartlib, Winstanley and others were more interested in equipping girls from the lower classes in crafts such as weaving.[25]

One of the few who did appreciate the danger of the divide was Basua Makin. Like Hannah Woolley appalled by the decline in education, Basua Makin, unlike Hannah, was concerned to restore or at least promote the study of Hebrew and the classics. She determined to run a girls' school guided by this principle.

Basua Makin had excellent credentials to found the most fashionable establishment, apart from the fact that she may have been associated with a set of girls' 'schools or colleges' at Putney in 1649, visited by John Evelyn. The sister, as we have seen, of John Pell the learned mathematician (another brother, Thomas Pell, had been Gentleman of the Bedchamber to Charles I), she had a particular claim on the loyalty of the newly Royalist society in that she had been governess to Princess Elizabeth, that sad little sister of Charles II who had died in captivity at Carisbrooke Castle. As a result, this Princess at least had enjoyed an elaborate education including Hebrew as well as Latin and Greek (unlike her aunt and namesake Elizabeth of Bohemia, denied the classics by *her* father, James I, because Latin had the unfortunate effect of making women more 'cunning').

The education afforded to the next generation of Princesses, Mary and Anne, daughters of James II, then Duke of York and heir presumptive to the throne, stood in astonishing contrast. How ironic that Basua Makin's passionate plea of 1673, *An Essay to Revive the Antient Education of Gentle-women, In Religion, Manners, Arts and Tongues. With an Answer to the Objections against this Way of Education*, should be dedicated to Mary, Princess of York, principal among all 'Ingenious and Vertuous Ladies'! For in the upbringing of Mary and her sister Anne, born in 1663 and 1665 respectively, domestic accomplishments were in fact stressed to the exclusion of virtually everything else. Yet these girls, as the children of the heir presumptive, stood in direct line to the throne from the moment of their birth, and in this age of high infant mortality there must always have been a distinct possibility that at least one of them would inherit it.

As a concession to their place in the Stuart family tree, it was thought important that these young Protestant hopes should be able to recite Anglican – as opposed to Catholic – prayers, but otherwise Mary and Anne could be safely abandoned to their favourite pastimes of whist and basset (another card game). Where education was concerned, the Princesses did learn French: Pierre de Laine's French grammar, published in 1667 when she was five, was written for Princess Mary, and a second edition for Princess Anne. Otherwise they were taught to sing and draw and dance (Mary was an especially graceful dancer), but that was the limit of their preparation for life. When Basua Makin wrote in anguish that all young gentlewomen were taught nowadays was 'to frisk and dance, to paint their faces, to curl their hair and put on a whisk'[26] she might have been describing the princesses' own fate.

Tragically late, it seems to have been borne in upon Queen Anne that she was lacking in some of the essential equipment of a monarch; it was said to be 'an unhappiness' to her that she was not much acquainted with English history and the reigns and actions of her predecessors: 'she beginning to apply herself to it but a little while before King William died'. For all these last-minute efforts, Queen Anne as a monarch, with no magisterial co-ruler, no William III at her side, did display a lamentable ignorance of history and geography; while her grammar and spelling were both deplorable. (Only her good grounding in French, that traditional female accomplishment, but also of course the language of diplomacy, was to be admired.)[27]

As for Queen Mary, in effect a consort not a ruler, it was hardly surprising that in adult life she displayed few intellectual ambitions. Instead she concentrated on those gentle pursuits such as 'knotting', bugle-work to make bead bags, crewel-work and other forms of embroidery beloved of well-bred English ladies of her time. These were the refined accomplishments, the study of which Hannah Woolley advocated in order that a gentle-woman would appeal to her mistress: skill in such matters was certainly essential to the ladies surrounding Queen Mary. Celia Fiennes gives a picture of the Queen and her Maids of Honour embroidering away for dear life at Hampton Court.[28] The poet Anne Countess of Winchilsea was aware that she was a scornful exception when she described herself as one who would not participate in such trivially pointless crafts:

> ... In fading silks compose
> Faintly, the inimitable Rose,
> Fill up an ill-drawn Bird, or paint on Glass,
> The Sovereign's blurred and undistinguished face.[29]

To many women, to Mrs Pepys for example, who adopted the new fashionable passion for decorating objects with shell-work, such accomplishments betokened the leisure to have mastered them, and such leisure, like the employment of a gentlewoman, was the outward symbol of their rising social status. In this way amateur music publications rose as amateur singing extended, and the pursuit of painting – ever considered a suitable hobby for a lady – increased too. It was true that in certain rare cases painting might lead to professional employment. But the real motive which inspired a young lady to learn to paint or 'limn' as *The Ladies Dictionary* phrased it in 1694 (where 'limning' headed the list of a lady's permitted recreations, followed by dancing and music and finally reading) was hardly to support herself; it was to bequeath 'rare moments of her ingenuity to posterity'.[30] The moments of her actual ingenuity may have been rare; but the hours of leisure which stretched about them were not. So the lady limner also bequeathed to posterity, along with her creative efforts, the message that she had been gracefully unsullied by any other occupation.

It will be seen that the Princess Mary was indeed an inappropriate dedicatee for Basua Makin's *Essay* of 1673, a work in which she was much concerned to break the tacit embargo by which women were not allowed to study the classical languages. 'Tongues are learnt in order to [learn] things', she cried. As for the old witticism: 'Many say that one tongue is enough for a woman', Basua described that angrily as 'but a quibble upon the word'. Furthermore Basua pleaded for education so that women could 'understand Christ'. She did not suggest that women of 'Low parts' (the poor) should be educated; what she was anxious to do was to break down that dreadful idle way of life common to women in society, by which they learnt when young 'merely to polish their Hands and Feet, to curl their Locks, to dress and trim their Bodies ...' and so were incapable of any finer way of life, including the enrichment of their own souls, when older.[31]

Moreover in her *Essay*, Basua Makin was already toning down considerably her original demands concerning the scope of female education. In 1663 she had called for a curriculum based on that of the celebrated Dutchwoman Anna van Schurman, with whom Basua Makin had kept up a correspondence (in Greek). This included the study of grammar, rhetoric, logic, physics, mathematics, geography, history, and all languages, with Greek and Latin stressed, as well as painting and poetry. Anna van Schurman, the friend of Descartes and Richelieu, as well as the exiled Elizabeth of Bohemia, was another Helena who had been well instructed by her father; the vigour of her intellect equalled its emancipation: 'By what right indeed are certain things alone apportioned to us? Is it God's law or man's?' she wrote. Her influential work appeared in England in translation in 1659 as *The Learned Maid*, in which Anna van Schurman even suggested that women should be able to study the theory of military discipline if they so desired.[32]

In one respect however the great Anna van Schurman was mistaken. Citing the celebrated women of the previous century, such as Queen Elizabeth I and Lady Jane Grey, she supposed Englishwomen to enjoy exceptional freedom. In fact this kind of high-born female concentration on learning and learned discussion, and thus by implication on the preparatory education necessary, was by this period to be found far more widely on the Continent than in England.

Madame de Maintenon, the austere mistress of Louis XIV whom he married privately after his Queen's death, was as keen an advocate of the education of poor girls of good family as Hannah Woolley or Basua Makin, but with a great deal more influence to bring to bear on the subject. She had set up several little schools before the famous school for 250 girls at Saint-Cyr was founded under royal patronage in 1686, Louis XIV taking a keen interest in the details. After the King's death in 1715, Madame de Maintenon chose Saint-Cyr as her own place of retirement.[33]

A passionate interest in female education was not a marked characteristic of any of the mistresses of King Charles II, nor would it be appropriate to regard the King himself as obsessed by this particular aspect of the female development (although he did patronize the education of poor boys, particularly in mathematics, leading to his own pet topic of navigation).[34]

In the end Basua Makin herself was forced to compromise. When she founded her new school at Tottenham High Cross, described as 'four miles out of London on the Ware road', for which the fees were to be £20 a year, she found that it simply was not viable without the inclusion of numerous pretty arts on the syllabus. Basua Makin's new proposition was that half the time was to be spent studying 'Dancing, Music, Singing, Writing and Keeping Accounts', with the other half dedicated to Latin, French, Greek, Hebrew, Italian and Spanish – but those who insisted might 'forbear the languages' and learn only Experimental Philosophy.[35]

Unfortunately most people did wish that their daughters should 'forbear the languages'. The accomplishments which would enable a single woman to survive in the world remained, however, regrettably from the point of view of female learning, those of Hannah Woolley. Where marriage was concerned the same standards prevailed. In vain Basua Makin protested against the contemporary belief that no one would marry an educated woman. Rather desperately she advanced the counter-proposition that learning in a wife was no disadvantage to a husband. Few gentlemen – and thus few parents – of the time would have agreed with her. In vain too Basua Makin denied that she was asking for 'Female Pre-eminence' and pleaded on the contrary that education would help women to understand even better that God had made Man 'the Head'. It was significant that she also denied that education would make women so proud that 'there will be no living with them'. Only in her proposition that since evil had begun with Eve and been propagated by her 'daughters', special care should be taken with their education, did Basua touch some kind of contemporary nerve.[36]

Even so, not many felt that Eve's daughters would be improved by a study of the classics or other serious topics. John Evelyn had his daughter Susanna taught Greek and Latin. Yet to his beloved Margaret Godolphin he gave the advice that she should read the Lives of Plutarch, Cyrus, Seneca, Epictetus, Virgil and Juvenal in English and French – 'More than this unless it be a great deal more, is apt to turn to impertinence and vanity.'[37]

John Locke benefited richly from the friendship of an educated woman: Damaris Cudworth, Lady Masham was the daughter of Ralph Cudworth, Master of Christ's College, Cambridge and Regius Professor of Hebrew (and incidentally the step-mother of Samuel Masham). She was Philoclea to Locke's Damon in a long personal and philosophical correspondence. She also provided him with a comfortable country retreat, despite a professed indifference to what she called 'the Impertinent Concerns of a Mistress of Family', which she assured Locke would never have 'Any place in my Heart; and I can at most do no more than submit to them'. As if in proof of this indifference, Lady Masham wrote two books herself as well as some very long letters indeed; 'you know I cannot write short letters'. It was Locke also who engaged Elizabeth Birch, who could speak Latin and Greek fluently, as governess to Lord Shaftesbury's grandson – another example of paternal encour-agement to learning, for Elizabeth Birch's father had been a schoolmaster. Yet Locke did not believe in the female need to study grammar. Lady Masham, deploring women's lack of real educational attainments in one of her books, put her finger correctly on the reason: 'so few Men...relishing these Accomplishments in a Lady'.[38]

Basua Makin, citing the usual historical stage army of eminent ladies to demonstrate the female's essential worth – Deborah and Hannah, down to Queen Elizabeth 'the Crown of All' – ended on some more recent examples including Rachel Lady Russell and Anne Bradstreet in America. Her reference to Margaret Duchess of Newcastle who 'by her own Genius rather than any timely Instruction, over-tops many grave Grown-Men' was perhaps in danger of destroying her own argument. Her tribute to her own pupil, Lucy Countess of Huntingdon, was more to the point, suggesting she was unique:

> A president for Ladies of this age,
> So noble, humble, modest and so sage;
> For French, Italian, Hebrew, Latin, Greek
> The ornament of our Sex; where may we seek
> Another like her self?[39]

It was generally felt that the rest of Eve's daughters, given

Lady Huntingdon's accomplishments, would sacrifice in modesty what they gained in learning. Better far to take no risks and educate the softer sex more softly.

Although the quality of education declined, the number of girls' schools increased after the Restoration as the middle classes increasingly made use of them. School under these circumstances was a worldly rather than an instructive experience. Of course there were exceptions – the Quaker schools were an exception, as the Quakers were the exception in so many things. There were the Quaker 'women's schools' (after all, if women were to be allowed to speak at Meetings they needed to be educated to do it), and there was also a Quaker co-educational boarding-school at Waltham Abbey, later moved to Edmonton, which George Fox visited in both localities. A Quaker school at Shacklewell in Hertfordshire under Jane Bullock was founded in 1667 on the advice of George Fox, for instructing 'young lasses, and maidens in whatsoever things were useful and civil in creation'; Rachel Fell attended it. There was another Quaker school at Chiswick under Ann Travers. Quakers apart, the overall figures for female literacy itself based on all classes also improved.[40] Nevertheless the ludicrously sketchy nature of lessons learnt in most schools provided the butt for satire in many Restoration plays.

A solemn young female cousin of Oliver Cromwell, born in 1654, who kept a private diary for 'the help of my Memory, concerning the work of God on my Soul, which I desire thankfully to commemorate', was placed by her father at school in London; she recorded that the sparks of religious life were almost extinguished within her as a result of this experience.[41] Little Molly Verney, on the other hand, daughter of Edmund Verney by his poor 'distracted' wife, who was sent to Mrs Priest's school at Chelsea at the age of eight, found there exactly the training she wanted.

She desired to learn to 'Japann', a special course which cost a guinea entrance and about 40s for materials. Edmund was quick to extend the paternal blessing: 'I approve of it; and so I shall of any thing that is Good and Virtuous, therefore learn in God's name all Good Things, and I will willingly be at the Charge so far as I am able – tho' they come from Japan and from never so far and look of an Indian hue and colour, for I admire all accomplishments that will render you considerable and Lovely in the sight of God and man...' But then Molly's fate, as planned by her father, was to be placed in the household of a lady of quality, with her own maid and her board paid, as a kind of finishing process; then she would be married off to a country squire.[42]

Part of the problem was the lack of adequate women teachers to instruct girls in anything remotely taxing, because they themselves had not been so instructed. 'From an Ignoramus that writes, and a Woman that teaches, *Libera nos Domine*' – so ran 'The New Letanie', a satirical jingle of 1647. This was the vicious circle to which Margaret Duchess of Newcastle drew attention: 'women breeding up women; one fool breeding up another; and as long as that custom lasts, there is no hope of amendment', she wrote, castigating the kind of 'ancient decayed gentlewomen' at whose mercy girls found themselves.[43]

At a lower level in society there was a strange lack of interest in the subject, compared to the attention paid to the boys' teachers; women teachers occasionally coming to prominence for some misdemeanour, as one Isabel Reun was presented to the ecclesiastical court at Ely in 1682 for teaching scholars and at the same time keeping company with a man not her husband. The ecclesiastical licensing system which was supposed in theory to concern itself with petty teachers as well as grammar masters does not seem in practice to have concerned itself with women. The tendency towards teaching girls what was immediately economically useful remained: as in the case of the dame of a village school in Sussex in 1699 who put her children to making clothes in school (much as the 'Red Maids' of Bristol were put to embroidery); she contracted out reading and writing lessons, taking a distinctly lower place, to visiting schoolmasters. There is no evidence that Basua Makin herself was licensed as a teacher.[44]

So the girls tripped in dainty slippers down the ornamental

paths of their education; so very different from the demanding
courses of classics and grammar set for their brothers. Whatever
the latter's application (Basua Makin answered the point that girls
did not desire education with the perfectly accurate riposte:
'Neither do many boys'),[45] the intellectual difference between the
two sexes was becoming ever more sharply defined; as the quality
of education offered to boys also improved, the gap only
increased. This had the makings of another vicious circle. A lady
who had received a lightweight education – in the words of Lady
Chudleigh,

> As if we were for nothing else designed
> But made, like puppets, to divert mankind

– such a one was generally only capable of filling her mind with
lightweight matters. Charges of frivolity against the sex were thus
all too easy to substantiate, summed up by Rochester's sneer:

> Love a Woman! you're an Ass
>   'Tis a most insipid passion
> To choose out for your Happiness
>   The silliest part of God's Creation.[46]

At the same time, such outward frivolity, indolence even, became
the mark of a lady, to be aped by those (not only Mrs Pepys) who
aspired to rise higher in society.

The growth of 'frivolity' in this apparently secure and certainly
leisured society following the traumatic period of the wars was
the subject of widespread comment. Halifax gave to his daughter
Betty his own zeugmatic picture of an idle lady of quality,
'wrapped up in Flattery and clean Linen'. Mary Evelyn, John
Evelyn's daughter, gives an amusing picture of the world of the
fashionable – and frivolous – in her *Mundus Muliebris: Or, The
Ladies Dressing-Room Unlock'd*, published after her death in 1690.
Her bedroom would include, in addition to its tea table, cabinets,
screens, trunks and silver plate:

An hanging Shelf, to which belongs
Romances, Plays, and Amorous Songs;
Repeating Clocks, the hour to show
When to the Play 'tis time to go,
In Pompous Coach, or else Sedan'd
With Equipage along the Strand …

Her 'Implements' would include, besides a mirror, 'one Glue Pot, One for Pomatum, and what-not Of Washes, Unguents, and Cosmetics', while of perfumes she would employ orange-water, millefleur and myrtle 'Whole Quarts the Chamber to Bequirtle'. As for the gallant courting this cosseted beauty, he must pursue her to 'the Play, the Park and the Music', even to Tunbridge Wells at the season of drinking the waters: 'You must improve all occasions of celebrating her Shape, and how well the Mode becomes her.'[47]

It was perhaps this kind of life that Rachel Lady Russell had led as a young married woman, haunting the theatre, choosing a church with a short sermon, impatient to reach the fashionable world of the park, and occupying herself with telling her mother-in-law malicious stories; many years afterwards she wrote of her frivolous conduct with regret.[48] But Rachel Lady Russell had to endure exceptional sufferings; most women, not subject to her tragic destiny, were also not subject to her regrets.

It is certainly a picture echoed over and over again in the plays of the period. Victoria and Olivia, daughters of Sir John Everyoung in Sedley's *The Mulberry Garden*, to give only two examples out of many, were said to dance and play at cards 'till morning'; they were described as 'more in their Coach than at home, and if they chance to keep the house an afternoon, to have the Yard full of Sedans, the Hall full of footmen and Pages, and their Chambers covered all with Feathers and Ribands'. In 1712 Addison, parodying the life of a society lady, began his account: 'Wednesday: from eight to ten drank two dishes of chocolate in bed and fell asleep after them exhausted by the effort.'[49]

There were plenty of prototypes in real life; when one reads an account of Ursula Stewkeley, daughter of Cary Verney by her second marriage, it is difficult to suppose these pictures were much exaggerated. This energetic young woman loathed country life and was furious if she could not dance twelve hours out of the twenty-four, and have music whenever she wanted. After eight months of pleasure in London, she returned to her country home in 1674 in the middle of the night, bringing a group of her friends with her, including a certain disreputable Mr Turner, who had been associated with a murder case; this uninvited party then proceeded to sit up till three in the morning loudly roistering. The next day Ursula borrowed a coach and took off for Salisbury races, returning that night with the same merry crew to sit up once more till the early hours of the morning.

'All this has sufficiently vexed me', wrote her mother, with feelings of parental indignation with which it is easy to identify even at a distance of 300 years. But in addition the unwelcome Mr Turner's linen had had to be mended and washed by her household and sent after him to London![50]

The first serious attempt to interest women in higher education as such was that of Mary Astell at the end of the seventeenth century (as opposed to Basua Makin's desperate avowal that she was only preparing women properly for marriage, or such isolated ventures as a sympathetic paper on the subject by the Anglican minister and writer Clement Barksdale in 1675). Mary Astell was born in 1666, to a prominent commercial family in Newcastle-upon-Tyne. Nothing is known about her own education, except that she came late to French; it seems it was her mother's death which brought her down from the north to London.[51] She lived in Chelsea, probably in Swan Walk, and included many of the clever socially prominent women of her time among her friends: Lady Betty Hastings, granddaughter of Lucy Countess of Huntingdon by her only son Theophilus and a tribute to the tradition of intelligent women in that family, was one. But the friendship which provoked Mary Astell into her first proposal for a form of women's college was a bird of a more gorgeous but less respectable feather. This was Hortense Mancini,

Duchesse de Mazarin, ex-mistress of Charles II, a flamboyant woman with the looks of 'a Roman eagle'. She had acceded with pleasure to the advances of Charles II, but had not subsequently managed to stabilize her career, being the subject of numerous scandals, each one leaving her rather worse off than before.[52]

It was Mary Astell's conviction that the 'unhappy Shipwreck' of her friend had been due to 'the dangers of an ill Education and unequal Marriage', the former contributing to the latter. Had Hortense been properly educated, wrote Mary Astell, there would have been a 'right improvement of her Wit and Sense, we should not have found her seeking Relief by such imprudent, not to say Scandalous Methods as the running away in Disguise with a Spruce Cavalier'. Perhaps in her generous assessment Mary Astell had not totally understood the character of her fallen friend; it is possible to argue that as long as there are spruce cavaliers, there will be at least some scandalous elopements. Nevertheless the conclusion which Mary Astell drew was in itself significant. She saw in her 'college' a refuge – an all-female refuge of course – where heiresses could elude the fate of an unwanted marriage, 'decayed' gentlewomen could teach, and daughters without dowries could be educated.[53]

Was there not something about Mary Astell's proposal which came very close to suggesting a kind of teaching convent? Of the sort only available since the Reformation to those Catholic girls like Mary Ward and her colleagues who were sent abroad. Ironically enough, this point was fully appreciated by Mary Astell's contemporaries, but only to denounce her suggested college for this very reason, as being 'Romanist'. Bishop Burnet in particular criticized her design on the grounds that it smacked of popery. It was only towards the end of his life, depressed by the 'ill methods' of the schools and colleges he saw around him, giving 'chief rise to the irregularities of the gentry as the breeding young women to vanity…' and being 'the source of corruption of that sex' that he came to see that Mary Astell had been right all along. 'Something like monasteries without vows would be a glorious design,' wrote the Bishop, 'and might be set on foot as to be the honour of a Queen upon the throne…'[54]

Mary Astell herself was already drawing a distinction between the two different kinds of women. Upon those who loved their 'chains' she poured scorn: 'Let them Housewife or Play, Dress and be entertaining in Company ...', these '*Very* women' as she termed them, whose accomplishments were 'most acceptable to all sorts of Men'. Then there were the other sort, who helped the poor and read pious books, who were accorded the honourable title of '*Good Devout Women*'. Mary Astell did not attack marriage as such, calling it 'the Institution of Heaven, the only Honourable Way of continuing Mankind'; it was however the plight of 'we poor Fatherless Maids and widows' which explicitly concerned her.[55] Yet by her distinction between the '*Very* women', acceptable to men, and those who were not, she helped to promote the notion of the learned lady as one who dwelt on the other side of some great divide; a more than slightly ridiculous figure, when viewed at a distance.

Elizabeth Elstob was that pioneer of Anglo-Saxon studies who had arrived at Oxford unofficially, by courtesy of her brother William's presence there. Described as 'the justly celebrated Saxon nymph', Elizabeth Elstob was responsible for the first Anglo-Saxon grammar, the first critical edition of one of Aelfric's sermons and the first attempt at a complete edition of Aelfric's homilies. With her brother, she formed part of a brilliant group at the university.[56]

Her work of 1709, *An English-Saxon Homily on the Birth-Day of St Gregory*, was dedicated to Queen Anne, hopefully relating her to such figures of history as Bertha the first English Queen, and the British-born Empress Helena. 'I know it will be said, What has a Woman to do with Learning?', she wrote. 'Why therefore should those few among us, who are Lovers of Learning, although no better account cou'd be given of it than its being a Diversion, be denied the Benefit and Pleasure of it, which is both so innocent and so improving? But perhaps most of these Persons mean no more than that it makes them neglect the Theatre, and long sittings at Play, or tedious Dressings, and visiting Days, and other Diversions, which steal away more time than are spent at study.'[57]

William Elstob died prematurely. Whereupon Elizabeth had at once to leave the university town. For many years subsequently she struggled in poverty. When she was trying to found a dame's school at Evesham the distinguished scholar was obliged to issue a nervous apology concerning her lack of certain skills: 'There are some things to be taught in such a school which I cannot pretend to; I mean the two accomplishments of spinning and knitting. Not that I would be thought to be above doing any commendable work proper to my sex', she added hastily. 'And as an instance of the truth of this, the gown I had on when you gave the favour of a visit was part of it my own spinning, and I wear no other stockings but what I knit myself.'[58]

At one point Elizabeth Elstob was to be found 'in her sleeping room, surrounded by books and dirtiness'; one who had 'pursued too much the drug called learning'. This brilliant woman would in the opinion of her contemporaries have enjoyed a happier life if she had pursued instead the two accomplishments of spinning and knitting. As it was she became dependent on the patronage of the (female) great: Queen Caroline, wife of George II, was persuaded to make her a small allowance. After the Queen's death, it was arranged that Elizabeth Elstob should enter the household of the Duchess of Portland – as governess to her children. And here in 1756, after eighteen years as a governess, the 'Saxon nymph' ended her days.[59]

CHAPTER SEVENTEEN

Petticoat-Authors

'I hate these Petticoat-Authors; 'tis false Grammar, there's no Feminine for the Latin word, 'tis entirely of the Masculine Gender, and the Language won't bear such a thing as a She-author.'

CHAGRIN THE CRITICK, IN
A Comparison Between the Two Stages, 1702

I f a woman did by any chance seek to educate herself, wrote Damaris Lady Masham, she was liable to be treated as 'a Scarecrow' by the Wits in London: Lady Masham (John Locke's 'Philoclea') added that in the country she would probably fare even worse. Scorn for the learned lady, generally expressed in cheerful ridicule rather than outright hostility but no less inhibiting for that, was one aspect of post-Restoration society with which every woman who pretended to achievements beyond the purely house-wifely – 'the dull manage of a servile house' in Anne Winchilsea's phrase[1] – had to cope.

Numerous English playwrights found in the idea of the pretentiously learned female an enjoyable inspiration for the stage. They included, it should be said, her whom Evelyn termed 'our Sappho ... the Famous Heroina Boadicia', Aphra Behn. In 1678 the character of Lady Knowall in Aphra Behn's *Sir Patient Fancy* was founded on that of Mary Astell. 'Oh, the delight of Books!' exclaims Lady Knowall. She goes on to describe her serious reading as Tacitus, Seneca and Plutarch or 'if in a Humour gay' Virgil, Homer or Tasso, all studied 'in the Excellence of their Original Language'. When the young Leander Fancy suggests that these authors can as well be read 'in our Mother Tongue,

Madam', Lady Knowall turns on him: 'Faugh, Mr Fancy, what have you said, Mother Tongue! Can anything that's great or moving be express'd in Filthy English ...?'² So much for Mary Astell and her plans, so much for Basua Makin and her desperate plea that 'tongues are learnt in order to [learn] things'.

The success of Molière's plays, crossing the Channel in English versions (Aphra Behn for example in *Sir Patient Fancy* drew upon *Le Malade Imaginaire*), added to the fun. Shadwell's *The Virtuoso* of 1676, an adaptation of Molière's *Les Femmes Savantes*, was itself pillaged by Thomas Wright in 1693 for *The Female Vertuosos*: Philaminte, Armande and Bélise emerging as Lady Meanwell, Mrs Lovewit and Catchat, three women of appropriately nonsensical achievements. Lady Meanwell has invented an engine to keep the streets of London dry and clean ('Tis only Setting up Timber Posts round about the City and then fixing a pair of Bellows on every one of 'em to blow the Clouds away!'). Catchat is teaching a flea to sing opera. Mrs Lovewit has made an exact collection of all the plays that ever came out, and has devised an alembic by means of which the quintessence of wit in them is to be extracted and sold to poets by drops. Congreve's *The Double Dealer* of 1694 included the character of Lady Froth: 'a great Coquet Pretender to Poetry, Wit and Learning', prone to apostrophize her servant in banal verse:

> For as the Sun shines every day
> So, of our Coach-man I may say
> He shows his drunken fiery Face
> Just as the Sun does more or less.³

At least Catchat in *The Female Vertuosos* was allowed to retort on the subject of female learning: ''Tis the partial, and foolish Opinion of Men, Brother, and not our Fault hath made it ridiculous nowadays ...' The trouble was that this 'foolish Opinion' grew rather than diminished in strength towards the end of the century. By 1702 the prevailing attitude of contempt for feminine achievement was summed up by the playwright and essayist Charles Gildon in *A Comparison Between the Two Stages*, through the mouthpiece of Chagrin the Critick: 'I hate these Petticoat-Authors; 'tis false Grammar, there's no Feminine for the Latin word, 'tis entirely of the Masculine Gender, and the Language won't bear such a thing as a She-author.' Although another character, Sullen, is more reasonable (a woman has recently won a prize for poetry in France, and even in England 'some of that Sex … have done admirably'), to Chagrin it is all rubbish: 'Let 'em scribble on, till they can serve all the Pastry-cooks in Town, the Tobacconists and Grocers with Waste-paper.'⁴

There is indeed a newly sour note about the mockery poured upon the generation of female playwrights following Aphra Behn (who died in 1689 in her fiftieth year). *The Female Wits*, a play of 1696, said to be by 'W.M.', took as its target a trio of women, Catherine Trotter, Mary Manley and Mary Pix, all of whom made their debut as petticoat-dramatic-authors about this time, and castigated them; although the author has not been identified, the piece was sufficiently appealing to the public taste to be published in 1704.⁵

In the following reign, all three of these women – Catherine Trotter (later Cockburn) at eighteen was the youngest, the others in their early thirties – would have to survive scathing male satire in pursuit of their profession; a fate predicted by Mary Manley in her Prologue to her first play:

> The Curtain's drawn now by a Lady's hand,
> The very Name you'll cry bodes Impotence,
> To Fringe and Tea they should confine their sense.

One traditional way of dealing with petticoat-prejudice was for a female author to issue her works anonymously. Conversely, if a play under a woman's name was successful, it would be suggested, in the words of Mary Manley's Prologue once more, that 'Some private Lover helped her on her way.' Aphra Behn, a woman of extraordinary enterprise who after her father's death supported herself by journalism and even more daring forays into the world of espionage, before turning to plays and poetry, had to suffer the indignity of this suspicion: 'the plays she vends she never made'.⁶

What Aphra Behn eloquently asked for was 'the privilege for my masculine part, the poet in me' to be heard; for assuming that females were so endowed, she saw 'no reason why women should not write as well as men'. In a sense Aphra was right, for in so far as her plays triumphed over the contemporary denigration it was because they were witty, full of good characters and thus loved by audiences. However not even Aphra's spirit and talents were totally proof against the handicap of an inadequate female education: that ignorance of Latin which she herself mourned meant that her poems lost their appeal as classically-based poetry became popular.[7]

Most women who felt in themselves the creative lust were not as bold as Aphra.† Theodosia Alleine, wife of Joseph Alleine, a minister living in Taunton who died in 1668, was more typical in her bashfulness. After her husband's death, Mrs Alleine wrote an account of his life and sent it to one of his colleagues, 'she not imagining it should be put forth in her own words', as the printer subsequently explained. 'But that worthy Person, and divers others, upon perusal, saw no reason to alter it [the manuscript], but caused it to be printed as it is.'[8] In general, petticoat-authors, far from stepping forward in challenge, were inclined to retreat still further within the veilings of conventional female modesty, as though hoping to atone for the sheer flagrancy of their endeavours.

Dorothy Lady Pakington, who died in 1679, had once presided over a kind of Anglican salon at her house Westwood in Worcestershire. She was sometimes thought to be the author of *The Whole Duty of Man* (in fact the work of the Anglican divine Richard Allestree), because the book arose out of discussions held at her house; although she may have assisted him with parts of *The Ladies Calling*. Here was one who basked posthumously in the approval of society, since it was said by Anne Winchilsea that Lady Pakington

---

† Wonderful Aphra fully deserves both her place in history as the first professional woman author, and her place in Westminster Abbey where she is buried; she lies in the Cloister, however, near the actress Anne Bracegirdle, not in Poets' Corner.

Of each Sex the two best Gifts enjoy'd
The skill to write, the Modesty to hide.

Sufficient modesty – and a sufficiently early death – could even gain undeserved reward: as Grace Lady Gethin, who died in 1696 at the age of twenty, was gravely admired for the essays *Reliquiae Gethinae* she left behind – in fact merely a number of Bacon's essays copied out.[9]

The most favourable kind of judgement was that accorded to Damaris Lady Masham, who herself gracefully eluded the hovering accusation of 'Scarecrow'; the existence of her books being somehow expiated by the parallel creation of a comfortable country house and the dispensation of hospitality not only to Locke but also to a wide circle of powerful connections. Aphra Behn's marble slab in Westminster Abbey was inscribed with the two lines:

Here lies a proof that wit can never be
Defence enough against mortality.

Damaris Lady Masham on the other hand was, on her tomb in the Abbey Church at Bath, described as one 'Who to the Softness and Elegance of her own Sex added several of the Noblest Accomplishments and Qualities of the Other.' Most petticoat-authors found it safer to be commemorated along the lines of Lady Masham rather than those of Aphra Behn.

Katherine Philips, an early example of the species, was known to her circle, according to the fashion of the time for slightly arch *sobriquets*, as the Matchless Orinda.[10] She was the author of one small volume of poems, one volume of letters and two translations from Corneille: *Pompey* and *Horace*. (Her version of *Horace* was the first woman's play to be professionally produced on the English stage, although it appeared after her death.) When *Pompey* was performed in Dublin – where Katherine Philips was then living – in 1663, the fact was celebrated in a cautious couplet:

Yes, that bold work a Woman dares Translate,
Not to provoke, nor yet to fear Mens hate.[11]

Throughout her life – she died in 1668 at the age of thirty-six – Katherine Philips showed indeed much care 'not to provoke' – as a result of which she was able successfully to avoid 'Mens hate'.

Katherine Fowler was born into the prosperous middle class, and educated at Mrs Salmon's school in Hackney, where she learnt both French and Italian. Her father had left her a respectable portion of £1,000 and in 1648 Katherine Fowler married James Philips of Cardigan. She was sixteen and he was fifty-four. Despite the disparity in their ages, it appears to have been a stable, happy marriage.

Katherine, being intelligent, was able to help her husband in business; thus the learning which enabled the wife to read Tasso, Michelangelo Buonarroti and Castiglione in the original (Florio's textbooks in the British Library have her name in them) caused no offence to the husband, himself benefiting from his wife's unusual qualities. Katherine Philips's French was even better than her Italian, John Davies dedicating his translation of *Cléopâtre* to her, 'a person so much above your Sex, in the command of those languages'. Nor did Katherine Philips's appearance present any kind of moral threat – 'very good natured … pretty fat; not tall; red pumpled [sic] face', wrote John Aubrey.[12]

Conventional in her happiness, Katherine Philips was also conventional in her griefs, the reiterated tragedies of the time; the death of her only child, that little boy Hector of whom she wrote in 1655 'I did but pluck the Rose-bud and it fell'; followed by the death of her step-son Francis who died in 1660 at the age of twelve: 'Ah, beauteous Blossom, too untimely dead!'[13]

The personality of 'Orinda' was born during the Commonwealth, when Katherine Philips formed a circle in London, at the centre of which was a coterie of devoted female friends, men being permitted to enter, but on slightly less hectically intimate terms. (James Philips featured as 'Antenor'.) In these friendships, as in her poetry itself, Orinda was carrying on that Platonic tradition which had flowered at the court of Queen Henrietta Maria before the wars: the poets she admired and followed being Cartwright, Suckling and Waller, luminaries of that earlier age. It is in this context of strictly non-carnal love that Orinda's eloquent addresses to her female friends, 'Lucasia' (Anne Owen), 'Rosania' (Mary Aubrey) and later in Dublin 'adored Valerie' (Lady Anne Boyle), should be seen.[14]

Orinda was capable of showing possessive disgust towards her friends' attachments. When Lucasia married the widower Lord Dungannon, Orinda saluted the occasion in verse:

> You are so happy in each other's love
> And in assur'd perfection from above
> That we no wish can add unto your bliss
> But that it should continue as it is.

Unfortunately this perfect bliss seemed to preclude a relationship with Orinda on the old terms; 'I find there are few Friendships in the World Marriage-Proof', she wrote crossly, 'especially when the Person our Friend married has not a Soul particularly capable of the Tenderness of that Endearment ... we may generally conclude the Marriage of a Friend to be the Funeral of a Friendship.' So 'lovely Celimina' (the Countess of Thanet) replaced the renegade Lucasia.

It would however be wrong to read anything covertly sensual into these relationships, however overtly passionate. That would have been quite outside the Platonic tradition. As Orinda herself wrote on the nature of friendship, such 'flames' were free from 'grossness or mortality'.[15]

Orinda's personality was sufficiently distinguished for Jeremy Taylor to ruminate on the whole nature of friendship in a work entitled: *In a Letter to the most Ingenious and Excellent Mrs Katherine Phillips.* Dr Taylor explained in advance how much he differed from 'the morosity of those Cynics – who would not admit your sex in to the communities of friendship'. Nevertheless in the body of the work, he himself differentiated carefully between the two sexes: 'a man is the best friend in trouble, but a woman may be equal to him in the days of joy: a woman can as well increase our comforts, but cannot so well lessen our sorrows: and therefore we do not carry women with us when we go to fight, but in peaceful Cities and times vertuous women are the beauties of society and the prettiness of friendship'.[16]

Where the merits of Orinda's poetry are concerned, it is unfortunately impossible to dissent from the view of her biographer: 'little enthusiasm is possible, even to one who has come to know her well'.[17] Although Keats was taken by her lines to Rosania:

> To part with thee I needs must die
> Could parting sep'rate thee and I –

the superbly banal wedding address to Lucasia and Lord Dungannon is quite as characteristic of Orinda's style: the touching simplicity of her grief for her dead son became her poetry best.

Her character is another matter. Katherine Philips, by dint of a personality which impressed but did not challenge, supported by a happily respectable private life, managed both to be known and to be respected as a she-author. She did so, unlike previous she-authors, without the benefit of aristocratic birth. This, in an age when it was the notion of the lady, with her carefully-nurtured, economically-protected languor, which captured the popular imagination, rather than that of her learned sister, was in itself a considerable achievement.

A gentle virtuous disposition in life, a life led none the less close to the highest in the land, an early much-lamented death leaving behind a deposit of poems to be printed thereafter in an atmosphere of mourning, these elements made of Anne Killigrew one she-author of whom it was not only safe but sentimentally delightful to approve. The fact that this Maid of Honour at court died in 1685 at the age of twenty-five unmarried contributed further to the sentimental picture: here was one who 'despised the Myrtle' (symbol of marriage) for the 'nobler Bay' (garland of the poet) in the words of Dryden. In an admonition to the reader the publisher of Anne Killigrew's work (to which Dryden wrote an introduction) drew attention to the same phenomenon, in slightly less graceful language:

> Know, that a Virgin bright this Poem writ,
> A Grace for Beauty, and a Muse for Wit!

But on the evidence of her secret poems, Anne Killigrew was a more complicated character than this salutation of 'a Virgin Bright' or Dryden's verdict – 'Wit more than Man, her innocence a Child' – would indicate.[18] An obsessional fragment called 'Cloris' Charms' described a journey to be taken by the love-lorn:

> First take thy Hapless Way
> Along the Rocky Northern Shore
> Infamous for the Matchless store
> Of Wracks within that Bay
> None o'er the Cursed Beach e'er crossed
> Unless the Robb'd, the Wrack'd or Lost
> Where on the strand lie spread,
> The sculls of many Dead
> Their mingl'd Bones
> Among the Stones,
> Thy Wretched Feet must tread...
> For there's no Light
> But all is Night,
> And Darkness that you meet...[19]

Throughout her poetry a thread of melancholy, even bitterness runs, particularly on the subject of female unrequited love, a hint that 'Love the Softer Sex does sorriest wound.' In one of her pastoral dialogues, Anne Killigrew portrays a maiden who has been betrayed. She exclaims:

> Remember when you love, from that same hour
> Your peace you put into your Lovers Power:
> From that same hour from him you Laws receive
> And as he shall ordain, you Joy, or Grieve.

Anne Killigrew's 'Paragon' was the beautiful and chaste Duchess of Grafton, wife of one of Charles II's bastards and daughter of his minister Arlington. Here was a woman who for all her beauty kindled 'in none a fond desire'; this virtuous wife, admired but not courted, bonded by reason not the chains of passion, was the type of heroine she envied.[20]

In general there is a fastidious rejection of the worldly values of the court against the background of which Anne Killigrew led the whole of her short life. A very long and very pessimistic poem 'The Miseries of Man' pleads that reason, not passion, shall hold the reins of the chariot, so that anger, fear, hope and desire may be harnessed. The poem, singularly modern in its approach to nature, points out:

> The bloody Wolf, the Wolf does not pursue;
> The Boar, though fierce, his Tusk will not embrue
> In his own kind, Bears, not on Bears do prey:
> Thou art then, Man, more savage far than they.[21]

'A Farewell to Worldly Joys' rejects among other things 'Ye Unsubstantial Joys, Ye Gilded Nothings, Gaudy Toys'. 'The Discontent' casts aside grandeur and fame, the pillars of the court, in favour of that repose which gold alone cannot purchase.[22] All of this suggests that the resignation saluted in another elegy on her death, probably by the poet and theologian Edmund Elys, was not achieved without emotional cost:

> O Happy Maid, who didst so soon Espy
> In this Dark Life, that All is Vanity.[23]

Anne's father was Dr Henry Killigrew, Almoner to the Duke of York, Chaplain to the King, and Master of the Savoy, one of three brothers all of whom combined an interest in the arts, specially the dramatic arts, with the royal service: Thomas Killigrew was manager of the Theatre Royal and head of the troupe of actors known as the King's Servants as well as Groom of the Bedchamber to the King; Sir William Killigrew, Vice-

Chamberlain at court, also wrote plays. It was these connections which led Dryden to describe Anne as 'A Soul so charming from a Stock so good.'[24] However, the good stock also included Thomas's son, dissolute Harry Killigrew, Groom of the Bedchamber to the Duke of York, whose bawdy exploits served to *épater* the court, as well as Sir William's more conventional daughter Mary, who by marrying an illegitimate son of the House of Orange, established still closer Killigrew royal connections. Anne herself entered the household of the Duke of York, as Maid of Honour to his second wife, Mary of Modena.

It was significant of the relative public attitudes to female painting (approved) and female authorship (suspected) that the recognition Anne Killigrew did seek during her lifetime was for her artistic talent, not her poetry. Applauded in royal circles as a portraitist, she was reckoned to be particularly successful in capturing the likeness of the Duke of York: 'Her Hand drew forth the image of his Heart,' wrote Dryden. From Dryden too we learn that Anne painted Greek and Roman scenes, and subjects such as Venus and Adonis, the Graces dressing Venus, and Judith and Holofernes.

Anne Killigrew looks out of her own self-portrait, displaying what Dryden described with not too much flattery as a 'well-proportion'd Shape, and beauteous Face'. In some ways this is the conventional late-seventeenth-century visage, so often painted by Lely, with its fine long nose, round cheeks, full mouth and lofty pure forehead, framed in thick curls; but there is something tighter and more disciplined here, compared to his flowering beauties (as well as a more restrained display of bosom). Anne Killigrew died of smallpox in the summer of 1685 and her father produced a memorial edition of her poems the following autumn. The modest yet firm self-portrait represents the public use of her talent. In private Anne Killigrew wrote poems like this *On Death*:

> Tell me thou safest End of all our Woe
> Why wretched Mortals do avoid thee so
> Thou gentle drier o' th' Afflicted Tears,

> Thou noble ender of the Cowards fears;
> Thou sweet Repose to Lovers sad despair ...[25]

But then painting and drawing were the agreed feminine accomplishments, were they not? Psychologically, it was always possible to regard the female artist as merely extending the talents of a refined education into a wider sphere, even when as in the case of Mary Beale, who was influenced by Robert Walker and Lely, she was actually earning a good professional income from her efforts. Joan Carlile seems to have been the first of such female artists, said to have been presented with artist's materials (ultramarine) by King Charles I, and by 1658 known as 'a virtuous example' of painting portraits in oils, as well as copying Italian masters in miniature.[26] Mary Beale, born before the Civil War, the daughter of a clergyman called Craddock, lived to the end of the century; she produced watercolours and crayon drawings, portraits amongst others of Milton, Lord Halifax, the Duke of Norfolk and Bishop Wilkins. With a house in Pall Mall, her earnings rose from £200 in 1672 to a peak of £429 pounds – from eighty-three commissions – in 1677; although as Lely's pupil, her popularity declined with his death.[27]

Mary Beale, like Anne Killigrew, wrote poetry; not for her however the kind of hostility which might be shown to the more ostensibly learned 'Scarecrow'. Her brother-in-law Samuel Woodforde, a Prebendary of Winchester and himself a poet, described her with affection as 'that absolutely compleat Gentlewoman ... the truly virtuous Mary Beale', and Woodforde included two of her works in his *Paraphrase to the Psalms*, saying that she had made 'Painting and Poetrie ... to be really the same'.[28] Where painting was concerned, the distinction between the professional and the amateur was not really perceived; no modest apologies were felt necessary for the presumptuous female pen so long as it was wielded in the cause of art not literature.

Elizabeth Capel, Countess of Carnarvon, who died in 1678 at the age of forty-five, was one of the large family of that Royalist hero Arthur Lord Capel, executed in 1648. All the Capels loved flowers (as the great family portrait of 1637 bears vivid witness): another sister, Mary Duchess of Beaufort, a keen botanist and a friend of Sir Hans Sloane, developed the gardens at Badminton and commissioned an important florilegium by Everhardus Kickius. Flower-painting, inspired by her parents' garden at Little Hadam, was Lady Carnarvon's speciality. There is a small gouache in the Royal Collection dated 1662 (which may however be a copy of an existing flower-piece), and Lely's double portrait with the Duchess of Beaufort shows Lady Carnarvon holding one of her own works. In both cases the signature reads 'E. Carnarvon *fec*...' under a coronet.[29] Here was a pursuit which no one resented: 'E. Carnarvon' would have many ladylike and floral-minded followers in the future, coroneted and otherwise, whom no one would think to criticize for being petticoat-painters.

There was another talented 'maid' at court who was an almost exact contemporary of Anne Killigrew.[30] That was Anne Kingsmill, later Anne Finch by marriage to Heneage Finch, a son of the third Earl of Winchilsea, and later still Anne Countess of Winchilsea when her husband succeeded to the title. (Heneage Finch was a great-nephew of that Sir Heneage Finch, Speaker of the House of Commons, who won the hand of the Widow Bennett in 1629.) Anne Kingsmill came of a good Hampshire family although both her parents died when she was very young; she began adult life as one of the six Maids of Honour to Mary of Modena, a body which included not only Anne Killigrew but also the witty and notorious Catherine Sedley, to whose very different use of her intelligence attention will be drawn in a subsequent chapter.

Anne's marriage was also made within the purlieus of the royal (York) household: Heneage Finch was Captain of the Halberdiers and Gentleman of the Bedchamber to James II, then Duke of York. The closeness of the connection meant that King James's flight from the throne threatened the Finch welfare: Heneage thought it prudent to take his wife to the family home of Eastwell in Kent, where his nephew Charles, fourth Earl of Winchilsea, gave his relations a retreat.

The secluded circumstances in which Anne now found herself, however galling in political terms, might be described as ideal for a serious (female) author. For one thing Anne lacked the joyous but distracting surroundings of a young family: she was childless and remained so, despite therapeutic visits to the spa at Tunbridge Wells. This was a negative asset. Then she had the positive advantage of a husband who was not only affectionate – 'They err, who say that husbands can't be lovers', she wrote – but also encouraging, making such gestures as asking her to write a poem for him ready for his return when he went to London. Heneage Finch was her 'Dafnis' and she was his 'Ardelia'.[31] Furthermore Heneage's nephew Charles, their young patron, also extended encouragement to Anne, before his death in 1712 left Heneage Finch to succeed to the title as fifth Earl of Winchilsea.

Anne certainly did not miss the busy life of the city. She said of herself that fashion meant nothing to her, wanting merely a new gown once a year in the spring and nothing more; her scorn for the feminine 'accomplishments' with which the idle and une-ducated beauties of society filled their hours has already been quoted (see p.394). What Anne enjoyed instead was the creative privacy of a country life, so much more conducive to the devel-opment of her poetry than the court where, as she pointed out, 'everyone would have made their remarks upon a Versifying Maid of Honour'. She wrote some melancholy lines on this theme:

> Did I my lines intend for publick view
> How many censures, wou'd their faults pursue …
> Alas! a woman that attempts the pen
> Such an intruder on the rights of men
> Such a presumptuous Creature, is esteem'd
> The fault, can by no virtue be redeem'd.[32]

Anne Winchilsea was right in her instinct that privacy was a further important asset to a she-author. For unlike Anne Killigrew, she lived out at least her natural lifespan, dying in 1720 in her sixtieth year. Chronologically if not stylistically (she was much influenced by Dryden) her poetry belongs to the eighteenth century; she first appeared in print in 1701, a small volume being published in 1713. Her reputation as a poet rests in consequence on more secure foundations: in the nineteenth century, Wordsworth fell in love with one of her poems, entitled 'Noctural Reverie', with its touching lines on the freedom of animals under cover of darkness:

> Their short-liv'd Jubilee the Creatures keep
> Which but endures, whilst Tyrant Man does sleep.

Commending its attitude to nature, he described 'Noctural Reverie' as 'often admirable, chaste, tender and vigorous'.[33]† But this also meant that unlike Orinda, a generation her senior, Anne Winchilsea survived to be printed in the keen-bladed age of Pope. And once her poetry was made public, it was open season for the hunt, as it was for the 'Female Wits'.

The trio of Pope, Arbuthnot and Gay together wrote a play, *Three Hours after Marriage*, in which Anne Winchilsea appeared as ludicrous Phoebe Clinket, ink-stained and with pens in her hair. Phoebe Clinket, unkempt as she might be, was also very much the lady of the house: she kept writing materials in every room in case inspiration seized her, and a compliant maid followed her about with a desk strapped to her back, so that Phoebe could even write on the move.[35]

Had Orinda been of a less charmingly tactful disposition, had Anne Killigrew cast modesty aside and made her secret feelings public, had both of them survived into the eighteenth century, one suspects that these ladies might have found themselves in the literary pillory along with ink-stained 'Phoebe Clinket'.

---

†In recent years she has been quoted with approval in a feminist context, as one who in Dale Spender's words protested against the idea of the 'natural' patriarchal order.[34]

Anne Finch, later Viscountess Conway, the little girl who had run about the gardens of Kensington House and worshipped her step-brother John, never did throw off those sick headaches which in her youth were ascribed to too much reading, unsuitable to her sex (see p.159). Yet despite a lifetime of crippling illness necessitating virtual social retirement towards the end, Anne Viscountess Conway survived to write a philosophical work admired after her death (when it was printed) by Leibniz; the editor of her correspondence describing her as 'the most remarkable woman of that remarkable age' and comparing her to that mystic of the twelfth century, the Abbess Hildegard of Bingen.[36]

It is too easy to say that Anne Viscountess Conway was able to develop her original intellect just because her illness cut her off from the world and enabled her to avoid the hostility generally shown to the learned lady. Just as it is far too simple to ascribe her torturing headaches merely to an unconscious desire to withdraw from the jovial society favoured by her husband; the pain which would cause her at one point to seek trepanning as the lesser of two evils was evidently real enough. Besides, diagnosis, whether medical or psychological, is notoriously dangerous in the absence of the patient, especially when all symptoms are described in the very different medical language of 300 years ago. Nevertheless the story of Anne Conway demonstrates that a perpetual acknowledgement of her own weakness was one way, albeit a very painful one, in which a clever woman could avoid disapproval; the physical doing very well in the judgement of the world as a metaphor for the intellectual.

Anne Finch, born in 1631, was the posthumous daughter of Sir Heneage Finch by the Widow Bennett. (She was thus linked to Anne Countess of Winchilsea by marriage not blood.) She had numerous intelligent and successful relations on her father's side, including a formidable grandmother in Elizabeth Heneage, first Countess of Winchilsea. But if we seek a matrilineal descent for her intelligence, we may also turn to her mother, that pretty well-heeled Penelope who held off all suitors till she secured the one she wanted, and who proved to be a far more astute character than was generally suspected (see pp.108–112). Or perhaps it was the cross between the two: the blood of the bright middle-class mother galvanizing into activity the more ancient strain of her father.

It was through her step-brother John that Anne first met the philosopher Henry More, and was introduced to his Cambridge Platonist circle, More being John Finch's tutor at Christ's College. Anne's first letter to More, which precedes her marriage, enclosed her own translation of a piece of Descartes:[37] for it was More who was responsible for introducing to England the Cartesian Rationalism which postulated that the general nature of the world could be established by demonstrative reasoning from indubitable premises (in contrast to the Empiricists like Hobbes, who held that knowledge of the world came through experience, and not through reason alone). Anne became for More 'my Heroine Pupil'. Under his influence she read Plato and Plotinus, and studied such mystical works as the *Desiderata Kabbala*.

In 1651 marriage to Edward Conway made Anne into the chatelaine of Ragley Castle, Herefordshire: a position which enabled her, like Damaris Lady Masham, to dispense hospitality to her philosophical friends, principal among them More. For all Conway's taste for London society, it would be wrong to regard Anne Finch and her husband as intellectually mismatched: here was no yoking of unhappy opposites. Edward, later third Viscount Conway, a man eight years older than his bride, was respected by More and himself a reader of Descartes. At Ragley he was happy to join in the discussions initiated by More on topics including spiritism and cabbalism as well as Rationalism. He was an early member of the Royal Society.

But Conway was also a man of action. The son of one of the principal Secretaries of State to James I and Charles I, he had distinguished himself in the north of Ireland in the recent wars. He could not see his own horizon, like that of his ailing wife, bounded by life at Ragley, whatever the stimulus of More's company. As a man pursuing a public career, his devotion to the social life at Whitehall was certainly defensible; one can also understand only too easily how a man with a taste for late-night suppers with the King and Nell Gwynn would not necessarily wish to spend every evening discussing Platonism in the country with a wife either crippled with or about to be crippled with a headache, a visiting philosopher and perhaps his wife's intellectually-minded gentlewoman – 'your library keeper Mrs Sarah'.[38]

Yet on the subject of Anne Conway's health, it should be remembered honourably in favour of Lord Conway, that he showed admirable stoicism when their only child, Little Heneage Conway, died at the age of two and a half of smallpox. (Anne caught it too, enduring still further impairment of her fragile health.) He was advised that his wife would suffer agonies if she 'bred' again, and therefore trained himself not to wish for children: a piece of self-denial most uncharacteristic of his age. When the news was brought that Anne was possibly pregnant again, Lord Conway commented: 'My thoughts were long since sealed against any impetuous desires after children, and my mind disposed to that which was more diffusive than gathering together an estate for an heir, and this [news] will not alter me.'[39] His stoicism stood him in good stead, for Anne Viscountess Conway never did bear children.

It was fortunate for Anne Conway that she also had the benefit of those other affectionate relationships – in both of which she was encouraged in her learned studies – with her brother John and with More. Her intimacy with More lasted thirty years and was both platonic and 'Platonick'. Early on, More dedicated *An Antidote against Atheism* to Anne, as one who in 'penetrant Wit' and 'speculative Genius' had so far outstripped all her sex. To More, Anne Conway was not only his 'Heroine Pupil' but also 'Virtue become visible to his outward sight'. Sir John Finch, a physician at Cambridge who ended his life there with his lifelong friend and 'chevalier' Sir Thomas Baines (they were buried in the same grave) led in between a successful life as a diplomat. Anne Conway's girlhood attachment to her brother never waned. Here More consoles her for her grief at his departure: 'What you speak concerning friendship in reference to your brother, and in the behalf of a more passionate kind of affection as an inseparable concomitant of it [that is, grief], is true', he wrote. All the same the philosopher felt bound to point out: 'reason moderates these emotions'.[40]

Today Anne Conway's recurring headaches would certainly be regarded as migrainous in nature, particularly as they were often accompanied by sickness (but migraine today, even if understood, is still something for which no absolute cause, let alone an absolute cure, can be given). In those days, as the Conway correspondence amply demonstrates, Anne Conway's existence was bounded by remedies tried and failed, doctors approached and abandoned, healers of infinite variety solicited, whose increasingly bizarre nature indicates all too eloquently the desperation of the uncured – but surely not incurable? – patient with the passing of the years.

There was 'a red powder' and 'a blue powder'. Mercury was resorted to three times (something which worried More), once in the form of an ointment prescribed by the celebrated physician Sir Theodore Mayerne, twice in the form of a powder taken orally, made up by Charles Huis, a well-known chemist. Robert Boyle made up another powder, to be taken in a solution of sack and canary, which he prepared himself. Opium – probably laudanum, at that time a novelty in England – was tried at the suggestion of Thomas Sydenham. Other doctors consulted included William Harvey and Sir Francis Prujean.

At one point Henry More proposed tobacco, which had a therapeutic reputation at that time and was not infrequently prescribed for headaches; he also suggested coffee.† Anne Conway's coach had to be stuffed with the softest down since even feathers threatened her acute sensibilities. She tried a special diet of 'husbandman's fare': woodcocks, pheasants and baked turkeys, and at the other extreme 'the experiment of water falling on your head.[42]

The gruesome suggestion of trepanning actually originated with Harvey in 1656 (although he did refer Lady Conway to a board of specialists). Nevertheless the patient, in what state of torment one can only guess, took a sudden decision to go to France and have the operation, involving the sawing open of a hole in the skull to relieve pressure, performed forthwith. In the

†Coffee has not lost its reputation: Oliver Sacks, in *Migraine*, 1981, suggests that migraine sufferers take caffeine tablets, for the 'management' of migraine attacks.[41]

event the French physicians did no more than open Lady Conway's jugular arteries, although it is not clear whether the doctors drew back or in the end the patient shrank from the ultimate ordeal. In any case, there was a further ordeal to be endured of quite a different nature: Lord Conway, coming to join his wife, was captured at sea by the Dutch and thrown naked into a filthy prison until such time as he was ransomed.[43]

The episode of the Irish faith healer Valentine Greatrakes was less traumatic (although equally unsuccessful in its results). Greatrakes, known as 'the Irish stroker', came of a good family in Youghal; he never took any money for his cures in Ireland. His visit did have therapeutic effects for a good many of the tenants at Ragley, who found their ills alleviated. To Lady Conway he arrived on a morning when the sun was shining: 'for the sun, Madam, is a great healer and composer'. Greatrakes laid his fingers on her head while all around waited for the headache to vanish. It did not. Day after day he repeated the process. Still the headache maintained its vicious grip. After a fortnight the 'Irish stroker' like the previous doctors, admitted failure and departed.[44]

Lady Conway's condition aroused sympathy beyond her own country. From the Grand Duke of Tuscany, at whose court John Finch held the post of Minister, arrived 'a very ingenious contrivance to sit at all heights in the bed, and have the use of a table. It goes upon screws, and everything is to be unscrewed. The glass within the bed-pan is to be taken out by unscrewing the handle and taking the handle quite off, for then it opens.'[45]

The particular stresses of Anne Conway's life, such as the death of little Heneage, naturally exacerbated her condition. 'Our passions are given us for certain uses and services which when they cease, our passions are to cease also,' wrote More.[46] That was easier advised than done. Yet it is notable and heroic — fully justifying More's praise of his pupil — that she pursued her studies throughout all these agonizing years; we find her for example attempting to learn Greek in 1665, when she was in the extremities of pain. In the winter of 1667 she was not only bedridden but reduced to an amanuensis in her correspondence with

More at Cambridge; by the autumn of the following year, however, she was rising gallantly once more.

All this while More the philosopher had to contemplate the physical purgatory of his friend, and could do nothing to help her to pass from it. 'The pious and virtuous' came out of their travails as 'gold purified out of the fire', he declared. In 1671 More wrote to Anne Conway: 'And I hope your body will not prove a Tomb to you, but rather an holy Temple, an hallowed edifice for your soul to work in, those bodies that are most vigorously in health are the most devouring sepulchres to swallow down the soul into and to bury all the nobler faculties.'[47] Reflections such as these can have been as little true consolation to Anne Conway's agonized friend as they were to the suffering woman herself.

Perhaps there was more comfort to be found when More turned to philosophy. Lady Conway's headache, he wrote, might be good for the whole on the grounds that what is good for the whole may not be good for the part, and Lady Conway's headaches were certainly not good for one part – 'her particular friends'. The sentence: 'if her body were as well as her mind, it would be better for us all' only applied after all to these friends. Or perhaps after all poetry provided the true consolation. More sent Anne Conway a scribbled translation, done in bed, of his own *Aphoria, or The Perplexity of the Soul,* and then *Euphoria, or The Extrication of the Soul,* in a friend's translation which Anne had learnt by heart and of which she desired a copy. These lines in *Aphoria* apostrophizing Father Jove may have found some dark echo in Anne's heart:

> 'Tis rare, we mortals live i' the clouds like thee,
> Lies, Toys, or some hid fate, us fix or move.
> All else being dark, what's life I only see ...[48]

In the autumn of 1670 Lord Conway and Henry More between them persuaded the Netherlander physician F.M. Van Helmont to visit Ragley. Van Helmont remained there for nine years, devoting himself to finding a cure for Lady Conway. Fresh medicines were sought from Germany; the headaches persisted but at least Lady Conway's general health, so much damaged by that fatal bout of smallpox which killed little Heneage, improved. At first Van Helmont's presence at Ragley had the agreeable side-effect that More could still visit the castle from Cambridge when Anne was too ill to receive him, since Van Helmont could act as host. But later Van Helmont's own interest in Quakerism reinforced Anne Conway's tendencies in that direction, and after some years of spiritual doubt she finally joined the sect in 1677. In the last years of her life she lived at Ragley surrounded by Quakers, and More's visits dwindled.

On several different levels, it is easy to see what attracted Anne Conway to the Friends; although the fact that Van Helmont regularly attended Quaker meetings from 1675 onwards was clearly relevant in view of Anne's physical isolation brought about by her sickness, More's estimate of his friend's character must also be borne in mind: 'she was one that would not give up her Judgment entirely unto any'.[49] Her first interest was in that sect known as the Familists and the cobbler-poet of Bohemia, Jacob Boehme. Then she came to study the Quaker arguments through their tracts: like several of her friends, including More, she was prepared to believe that religion had been choked with irrelevant detail and speculate how it might be resuscitated.

Lady Conway was of course cut off by illness not only from the Quaker Meetings, but also from the more violent public manifestations of their religion, exactly those aspects which revolted her contemporaries. Thus Lady Conway did not perceive in the Quakers uncontrollable spirits who might interrupt a preacher in the midst of his sermon, but rather 'lovers of quiet and retirement'. On this ground, she sent away to London for Quaker maids: 'for if they prove what they seem to be … they will fit the circumstances I am in (that cannot endure any noise) better than ordinary domestics'.[50] And she seems to have been lucky in her finds: for Quaker maids could be unreliable, suddenly inspired by the Lord to leave their position and go preaching; Lady Conway's maids on the contrary stayed with her to the end.

Lady Conway was also convinced that the Quakers

understood the loneliness of pain and could comfort her when 'Reason' and 'Philosophy' could not, just because of their own frequent ordeals in the Lord's service: 'they have been and are a suffering people'. She wrote: 'The weight of my affliction lies so very heavy upon me, that it is incredible how very seldom I can endure anyone in my chamber, but I find them so still and very serious'; the Quakers' company would be acceptable to her so long as she could bear any company at all.[51] So in her dark room surrounded by luxuries which could not cure, she harkened to their consolations and listened to their sufferings.

More, who had warned Anne against 'melancholy' (which has been described as the contemporary atheism), had failed to predict that she would turn to 'enthusiasm' (the contemporary fanaticism).[52] Before her death Anne did somewhat reconcile More to the Quaker cause: at least to understand her own attraction to it. Conversions, especially those to 'enthusiastic' or fanatical religions, are however notoriously difficult for the previous intimates of the convert. Lord Conway was by now occupying an important administrative position in Ireland; Anne dispatched a parcel of Quaker books to him 'to chalk out the way, by which all serious seekers after God may attain their desired satisfaction and true rest'. She signed her covering letter for the first time in Quaker style: 'Thine'. Although Lord Conway tried to plough his way through the books, despite eye-strain, and although he attempted honourably to assist the Quakers in Ireland (just as his wife in England tried to get George Fox out of gaol), he still pronounced them from the point of view of a government official a 'senseless, wilful, ridiculous generation of people.'[53]

At his last visit to Ragley in Anne's lifetime, Lord Conway was dismayed to find how the situation had changed: 'all the women about my wife and most of the rest are Quakers and Mons. Van Helmont is governor of that flock, an unpleasing sort of people, silent, sullen and of a removed conversation'. George Fox on the other hand, the Friends' leader, found Lady Conway 'tender and loving', and in 1678 willing to detain him longer than he was ready to stay, in view of the call of his mission in other parts of the country.[54]

In February 1679, after days of terrible pain, Anne Conway was released into death; in her last agonies, she stoically refused to have Lord Conway sent for from Ireland, but her tiny wasted body was encased in an inner coffin of wood and glass so that he could see her face on arrival before she was wrapped in her outer covering of lead. A codicil to her will, clearly written with much physical difficulty, asked that the customary ostentation at the funeral of a lady of her quality should be forsworn, in accordance with Quaker practice. In addition, 'My Lady would have no Cerecloth to avoid the coming of any men about her, but desired that only Her Women with the two maids should lay her in the coffin'. In her will Lady Conway left £500 to Sir John Finch, £400 to Henry More, and £300 to Van Helmont, representing three stages of affection in her life.[55]

More spoke this epitaph upon her: 'I perceive and bless God for it, that my Lady Conway was my Lady Conway to her last Breath; the greatest Example of Patience and presence of Mind, in highest Extremities of Pain and Affliction, that we shall easily meet with: Scarce anything to be found like her, since the Primitive times of the church.' But the most telling judgement on Anne Viscountess Conway, at least by the standards of the century in which she lived, was pronounced by her brother Sir John Finch: 'I must never hope to see again in this World, knowledge enough to have made a Man of Parts proud, in a more talkative Sex to be possessed without noise.'[56]

The Principles of the Most Ancient and Modern Philosophy by Anne Viscountess Conway is thought to have been written by her when Van Helmont first lived with her and her general health temporarily improved: it was noted down with 'a Black-lead Pen' in 'a Paper-Book'.[57]

Like many others in the seventeenth century, Lady Conway was interested to try and reconcile the findings of the new science with the truths of the Christian religion. She put forward a great many notes on Hebrew and cabbalistic beliefs. Her work also included a disquisition on the nature of God, who had created the world out of goodness, not out of necessity. 'In God there can exist no Passion... For every Passion is something Temporal.' She proposed that the time passed since the beginning of Creation must be infinite (not 6,000 years as was popularly believed), as could be demonstrated from the infinite goodness of God: 'Now how can it be, that this Fountain shall not always plentifully flow, and send from itself Living Waters?' As it was 'an Essential Attribute' of God, to be a Creator, 'so by Consequence God ever was a Creator, and ever will be a Creator'; otherwise his nature would be changed. Creatures themselves ever were and ever would be: 'yet this Infiniteness of Times is not equal to the Infiniteness of God's Eternity, because the Eternity of God himself, hath no times in it'. Christ she described as 'the Middle Being, not subject to decay'.[18]

Lady Conway was of course a resolute opponent of Hobbes, who with his associates 'grievously' erred in teaching that 'Sense and Knowledge' were no more than 'a reaction of Corporeal Particles' one upon another. Sense and knowledge, she wrote, were 'a Thing far more Noble and Divine; in any Local or Mechanical Motion of any Particles Whatsoever'. Rejecting Hobbes utterly, she described every creature as comprising both a body and a spirit, or *Principium magis Activum, et magis Passivum* (a more active and a more passive principle). Lady Conway thought these two principles 'may fitly be termed Male and Female, by reason of that Analogy a Husband hath with his Wife: For as the ordinary Generation of Man requires a Conjunction and Co-operation of Male and Female; so also all Generations and Productions whatsoever they may be, require an Union.'[19]

More was probably responsible for the Latin translation of Lady Conway's *Principles*, in which form it first appeared in print in Amsterdam in 1690; two years later the book, re-translated into English, was printed in England. The English edition referred to a certain English Countess (Lord Conway was raised to an earldom in the year of his wife's death), 'a Woman learned beyond her Sex', whose work, found after her death inscribed 'in a very dull and small character' could only be read with the greatest difficulty. Leibniz probably heard of her work through Van

Helmont: he declared himself greatly influenced by her and expressed his approval of her principles over those of Locke – '*Les miens en philosophie approchent un peu d'avantage de ceux de feue Mme la Comtesse de Conway.*'[60]

A postscript may be added concerning the fate of Lord Conway. He was now in his mid-fifties, a man with an important position in the world; in 1681, two years after his wife's death, he was created one of the Secretaries of State. Yet his house had no mistress and he himself had no heir. However valiantly Lord Conway may have reconciled himself to this disappointment twenty years earlier, he was now generally judged to be in need of a wife who would provide a son. Nor did the Finch family shrink from the prospect. Anne Conway's sister, Lady Clifton, was pleading with her brother-in-law to marry again only two months after Anne's death. Sir John Finch was also prominent in his persuasions, invoking the very name of his dead sister: let him remarry 'for her sake (whose dust could it speak, would join with me I am sure)'. Sir Thomas Baines, as the lifelong 'chevalier' of Sir John Finch, also interested himself in the affair: he gave it as his opinion that the ideal 'widower's wife' was small, thin and pale, albeit very healthy and coming of fruitful parents; she should also be 'of a feminine lax temper'.[61] A stream of young – or youngish ladies, generally in their early twenties, was paraded, most of whom possessed large or largish portions.

What did Lord Conway now do? Ignoring the parade (and the advice) he fell violently in love with a most unsuitable chit of seventeen – unsuitable because she was flighty – Margaret Poulett, daughter of the second Lord Poulett and niece of the Speaker of the House of Commons. What pent-up emotions, suppressed during his wife's long illness, what middle-aged desires, long believed quiescent, surged through the bosom of the admirable Lord Conway during this unexpected Roman spring?

Lord Conway's friends, trained to believe that a fifty-six-year-old widower was indeed a proper spouse for a young girl if his rank was sufficiently august, suggested various modes of attack, in all of which ultimate victory was assumed.[62] Perhaps he should emulate the methods of Julius Caesar who came and saw and conquered: cry *Veni, Vidi, Vici*, and then all the young gallants who surrounded Mistress Margaret would be blown away. Another friend advised him first to prepare his 'Wooing Countenance' and then reflect on St Matthew, Chapter One (this, which begins with a long recital of the begetting of the generations before Jesus, was presumably to be regarded as some kind of fertility chant). For this elderly Romeo a further confidant recommended 'a Handsome Dress'.

So Lord Conway had 'a riding-suit' ordered in order to call on his beloved at Bath. It was to be lined with black satin, and embroidered with black and silver; apart from the other black touches it was to be laced with black and white love lace, 'both mourning enough and fine enough for this expedition', a delicate way of emphasizing Lord Conway's status, at once a widower and a lover. Fifty pounds was disbursed on this outfit, not counting the sword and hat which were extra. But the whole effect was wasted, at least in Bath, when Margaret Poulett's brother would not let Lord Conway call upon her; he was himself perversely backing the suit of his own friend (and contemporary), the young Lord Arran. Lord Conway had to wait till London to call upon his beloved.

Gradually, very gradually, it was borne in upon Lord Conway that Margaret was merely playing with his attentions. He withdrew from the field. He did not however deny the force of that sweet fever which had ravaged him. He could have had many richer, nobler, handsomer and more discreet wives, he wrote, but 'I have still more inclination for her [Margaret] than for any woman that ever I heard of...I believe there is a fate in such things which I can give no account of'.

Lord Conway did marry again a considerably older woman, someone presumably much closer to Sir Thomas Baines's recipe for the widower's ideal. But this second wife died in childbirth, as did the son she bore. Less than six weeks later Lord Conway married for the third time, a woman who brought him a portion of £30,000. By now Lord Conway's own race was almost run. He died in August 1683, only four years after the death of Anne. He died without an heir; but then he had long ago braced himself to accept that defeat rather than increase the physical burdens placed upon his precious jewel of a first wife; she who in the words of her brother possessed 'knowledge enough' to make the most intelligent man proud – and all 'without noise'.

CHAPTER EIGHTEEN

Helping in God's Vineyard

'Here will be work and business enough for us all that
none need to be idle in God's vineyard, but as we have
everyone received a measure of God's spirit and grace
some may be fellow helpers and workers together with
our brethren…'

LETTER OF ISABEL (FELL) YEAMANS, 1676

Anne Viscountess Conway desired to have Quaker servants
about her because this 'suffering people', so 'still and very
serious' in their behaviour would make ideal sympathetic
attendants for an invalid. Lord Conway on the other hand, in
Ireland where he had to cope with the Quakers' sudden demon-
strations according to the dictates of 'the Inner Light', found
them 'senseless, wilful, ridiculous'.[1]

Certainly the stories of the early Friends, and their persistent
testifying under the most hostile circumstances, more than justify
Lady Conway's description of them as 'a suffering people':
although her belief in their stillness might have been shaken by
some of the events in the 'steeplehouses' and elsewhere when
'the Inner Light' inspired a Friend to interrupt proceedings. In
the 1670s for example the charge brought against a Quaker
woman called Ann Blaykling was that she had called the minister
'Priest, hireling and deceiver, greedy dumb dog, with many words
of the same nature':[2] a by no means uncharacteristic selection of
insults for an early Friend. In their opposition to the payment of
tithes, because they believed in the separation of Church and
State (hence Anglican ministers were 'hirelings'), their refusal to
swear an oath (including an Oath of Allegiance in court), and in

their insistence on their own form of marriage, the Friends, as Lord Conway discovered, also posed other problems to the State, beyond an awkward tendency to extemporary prayer.

At the same time the Society of Friends increased: it has been estimated that when its founder George Fox died in 1691, there were 50,000 Quakers in England, one in every 100 of the population.[3] In all of this, the sufferings, the agitations and the responsibilities, women continued to play that prominent role which had been theirs from the first inception of the sect. In 1656 George Fox had defended the spiritual equality of women with men (see p.322): there was not only natural justice in this, there was also a practical recognition of the support women – including that despised, feared, disliked class, elderly women – gave him from the first.

Quakers were of course not alone among the sects which were nourished by the enthusiasm and energies of women. The force of women preachers, the original Baptists and Anabaptists of the 1640s, bore witness to that aspect of so-called heretical sects which enabled women to find liberation, both spiritual and social, in their midst. There were other examples, and early evangelism (unconnected with Quakerism) would continue to find women prominent. The history of the Quakers does however provide a microcosm of that liberation, with all the problems, as well as fulfilment, it brought. For one thing, their adoption of the Quaker religion hardly freed such women from the pressures to which their condition made them already subject. An 'ancient' widow inspired to step outside the traditional woman's role and speak publicly was for example more, rather than less, likely to be suspected of truck with the devil. As Margaret Fell, one of the most prominent of the early Quaker women, pointed out, there was always the danger of the Inner Light being mistaken for witchcraft; just as the prophetess Anna Trapnel, another female of independent voice, had been subject to the scrutiny of the 'witch-trying woman' (see p.316). Barbara Blaugdone of Bristol, for example, who spoke out both in the West Country and Ireland, was forty-six when she was 'convinced'; in Cork some of her former friends termed her a witch and had their servants turn her out of doors. (But convincement brought strength: for all her sufferings, the dour sharp-tongued Barbara Blaugdone lived to the age of ninety-five, dying in 1704.)[4]

Nor did the presence of vociferous women in the Quaker midst allay hostility to a religion which relied on the worrying instrument of extemporary prayer – uncontrollable from the outside. In 1677 in *The Countermine*, the Royalist pamphleteer and historian John Nalson used this suspicious combination to deduce that such impromptu manifestations were in fact inspired by the devil. He gave an instance of a woman who had become generally admired for being 'so eminent especially in this Gift of Prayer'; subsequently she went to New England where she was discovered to be 'a most Abominable Witch'. At her trial she confessed that she had given up her soul to the devil in return for the gift of extemporary prayer. Concluded Nalson with satisfaction: 'Either now we must believe that this Extempore Way is not an infallible sign of the Spirit of God: or that the Devil has the Power of disposing of the Gifts of the Spirit'. Had not St Paul himself issued 'an express Command' against 'these Female Doctresses'?[5]

As against this, George Fox, with that power which great conviction allied to great personal strength always bestows, never ceased to push forward the view that there was work for Quaker women to do as well as men. He admonished the Women's Meetings: 'Encourage all the women that are convinced, and minds virtue, and loves the truth, and walks in it, that they may come up into God's service, that they may too be serviceable in their generation, and in the Creation ...'[6]

On the one hand therefore the Quaker women were able to exercise responsibilities within their own religious organization denied to any other Englishwoman of their time (and for a long time thereafter, if granted at all). These women as a result were able to practise a certain kind of admirable Nonconformist philanthropy from which so much reforming richness has flowed in English social life. On the other hand where the Inner Light drew Quaker women into a more challenging and adventurous way of life, not only did they themselves suffer hideously, but they also pulled down upon their whole sex still viler imprecations concerning the nature of womankind.

Into the latter category of adventuresses falls the heroic Elizabeth Hooton – it is surely impossible to deny her the epithet, on grounds of her age alone.[7] She was nearly fifty when she first met George Fox, and over seventy when she came to her death in a foreign land, still serving the cause which she had made her life. Her age was indeed much remarked at the time: most allusions refer to her as old or 'ancient'.

To George Fox Elizabeth Hooton was however 'a very tender woman'.[8] The wife of a prosperous Nottinghamshire farmer, she was in fact George Fox's first convert and his first preacher; that in itself was an indication of the prominent role women would play in his mission. George Fox met Margaret Fell a few years later. Elizabeth Hooton was then a Baptist, and had probably been a preacher among the Baptists before her 'convincement'. Although Fox, like the Baptists (and other sectaries), shared in the denunciation of tithes, he criticized them in his journal for being 'Jangling Baptists'; Elizabeth Hooton now testified against their 'deceit'. By the end of 1648 Elizabeth Hooton had left her husband and family to become a Quaker preacher. Carrying out in church, when moved by the spirit, those kinds of interruptions which brought the Quakers their early notoriety, Elizabeth Hooton suffered as a result a series of imprisonments.

As with all problems of civil order, when the disrupter absolutely declines to promise amendment, one can certainly feel sympathy for the authorities in the administrative problem which the Quakers presented.† How were these interruptions – often of a frenzied and highly insulting nature – to be handled? On the other hand the rigorous treatment of the Quakers in prison can

---

†Although one would hardly today go as far as Mabel R. Brailsford who, writing in 1915 in *Quaker Women 1650–1690*, was influenced – but unfavourably – by the actions of the suffragette movement; she compared the plight of the 'priest' faced by a Quaker woman to that of a Cabinet Minister faced by a suffragette, her sympathies being with the politician.[9]

command no such understanding. George Fox was first imprisoned in Derby in 1650. This term initiated a period of close on forty years in which the Quakers were regularly confined for disturbing the public peace until the exemption of Dissenters (including the Quakers) from the penal laws in 1689 gave them relief: a Declaration of Loyalty was allowed to replace the Oath of Allegiance in court which the Quakers' religion would not permit them to swear.

There were periods of remission: at the Restoration a number of Quakers imprisoned under the Commonwealth were released from gaol. At the Declaration of Breda King Charles II had after all promised a liberty to 'tender consciences'. What happened however if liberty of conscience led to a breach of the peace – and some even more menacing manifestation such as rebellion? It was ill luck that the Quakers should become identified in the mind of authority with those rebellious millenarian relics, the Fifth Monarchists; a foolish rising of 1661, headed by a wine-bottler named Thomas Venner, led to wide-scale Quaker imprisonment. The tough Quakers' Act of 1662 followed, which imposed severe penalties on their Meetings, with transportation for a third offence. Then the first Conventicle Act of 1664 curtailed the activities of all Nonconformists by making it illegal for more than five persons outside a family to gather together for religious purposes. The Conventicle Act lapsed in 1668 but was re-enacted in 1670, bringing a fresh wave of imprisonments. As a result, thousands of Quakers passed through the prisons of England.

It was however from this experience, this wholesale incarceration of people who were not themselves members of the criminal classes, that the honourable Quaker commitment to prison reform sprang. It has been pointed out that in her letters from prison Elizabeth Hooton herself anticipated by 150 years the demands of the nineteenth-century Quaker reformer Elizabeth Fry.[10] Elizabeth Hooton's earliest extant letter to the Mayor of Derby contrasted the state of the prisoners with his own comfort and honour, warning him of the fate of Dives 'if he will not regard the poor and in prison'. Elizabeth Hooton was first shut up in the Fen Country; then in York prison (where she found a number of other Friends) on and off for two years; then in Beckenham prison for once again 'exhorting the people to repentance' for five months; finally she was imprisoned in Lincoln Castle, and here she found herself entirely among felons.

At Lincoln Castle too Elizabeth Hooton encountered a further hazard in the shape of a particularly malevolent female gaoler. The law permitted the magistrates to send Quakers to prison, but they were not obliged to make provision for the Quakers' maintenance (nor for that of other prisoners of course). The Quakers then had to find their own board and pay fees for their lodging, something which brought them squarely within the power of their gaolers if malevolently inclined. It was easy for 'a malignant woman' like the gaoler of Lincoln Castle to persecute her Quaker prisoner, and also to whip up the other prisoners against her. *Elizabeth Hooton, Prisoner in Lincoln Castle, pleads to him in Authority to reform the Abuses of the Gaol* drew attention not only to the system of 'fees' but also to Brueghel-like conditions within the prison itself. Elizabeth Hooton described 'in drinking and profaneness and wantonness, men and women together many times part of the night…' She asked that strong drink at least should be removed from the gaols.[11]

One of Elizabeth Hooton's fellow prisoners in York prison had been a Quaker servant-girl, originally from Pontefract, called Mary Fisher. She had probably been converted by George Fox in 1651 when she was about twenty-seven.[12] It was this Mary Fisher who was inspired by the Inner Light to carry the Quaker message to New England. Accompanied by Anne Austin, she reached Boston in July 1656. Her reward was to be 'searched' for being a witch. The hundred or so books on Quakerism which filled her baggage were confiscated. She was then flogged at the orders of the Governor of Massachusetts and expelled. In 1657 and 1658 the General Court of Massachusetts passed laws against Quakers' landing. Elizabeth Hooton, once more at liberty, was moved in her turn to set forth for New England. She intended to carry on the work of Mary Fisher and the other Friends, regardless of the Governor's prohibition.

The death of Oliver Hooton in 1661 placed 'old Elizabeth' in that traditionally strong position of a widow of considerable property at her own disposal. At the age of sixty she determined, despite the opposition of her children, to set forth for Boston; Joan Brocksoppe of Derbyshire, reputedly about the same age, 'freely resolved to be her companion'. The two women, having taken this resolve, were however forced to kick their heels for a considerable time before a passage to New England could be secured; this because a new law had been passed in Boston fining the captain of any ship bringing a Quaker within its jurisdiction £100.

When Elizabeth Hooton and Joan Brocksoppe did reach Boston, by a sea and land route, they entered a town where one Quaker woman, Mary Dyer, had already been hanged on Boston Common in 1659, to say nothing of those who had been whipped at the cart-tail from town to town. None of this prevented the two 'ancient' Quakers from interrupting the preachers when moved to do so. Soon enough, therefore, old Elizabeth and old Joan found themselves shut up in that 'Lion's Den', Boston prison.

From here they were taken to confront the dreaded Governor Endicott. He roundly called both these women witches, and asked them why they had come to Boston.

'To do the will of Him that sent me,' was the reply.

'What do you understand by that will?' demanded the Governor.

'To warn thee of shedding any more innocent blood,' answered Elizabeth Hooton. When the Governor countered that he would hang many more yet, Elizabeth Hooton pointed out that the Lord might spoil his plans by choosing to take him away.[13] Awaiting this happy event, she was put back into the Lion's Den, expecting to meet the same fate as Mary Dyer. In prison at the same time lay a Quaker man, Wenlock Christiansen, who was himself due to be hanged on 13 June. Unexpectedly all the Quakers – including Christiansen – were released the day before. It transpired that the execution of Mary Dyer was regarded with displeasure in England; for while no one could work out a plan for muzzling the Quakers, hanging was certainly considered an inappropriately harsh solution.

Perhaps there were moments when Elizabeth Hooton wondered if the fate which was substituted for it was not even worse than the gallows. Or on second thoughts, since there is no record of despair, we must assume her remarkable faith sustained her through the ordeal which followed. In Elizabeth Hooton's own words, another jury was called 'which condemned us all to be driven out of their jurisdiction by men and horses, armed with swords and staffs and weapons of war, who went along with us near two days' journey in the wilderness, and there they left us towards the night amongst the great rivers and many wild beasts that useth to devour and at night we lay in the woods without any victuals but a few biscuits that we brought with us and which we soaked in the water'.

By degrees the two old women reached Rhode Island, the centre of religious toleration since its foundation by the liberal-spirited Roger Williams. From Rhode Island they proceeded to Barbados, where Mary Fisher had also brought the message of Quakerism, and there were in consequence a number of Friends to receive them. Even at this point the two women were convinced that it was their duty to return to Boston; but having sailed back to New England, they were once more arrested in Boston and deported to Virginia. From here at last they took ship again for home.

In England however old Elizabeth's problems hardly diminished. She found herself returned to a land where Quakers were beset by the problems posed by the recent Acts comprised in the 'Clarendon Code' (which included the harsh Conventicle Act). A magistrate summoned Elizabeth's son at harvest-time, and when he would not take the oath in court, according to Quaker practice, fined him £5. When the son refused to pay, Elizabeth Hooton's property – to the value of £20 – was confiscated; to meet such demands the old woman was further forced into selling her farm at a severe financial loss. Then Elizabeth Hooton herself was imprisoned for twelve weeks, for not taking the oath.

At this point Elizabeth embarked on a relationship with King

Charles II based – in her opinion – on her crying need for temporal mercy and his equally pressing need for spiritual conversion. Even if somewhat one-sided, this relationship does at least give some kind of lighter touch to her otherwise painful story. This lightness was not entirely due to the piquant combination of the earnest old Quaker woman with the playful womanizing monarch: 'king charles,' she would exclaim some years later, 'how oft have I come to thee in my old age, both for thy reformation and safety, and for the good of thy soul, and for justice and equity. Oh that thou would not give up thy kingdom to the papists nor thy strength to the women…' Lightness was often King Charles's way with solemn events, as though good-natured mockery might palliate those ills which could not be eliminated. Pepys witnessed a scene when a pretty young Quaker presented an extremely long petition to the King. (She was probably the Kentish Quaker's wife who was debauched by an adventurer called John Scott; he got hold of her entire fortune to purchase an imaginary estate in Long Island, and then fled to America himself, taking with him her jewels and her eldest son.) Charles II listened to the petition and then observed that 'if all she desired was of that length, she might lose her desires'. The pretty Quaker declined to join in a conversation of such immodesty; it was not until it had returned to a more serious level that she began again. 'O King!'[14]

Yet the compassion of the King towards his 'tender consciences' was genuine enough, a feeling of mercy strengthened by his own sufferings in exile – so long as he did not consider that their deeds were threatening the security of the newly established stable state. The King frowned upon any possible connection between the Quakers and the Fifth Monarchists. But he chided his brother the Duke of York for an explosion against the Quakers and suggested that they might do better instead to amend the quality of their own lives. When the brave Baptist girl from the West Country, Hannah Hewling, presented a petition to James II in 1685 on behalf of her brothers William and Benjamin, implicated in the Monmouth rising, Lord Churchill warned her of the hardness of King James's heart: 'marble is as capable of feeling compassion'. (Nor did Hannah's pleas save the boys: both were hanged, although Hannah's money did at least spare their corpses the indignity of 'quartering'.)[15] There was nothing of this chill quality about the heart of Charles II.

Elizabeth Hooton first thought of coming to court in response to a revelation she had had at sea 'and in great danger of my life, that I should go before the King, to witness for God, whether he would hear or no …' But now she also asked for justice concerning the confiscation of her goods towards her son's fine. With the cry 'I wait for Justice of thee, O King', she now proceeded to follow Charles II wherever he went, including two visits to his tennis court, when she spoke to him as he went up into his coach, 'after he had been at his sport', and an encounter in another favourite place of royal relaxation, St James's Park, when she presented the King with two letters.

Familiarity bred in the soldiers round the King a rough sympathy for the persistent old lady, and the King's coachman actually read aloud one of her letters. In the park, the ordinary people murmured because old Elizabeth did not kneel before her sovereign. But one of the kindly soldiers did eventually get Elizabeth a kind of informal audience. She used it of course for a lengthy bout of preaching; and was in the end put once more outside the palace gates. The next morning Elizabeth Hooton returned, having devised a costume of sackcloth and ashes for herself in the meanwhile; once more she was pulled away from her preaching, but as she was being ejected, she continued to preach all the way through Westminster Hall and the palace yard, denouncing in particular the lawyers (who made professional use of that area).

Elizabeth Hooton's master-plan, apart from the need for justice, was to be able to buy a house and land within Boston itself, so that the Quakers of New England would have at once a meeting-house, a resting-place and a burial ground, all three being denied to them by current laws. The fact that Charles II eventually granted the old woman a certificate to settle in any British colony will not surprise anyone who is familiar with the parable of the importunate widow (even she did not think to accost a man exhausted after his favourite sport). So Elizabeth Hooton sold her farm, and armed with the King's certificate succeeded in sailing to Boston, the certificate preventing the captain of the ship from being fined for transporting a Quaker. But the royal backing did not prevent her from having to pay up to 20s a night for her lodging – to cover the fine which might be levied.

Elizabeth Hooton's subsequent experiences in New England, where she wandered about North Massachusetts preaching, were indeed even more harrowing than her previous ones, certificate or no certificate. In Cambridge, Massachusetts, the college boys, never as a class very sympathetic to Quakers, as 'Little Elizabeth' Fletcher found at Oxford (see p.321), mocked and pelted her.[16] She was then put into a stinking dungeon and left for two days and nights without food, before being sentenced by the court to be whipped through three towns and finally expelled from the colony. So she was tied to a Cambridge whipping-post and lashed ten times with a three-stringed whip, three knots in each string. At Watertown willow-rods were used; at Dedham, on a cold frosty morning, she received ten lashes at the cart-tail. Once more, but this time 'beaten and torn' she was carried into the wilderness: 'towards night they left her there, where there were many wolves, bears and other wild beasts, and many deep waters to pass through'. Once again, as on her first visit, Elizabeth Hooton made her way to friendly Rhode Island; she ascribed her preservation to the guidance of 'an invisible hand' and thanked God fervently that for His sake she had been able to endure 'beyond what her age and sex, morally speaking, could otherwise have borne'.

Still Elizabeth Hooton did not abandon her mission, continuing to assail Boston with her fervour, before being assailed in turn by the authorities and returning to Rhode Island to recuperate. A rare treat was provided by the funeral of Governor Endicott, taken away by the Lord just as Elizabeth had predicted five years earlier, in 1665. Elizabeth Hooton attended the ceremony; but since the Lord guided her to preach at it, she was removed from there to prison once more.

Elizabeth Hooton never succeeded in buying a house and

land; after five years therefore she returned to England. Her experiences were summed up by her son Samuel, who later tried to continue her mission and told the justices: 'I had an old mother who was here amongst you and bore many of your stripes and much cruelty at your hands!' Back in England, Elizabeth Hooton was in time to witness the fresh wave of Quaker imprisonments consequent upon the second Conventicle Act of 1670, the penalties of which were still more severe than those of the previous one; Margaret Fell was one of these victims and Elizabeth Hooton lobbied her old friend the King on her behalf. In 1671 a London Meeting of the Friends made her one of the Overseers of the Fleet prison, to help care for the Quakers therein.

For all this useful work, the call of the New World still rang in the old woman's ears. When she learnt that George Fox intended to visit the West Indies in order to straighten out the somewhat chaotic affairs of the Quakers there, she decided to accompany him, one of twelve Friends to do so. She sailed with the rest on 12 August 1671, and arrived after a troublesome journey at Barbados on 3 October. In January the following year George Fox set off again for Jamaica where Quakerism, introduced in 1658, had recently been languishing. He was accompanied by Elizabeth Hooton and three male followers. This was to be old Elizabeth's last journey. A week after they landed, she died.

She went very suddenly, well one day and dead the next, according to George Fox's journal: 'in peace like a lamb'. A fellow Quaker, James Lancaster, was beside her when she died, and heard her give her last testimony 'concerning Truth'. But Elizabeth Hooton had spoken her own best epitaph when she explained, a few years before the end of her life: 'Yes, the Love that I bear to the Souls of all Men, makes me willing to undergo whatsoever can be inflicted on me.'[17]

Mary Fisher, the Yorkshire girl who introduced Quakerism to New England before being banished from it, was another of those early Friends whose travels 'for the Service of Truth

Abroad' compel one's awe.[18] Her early spell in York prison had had one beneficial effect: she learnt to write while she was there. On her release Mary Fisher left Yorkshire for East Anglia. It was within the university town of Cambridge that Mary Fisher and her companion Elizabeth Williams met with an experience parallel to that of Elizabeth Hooton at Cambridge, Massachusetts, although some small provocation can be argued in this case. Observing the 'Froth and Levity' of the undergraduates' behaviour at Sidney Sussex, the two women told them that they were 'Antichrists' and that their college was 'a Cage of Unclean Birds, and the Synagogue of Satan'. As a result the women were abused and pelted with stones.

Examined by the Mayor, Mary Fisher and Elizabeth Williams presented that familiar conundrum where problem women were concerned: under whose legal protection were they? He asked their names: They replied, their Names were written in the Book of Life. He demanded their Husbands' names. (It was in essence the same question as that posed by the magistrate to the Catholic nun Sister Dorothea in 1617 – see p.179.) The two women told the Mayor 'they had no Husband but Jesus Christ and he sent them'. At this the Mayor grew furious, denounced them both as whores, and ordered them to be whipped by the constable until the blood ran down their bodies. They were probably the first Quakers to suffer under the brutal application of the Elizabethan Act against rogues and vagabonds to the members of their religion. Throughout this ordeal Mary Fisher and Elizabeth Williams managed to sing: 'The Lord be blessed, the Lord be praised.'

In New England, as we have seen, Mary Fisher was flogged before being expelled. Curiously enough it was in her encounter with the 'Grand Seignior', as the Sultan of Turkey was known, that Mary Fisher suffered no ordeal beyond that imposed by her own adventurous progress. There was a certain irony in the fact that the low position of women in the Moslem world enabled the Turks at least to appreciate exactly how remarkable an individual Mary Fisher must be; they accorded her that amazed respect denied to her in the Christian world. On the other hand it is only fair to say that the converse is also true; Mary Fisher displayed a tact in handling the claims of Mahomet to divinity which she certainly did not choose to exercise when denouncing the frothy and light-hearted undergraduates of Sidney Sussex College.

Be that as it may, it is undeniable that this strange episode, like some kind of 'Turkish Nights' is one from which Sultan and Vizier of Turkey alike emerge with a credit quite alien to Governor Endicott of Massachusetts. The fate of Mary Fisher in Turkey was also a great deal preferable to that of two fellow Quakers, Katherine Evans and Sarah Chevers, who embarked for Alexandria but only got as far as Malta, where they were imprisoned by the Catholic Inquisition. There they remained for three and a half years until the efforts of the English Catholic Seigneur d'Aubigny, almoner to Queen Catherine, who had Maltese interests, effected their release in 1664. The two women then offered to serve d'Aubigny should it be in their power. He courteously replied that it was enough that he should be remembered in their (Quaker) prayers.

Mary Fisher originally set out for the Mediterranean in 1657 as part of a Quaker mission of six people: three men including the Irish Quaker John Perrot, another ex-Baptist, and two other women, Mary Prince and Beatrice Beckley. Hoping to reach Jerusalem, they got as far as Smyrna where the idea of converting the Turkish 'Grand Seignior' along the way seems to have first occurred. The English Consul, if amiable, was also discouraging, and sent the party back towards Venice by sea. However, Mary Fisher took the opportunity of a call along the coast to Morea to land and head none the less for the Sultan's court. Beatrice Beckley seems to have accompanied her at the landing, but Mary Fisher made her final prodigious journey alone. The first account published (by a Dutch Quaker in the early eighteenth century) said that she made it entirely on foot, which would have meant walking 500 to 600 miles through Greece and Macedonia and over the mountains of Thrace: this during a period when the prolonged war between Venice and the Ottoman Empire (and internal feuds within Turkey itself) caused either terror or xenophobia at the mere sight of strangers. It is more probable that the Friends took a Greek boat across the Aegean, before Mary Fisher set off alone on foot on her divinely appointed mission to the 'Great Turk'.[19]

The Sultan – the 'Great Turk' – was at this point lying together with 20,000 men at Adrianople, along the banks of the river Maritsa, whither he had repaired from Constantinople. The Sultan's tents were hung with rich gold embroideries: 'the magnitude of these Pavilions is such', wrote Henry Marsh in a survey of the Turkish Empire a few years later, 'that afar off they seem no less than Cities'. The Sultan himself, Mahomet IV, aged sixteen, was also gorgeously attired in gold and sable as he sat surrounded by his eunuchs. His appearance was however more terrifying than dazzling. The son of a half-witted father, he had been permanently marked by his father's savage attack on him as a child. For all his majestic trappings here was 'a monster of a man' in the words of another English observer, 'a deformed sight both in body and mind, as if one strove with the other how to offend; stupid, loggerheaded, cruel, fierce as to his aspect'.[20]

Mary Fisher, on the other hand, was a thirty-five-year-old 'maid'; one whose 'intellectual faculties' were in the opinion of a contemporary 'greatly adorned by the gravity of her deportment'. Even to be granted an interview was in itself an achievement. Mary Fisher succeeded in persuading the Grand Vizier, to whom the Sultan left all business matters so that he himself could 'follow the chase of fearful and flying Beasts', to introduce her, despite the fact that the Grand Vizier, generally speaking, recommended the Sultan never to listen to women's 'Counsels and Advices'.

Surrounded by dragomans, who waited to interpret for her, Mary Fisher was introduced into the Sultan's presence. She then stood in silence. She was after all waiting for the guidance of the Inner Light. When the Sultan, mistaking her silence for modesty, offered to dismiss some of his suite, she declined his offer. Finally she spoke 'what was upon her mind'. The Turks listened to her 'with much attention and gravity' until she had done. The Sultan asked Mary if she had anything more to say, and she in return asked whether he had understood her message. According to the Quaker account which may have come from Mary herself, he answered, Yes, he had understood every word, 'and further said, that what she had spoken was truth'.[21]

The Sultan then pressed Mary Fisher to stay with them, saying that they could not but respect one who had taken so much pains to come to them so far from England, with a message from the Lord God. In view of the danger of travelling alone, he also offered her a guard to get back to Constantinople, if she persisted in that plan. Mary Fisher declined both offers: It was at this point that the Turks asked Mary Fisher what she thought of their prophet Mahomet, and she replied warily 'that she knew him not' although she knew Christ the true prophet. Concerning Mahomet she suggested that they should judge him to be true or false according to the words or prophecies he spoke: 'If the word that a prophet speaketh comes to pass, then shall ye know that the Lord hath sent the prophet; but if it come not to pass, then shall ye know that the Lord never sent him'. The Turks acknowledged the truth of what she said.

It is impossible to know exactly what interpretation the Sultan and his entourage put upon this amazing visitation; just as it is impossible to know exactly how Mary Fisher's words – and those of the Sultan – were transformed in translation. The Sultan never did mend his ways towards other Christians, or show any practical appreciation of Mary's message. Nevertheless Mary Fisher herself did return to Constantinople 'without the least hurt or scoff'.

Her gracious treatment at the Sultan's hands inclined her to believe of the Turks that 'there is a royal seed amongst them which in time God will raise'. 'The English are more bad, most of them', wrote Mary grimly. For in Constantinople the Quakers, including Mary, were treated much as they were in England and America, as a pernicious nuisance. The English Ambassador, Sir Thomas Bendish, drew weary attention to the Quakers' 'insufferable' disturbances of 'our divine exercises'. His successor was the third Earl of Winchilsea (father-in-law of Anne Countess of Winchilsea, and Anne Viscountess Conway's first cousin). He too complained that 'the carriage of that sort of people is ridiculous and is capable to bring dishonour to our Nation...' when ordering the removal of the English Quakers.[22]

This particular Earl of Winchilsea, a man of great magnificence, was certainly not predisposed by his way of life to appreciate the Quaker message, unlike his cousin Anne. He was married four times and had twenty-seven legitimate children, of whom sixteen lived to maturity. His second wife, who accompanied him to Turkey, bore eleven of them. But Lord Winchilsea also kept a number of other women in Turkey, building little convenient houses for them, by whom he produced still further progeny. 'My Lord, you have not only built a town, but peopled it too', observed Charles II on Lord Winchilsea's return to England in 1669. 'Oh Sir, I was your Majesty's representative', retorted the prolific Earl.[23]

As for the grave and fearless Mary Fisher, she eventually reached England safely, where she later married a fellow Quaker, the master-mariner William Bayly, a romance begun when he was in Newgate. It was a very happy marriage, blessed by three children, and Mary Fisher preached no more. But in 1697, as an old lady, she was still pointed out as 'one whose name you have heard of, Mary Fisher, she that spoke to the Grand Turk'.

'God is thy Witness', wrote Elizabeth Hooton to Margaret Fell in 1671, 'thou hast suffered more than many have expected ...'[24] It was true that Margaret Fell, born Margaret Askew in 1614, might legitimately have expected a comparatively easy life by the (female) standards of the time. As a girl she had a portion of £3,000; she was married at sixteen to a much older man, Judge Fell, and left a wealthy widow on his death in 1658. Margaret Fell also enjoyed the blessing of an extremely large and affectionate family: she had no less than seven remarkable and intelligent daughters. Against these one ungrateful son weighed lightly in the emotional balance; although the practical consequences of his ingratitude, in the light of his sex, were heavy. She was blessed in addition with a constitution which would enable her to survive into her late eighties.

Nevertheless Margaret Fell from the first moment she heard George Fox preach 'saw it was the truth and I could not deny it'.

Judge Fell on his return home was told that Margaret and her daughter Sarah had been bewitched. As Margaret Fell wrote: 'any may think what a condition I was like to be in, that either I must displease my husband, or offend God'. She chose to displease her husband (although Judge Fell was in fact to show himself remarkably tolerant of his wife's earnest convictions). Now many of the Fell female household, including 'little Mabby', Bet Drinkall, Peg and her sister 'Old Jane', became Quakers. Margaret Fell herself was to be, in George Fox's own words 'the nursing mother' of Quakerism.[25]

Her role as a nursing mother (she is addressed on occasion by her fellow Quakers in quite lyrical language: 'O thou daughter of God, thou art comely in thy beauty, clothed with the sun and moon under thy feet')[26] was however essentially different from that of the itinerant Elizabeth Hooton and Mary Fisher. Margaret Fell did not preach. She did not travel the country. She did not venture abroad. The presence of this established socially unassailable woman in the Quaker midst emphasized that other side of female Quakerism: its organizational philanthropy towards its own members. The hospitality which Margaret Fell dispensed, with her daughters, at Swarthmoor Hall in Lancashire, stood for more than mere material need gratified, though that was important too; it also indicated that not all female Quakers could be classed as wild spirits or even witches in the grip of the devil's 'Extempore Way'.

It is suggested by Margaret Fell's biographer, Isabel Ross, that the emotionalism of her first response to George Fox, and that of her daughters, enabled her to understand and cope with this phenomenon in Quakerism later. Postscripts in letters to Fox give some indication of the flavour of this. Susan aged two [sic]: 'O my dear father, when wilt thou come'; Mary aged five: 'thou art the fountain of life'; and Margaret Fell herself: 'We thy babes ... O thou bread of life ... O our life ... O our dear nursing father ... O our life, our desire is to see thee again that we may be refreshed and established'.[27]

But more practically it was Margaret Fell who led the first Women's Petition of 1659, a supplement to the general Quaker protest against tithes. She protested against the imprisonment of George Fox at Lancaster, and was instrumental in securing from Charles II that release of Quakers which attended the Restoration. Margaret Fell's social position enabled her to write to such high-born ladies as Mary Princess of Orange and Elizabeth of Bohemia (rumoured to have Quaker sympathies); she even tackled the arch-Catholic Dowager Queen Henrietta Maria, presenting her with Quaker books.

Even these connections could not free Margaret Fell from the problems posed by her own conscience. She could not – would not – take an oath. At the March Assizes of 1664 Margaret Fell was summoned for allowing illegal meetings in her house. She refused to take the necessary oath in court. Although Margaret Fell was courteously granted a stool and a cushion by the judge (something not offered to Elizabeth Hooton and Mary Fisher), she was none the less threatened with the forfeiture of her estate, as well as life imprisonment, if she would not swear. At the death of Judge Fell, Margaret Fell had inherited Swarthmoor Hall for herself and her daughters; her son George received her own dowry of Marsh Grange, where he was probably already living. At this threat of forfeiture therefore Margaret Fell spoke up boldly: 'I am a widow, and my estate is a dowry, and I have five children unpreferred [unplaced]; and if the King's pleasure be to take my estate from me, upon the account of my conscience, and not for any evil or wrong done, let him do as he pleaseth'.[28]

Refusing to take the oath, or remove her glove, or promise to hold no further Quaker meetings, Margaret Fell was duly imprisoned in Lancaster Castle (where George Fox was already installed). There, in lodgings which let in the rain and the snow, she remained until the summer of 1668; she lay under sentence for *Praemunire*, that is, for rejecting the authority of the English courts in favour of some other (spiritual) authority. It was finally on the orders of the King and Council that she was set free.

Gossips had long connected the names of George Fox and the widowed Margaret Fell: 'I am so well used to them I know how to bear them', she told one of her daughters.[29] Contemporary satire was always rich – or poor – in jokes about the sexual morals of the Quakers. Some of this was owing to the unrestrained behaviour of the group surrounding James Naylor under the Commonwealth. Quaker inspiration was also mocked. Chapbooks (cheap popular fiction) of the 1680s included one story entitled *Love's Masterpiece* which ended with a Quaker suggesting to his mistress that they should retire to the coal-hole: 'there only the light within will shine'. Quaker marriage was another fertile source of allusions, since the Quakers persisted in having their own form of ceremony at a Quaker Meeting, when the couple simply testified in the presence of the Friends. This led to accusations that the Friends 'went together like brute beasts', as was asserted at the Nottingham Assizes.[30]

Quaker marriage also led to troubles about inheritance: if the Quaker ceremony was not valid, then were the children of the marriage illegitimate? At Nottingham, where the inheritance of Mary Ashwell, daughter of the Quakers William Ashwell and Ann Ridge, was in doubt, the judge found for the Quakers. He compared the Quaker marriage to the union in paradise when Adam took Eve and Eve took Adam: 'it was the consent of the woman that made the marriage'. The general vagueness of the time about the state of marriage and the status of the ceremony which introduced it acted in this case to the benefit of the Quakers. Even so it remained a source of popular anxiety. At the end of the century *The Athenian Oracle* was asked whether a Quaker marriage was valid. The reassuring answer was that it *was* valid, if not strictly legal, and 'accordingly their children are for inheritance'.[31]†

When George Fox did marry Margaret Fell – in October 1669 – he was forty-five and she was fifty-five. It was a spiritual match. According to the Quaker custom for the preliminary examination of the parties concerned (which meant that Quaker marriages, far from being more loosely performed, were actually more carefully contracted) Fox was questioned on the subject of his bride's age. Surely marriage was only for the procreation of children? Fox answered his interlocutor: 'I told him I never thought of any such

†Between 1753 and 1837 the marriages of the Quakers and the Jews were the only ones performed outside the Church of England which were legal.

thing [marriage] but only in obedience to the power of the Lord...' He added: 'I had no command to do such a thing till a half year before, though some people had long talked of it.' He also took the trouble to make it clear that he was not interested in marrying a rich widow; carefully asking his future step-children whether their rights under their father's will had been respected. Fox also engaged himself never to meddle with the estate.[32]

The intention of George Fox and Margaret Fell to marry was published at three separate Meetings: a Man's Meeting where Margaret, her daughters and twelve women Quakers were also present: a Meeting of men and women Friends; and a public Meeting. They were eventually married at a very large public Meeting.

At the first of these Meetings, one of Margaret's daughters, Rachel, testified: 'And I do believe, that the thing [the marriage] is of the Lord'. Unfortunately George Fell, Margaret's only son, and his wife Hannah, who were not Quakers, held the very opposite belief. George Fell felt humiliated by the union of his mother with this weird and wild itinerant preacher, *habitué* of prisons, and there were financial considerations as well, for all Fox's precautions. Margaret Fell was after all in possession of Swarthmoor. There is reason to believe that George and Hannah Fell were instrumental in securing Margaret Fell's return to prison in 1670 when the Conventicle Act was renewed.[33] And when George Fell died in 1670, he specifically bequeathed the Swarthmoor Estate to his infant son, although his father in his will had left it to Margaret to provide for the girls. Hannah Fell, established at Marsh Grange, continued the vendetta. Whatever the rights and wrongs of the legal position (by no means clear in view of a wife's weak position at law), where Hannah Fell is concerned, it is difficult to disagree with the incensed judgement of old Elizabeth Hooton: 'What a rebellious daughter-in-law art thou! Was there ever such a wicked thing done in England or in any age before, that thou should ruinate thy husband's mother? The same hand that cut off thy husband will do the same by thee and leave thee neither root nor branch if thou do not speedily repent.'[34]

In April 1671 Margaret Fell was released on the orders of the King, and her part of Swarthmoor Estate was granted to her daughters. The odious Hannah lived on at Marsh Grange. Nor was this family dispute thoroughly settled until 1691 when Daniel Abraham, husband of Rachel Fell, 'bought' the Swarthmoor Estate.

It would be wrong, however, to see life at Swarthmoor as dour, or Margaret Fell herself as priggish. She besought the Friends to think where dress was concerned, that uniform dress and colour did not necessarily bespeak a pure life within. When disapproval of coloured and striped apparel was minuted at a Yearly Meeting (the beginnings of the so-called Quaker look of plain dressing) Margaret Fell exclaimed: 'This is a silly poor Gospel. It is more fit for us to be covered with God's eternal Spirit, and clothed with his Eternal Light.' She was probably less rigid in this respect than Anne Countess of Winchilsea, groaning at the demands of the fashionable life. Her clever eldest daughter Sarah wore red stockings and others of sky-coloured worsted. White wine, claret and brandy featured in the household accounts at Swarthmoor. Luxuries like oranges were sent for from London as were gloves and even frivolities like vizard masks,[35] so frequently employed by the courtesans of the capital to conceal their countenances, that the term 'vizard mask' became synonymous with their profession.

It was in 1666, during Margaret Fell's first spell in prison, that she wrote her defence of female preaching, *Womens Speaking*. Even among the Quakers themselves, the revolutionary proposition that a woman's voice might be heard in public on religious matters met with opposition.[36] Margaret Fell met the challenge boldly with quotations from the Acts of the Apostles and also from Joel: 'And it shall come to pass, in the last days, saith the Lord, I will pour out my spirit upon all Flesh; your sons and daughters shall Prophesy.' Her basic message was that 'God hath put no such difference between Male and Female as man would make.' She firmly blamed the devil – 'the Serpent' – whose ancient enmity towards Eve had led to the general silencing of women since the Fall: 'and if the seed of the Woman speak not, the Seed of the Serpent speaks; for God hath put enmity between the two seeds, and it is manifest that those that speak against the Woman and her Seeds speaking, speak out of the enmity of the old Serpent's seed'. In short: 'all this opposing and gainsaying of Women's Speaking: hath risen out of the bottomless Pit...'[37]

As for the message of St Paul, why should women be specifically ordered by the Apostle to have their heads covered when they prayed or prophesied, if the latter activity was not to be permitted? Margaret Fell was also free in quoting many texts in which Jesus – or his predecessors the prophets – compared the Church to a woman: from that of Isaiah ('I have called thee as a Woman forsaken'), via David ('The King's Daughter is all glorious within') to the vision of St John concerning heaven ('a Woman clothed with the Sun, and the Moon under her feet...') She also pointed out that the most important revelations concerning Himself were spoken by Jesus to women, including that to Martha at Bethany: 'I am the Resurrection and the Life'. And was it not to a woman that Jesus first appeared on earth *after* the Resurrection?[38]

Like George Fox, who had early on pointed to the Magnificat as the supreme example of a woman 'speaking', Margaret Fell pointed triumphantly to the use of the words of Elizabeth, the mother of John the Baptist, and the Virgin Mary in the *Book of Common Prayer*: 'Are you not here beholden to the woman for her sermon to use her words to put into your Common Prayer? And yet you forbid women's speaking.' But perhaps Margaret Fell's most telling point, at least from the modern point of view, was that men were trying to limit the power of Almighty God, by contending that it existed only in the male sex.[39]

The first organization of the Quaker movement was developed by George Fox out of sheer necessity to combat the effects of persecution (although there were those who continued to criticize him for abandoning his original conception of an unorganized religion). In some places women featured in this at an early stage; in about 1656 two Women's Meetings developed in

London, the Box Meeting (for succouring the poor, so called because money was gathered in a box) and the Two Weeks' Meeting, on the model of the Men's Two Weeks' Meeting. Elsewhere in the country the participation of women was dependent on local prejudice – and no doubt on the availability of energetic women. It seems that it was not until 1671 that George Fox set in train the formation of the Women's Monthly and Quarterly Meetings to come together at the same time as the Men's. Fox, constantly using the word 'helpmeet' where the women were concerned, believed that they were intended for special work such as the care of Quaker servants and the examination of future spouses as well as the tending of the poor.[40]

It was a point of view well expressed by one of Margaret Fell's married daughters, Isabel Yeamans, writing from Swarthmoor in 1676 on the subject of Women's Meetings.[41] She thought these should be 'constant and frequent … to wait upon the lord to feel his power to administer counsel, wisdom and Instruction that thereby your minds may be seasoned and fitted for the lords business'. This business was 'to inquire into the necessities of the poor and to relieve the widows and the fatherless and to visit the sick and the afflicted which is the pure practice of the pure religion'. The fallen should be reproved – but mildly. A private warning about 'undue conduct' should precede the reproof of the Women's Meeting. In general it was the duty of the 'elder and honourable women', in the footsteps of the holy women gone before, to be 'teachers of good things that they may teach the young women according to the holy apostles' exhortation and so to be good examples and patterns of prudence …'

Isabel Yeamans continued: 'Here will be work and business enough for us all that none need to be Idle in God's vineyard, but as we have everyone received a measure of God's spirit and grace some may be fellow helpers and workers together with our brethren in the work of the lord in these gospel days …' It was the distinguishing Quaker argument, first laid down by George Fox, that women too should be allowed to be 'serviceable' in their own 'places and stations'. Isabel Yeamans wrote: 'So every member of the body whereof Christ our lord is head may be serviceable and although we may be many members and some much more honourable than others yet no member though it be small is to be despised.'

George Fox himself defended his original contention concerning women's right to speak, both in England and on his travels abroad. In Flushing, New England, for example a minister's son disputed the subject with Fox at the end of a meeting in 1672. 'And as for women's speaking, such as the apostles did own, I owned, and such as they did deny, I did deny', was Fox's reply. In 1673 one Nathaniel Coleman spoke up against the whole principle of the Women's Meetings at Slaughterford in Wiltshire. Eventually Coleman flung out of the house 'in a rage and passion' vowing that 'he would rule over his wife' and so on and so forth.

To combat this, Fox explained that woman's lack of authority was part of the bad order of things, and had not existed in a state of innocence. Eve, by her transgression, her evil 'teaching' of her husband, had brought that about, but in the restoration, brought about by Jesus Christ, 'all the family of God, women as well as men, might know, possess, perform and discharge their offices and services in the house of God'. He also made the point, which arose in different forms throughout the seventeenth century, that if husbands such as Nathaniel Coleman could rule over their wives, which he did not seek to deny, 'neither he [Coleman] nor they must rule over widows and young women, and other men's wives'.[42]

In general, however, Fox attempted conciliation rather than provocation. So the arguments about the Women's Meetings and their precise purpose, and women's right to speak, continued within the Quaker movement itself: the very existence of such a controversy at that period being of course a tribute to the movement's early ideals concerning the spiritual equality of women.

Margaret Fell did not only enrich the Quaker movement with her own stalwart example of a woman whose conscience was unshackled by wealth, uncowed by adversity; she also bequeathed to it those further crusaders, her brilliant daughters. The possible influence of the mother for good at a period when few women were subject to influence outside the home is demonstrated at its fullest by the lives of the Fell girls. Sarah Fell, later married to William Meade, was said in her preaching to ravish 'all her beholders and hearers with admiration and wonder'. Margaret Fell herself had long shown an interest in Hebrew literature and teaching, leading towards the possible reconversion of the Jews. Sarah taught herself Hebrew to confound her critics, who claimed that she could not understand the biblical texts.[43] Isabel Yeamans accompanied her step-father on his travels to Europe.

George Fox died in January 1691 but Margaret lived on another eleven years, to benefit from the expanding atmosphere of toleration following the accession of William III. She was not bereft of the traditional joy of old age. Her eight children gave her twenty-four grandchildren, fourteen of whom survived childhood. As little John Abraham, son of Rachel, wrote in 1687: 'Dear Grandmot thou art oftener in my mind than I can menshon.'[44]

As for Margaret Fell's spiritual convictions, as late as 1695 she was reminding the Women's Yearly Meeting in London that the 'seed is one in male and female'.[45]

CHAPTER NINETEEN

The Delight of Business

'Business is her sole delight in this world ... It is
charity to keep her in full time employment.'

MRS CONSTANCE PLEY TO SAMUEL PEPYS,
Calendar of State Papers, Domestic, 1666

'It is the Lord that creates true industry in his people ...'; thus
Joan Dant, a pedlar, or rather a pedlar-extraordinary, and one
of the few women *entrepreneurs* of the seventeenth century
about whom some personal details are known. A woman pedlar
in the seventeenth century was of course not necessarily indigent
or despised, as the name might seem to indicate today. At one
end of the market there did exist those women, close to beggars,
who if sufficiently unsuccessful, old and quarrelsome, might be
in danger of being accused of witchcraft. But at the other end
were those enterprising women who travelled the country supplying haberdashery or provisions to the good wives unable or
unwilling to make the journey to market. There was the Widow
Elizabeth Doddington of Hillbishops, licensed by the Somerset
justices in 1630 to use up to three horses in her work as a 'badger'
of butter and cheese in Somerset, Wilts, Hants and Devon; or
Hester Pinney, the unmarried daughter of a Puritan minister in
Dorset who was ejected from his living at the Restoration: she
sold lace in London, first as part of the family business (keeping
in touch with her relations by letter) and then on her own
account.[1]

When Joan Dant, who died in 1715 at the age of eighty-four,

came to make her will she was worth rather more than £9,000. 'I got it by the rich and I mean to leave it to the poor,' she observed. In a letter to her executors she described herself as having 'through the blessing of God, with honesty and industrious care, improved my little in the world to a pretty good degree'. She therefore wished to help 'the fatherless and the widows in the Church of Christ'.

Joan Dant was a Quaker. Her husband had been a weaver who worked in Spitalfields. It was after his death that she took up work as a pedlar; carrying haberdashery, hosiery and the like from house to house in London and thereabouts. As a Quaker, and incidentally a woman of resolutely upright life, she was able to make good business use of her connections among the Friends. Soon the frugality of her own lifestyle (which she never altered) combined with the expanding nature of her business enabled her to save enough to start trading abroad. At her death, her executors found debts incurred due to business pending, as far away as Paris and Brussels; while the amount of her fortune surprised even those who knew her well.

Joan Dant's industry – that 'true industry' whose creation she ascribed to the Lord – is an example of the fact that religions which encouraged women as well as men to work 'in God's vineyard' often encouraged them by implication to toil in other more commercial fields. The medieval abbesses of the great convents, confident in their religious office, had also been great businesswomen; in the same way Quaker women were sustained rather than depressed in the world of business by their beliefs; the knowledge that God intended them, in the words of George Fox, to be 'serviceable in their generation'.[2]

Katherine Philips, the Matchless Orinda, had been able to help her husband in his business as well as write plays and poetry, in which capacity, wrote Ballard in the eighteenth century, 'few wives are supposed capable of serving their husbands'. But a Quaker dynasty, such as that of the Gurneys of East Anglia, would produce without comment women like Elizabeth Gurney, who in the 1680s kept the books of her husband's and brother's mercantile affairs, and acted as chief clerk. This energy can hardly be ascribed to lack of employment on her part; Elizabeth Gurney also bore eight sons, four of whom lived to adulthood.[3]

In part this ability was due to the Quaker emphasis on schools and education for both sexes, which meant that arithmetic was not a closed book to the female Friends. But since this emphasis on education was in itself due to the Quaker conviction that the Lord might move in any spirit, regardless of sex, one is back with the confidence granted at source, that is with the esteem given to women within the Quaker religion. Sarah Fell, Margaret's brilliant eldest daughter, had a good head for business, as well as being a 'ravishing' preacher, as the account books for Swarthmoor Hall show, during the years when she ran it.[4]

Where the women of the other dissenting sects were concerned, the connection, traced by the Puritans, between worldly success and divine approval, meant that there was nothing inherently abhorrent about the amassing of profits, particularly when they were used to forward God's purposes. (We detect a note of this in Joan Dant's letter to her executors, even if she was herself a Quaker.) But it is also noticeable in general that those women – often but not always widows – whose circumstances led them to indulge in business, could, whatever their rank or religion, expect approval if their efforts were successful. There was no trace here of that execration which attended the public endeavours of the 'petticoat-authors'. After all business practice in a woman could be seen as an extension of her role as the mainstay of her household, whereas learning and authorship were dangerously unfeminine pursuits. Just as the arithmetic necessary to do accounts (household accounts) was an esteemed part of female education, whereas the study of the classics drew forth angry male expostulations.

In the conduct of their affairs therefore, women paid far less lip service to the gospel of female modesty than they did, perforce, in the pursuit of a literary career. The melancholy withdrawal of Anne Countess of Winchilsea, fearing contempt for poems from a woman's pen, may be contrasted, with the zest displayed by Anne Russell, Countess of Bristol, in the exploitation of her wine licence. Sister of William, fifth Earl and first Duke of Bedford, wife of George Digby, Earl of Bristol, the Countess was one of those rewarded with a licence to import goods at the Restoration, her husband having formed part of the Royalist administration-in-exile. She set to and sold her wine with a will, the Earl of Bedford being among her early customers. In 1691, when she was nearly eighty, the Countess of Bristol still managed to sell her brother six dozen bottles of red port for the sum of £5 8s.[5]

It was true, as the editors of Alice Clark's seminal *Working Life of Women in the Seventeenth Century* (recently reissued with a new introduction) point out, that women's 'productivity and talents' depended on 'the domestic conditions which fostered them or precluded them'.[6] Pepys's diary provides an excellent insight into a world in which a variety of women were to be found working as shop-keepers, booksellers, ale-house keepers and the like. Nearly always family circumstances played some part in their situation.

The connection of women with the Stationers' Company and printing referred to earlier (see p.119) found its natural extension in the existence of women booksellers, either independently or in working partnership with their husbands. One of Pepys's earliest entries concerns 'my bookseller' Mrs Ann Mitchell, who with her husband Miles sold not only books but pamphlets and newspapers in Westminster Hall. After Miles Mitchell died of the plague in 1665, Mrs Mitchell carried on the business. Also in Westminster Hall, plying their trade as linendrapers (not linendrapers' assistants) were the sisters Betty and Doll Lane, to whose activities as Pepys's unofficial mistresses we shall return.[7]

There had always been women among the brewers and the ale-wives, with special rights to brewers' widows; ale-houses themselves being then enjoyed as meeting places by women as much as men, at a time when ale was the drink of the poor and tea and coffee the luxuries of the rich.[8] Just as women might enjoy a pipe, there were numerous women among the tobacco-sellers (frequently unlicensed) keeping murky establishments where it was said of the inhabitants: 'there communication is smoke'. The mistress of the ale-house was a stock character in the popular chapbooks. Then of course at a less commanding level there was a 'lily at the bar' as the playwright and Wit Sir George Etherege described the barmaid at the Rose Tavern in Russell Street. Sometimes the lily was the ale-wife herself; Richard Gough, in his *The History of Myddle*, a portrait of a Shropshire parish begun in 1670, describes the lovely girl – 'very fair' – who helped her husband Samuel Downton keep an ale-house.[9] She was known as White Legs because she wore no stockings, and drew the customers irresistibly from miles around to the great benefit of her husband's business.

White Legs was actually the second Mrs Downton, Samuel Downton's first wife having left him a fair amount of money. She had been a maid. Unfortunately White Legs's character was not as fair as her complexion. First she decamped with her husband to Staffordshire, leaving behind three children to be maintained by the parish. Then the Downtons descended to becoming beggars; he 'an old decrepit person' and she with a box of pins and laces to sell. How unlike the worthy Joan Dant did White Legs show herself in her attitude to her trade! There was little of the 'true industry' given by the Lord to be seen here. Soon White Legs left her elderly husband for 'a new Sparke' who travelled the country. Old Samuel went back to Shropshire to be maintained by the kindly son of his first marriage.

Women, as we have seen, had always had strong connection with the provision business, where their work naturally complemented that of their male relations. In June 1690, a certain Widow Long was discovered who was prepared to give evidence to explain the adulteration of the soldiers' and sailors' provisions the year before. 'Bloody arts' had been practised, as a result of which many had become sick. The widow would give her evidence so long as she was protected from the consequences, since 'one of her nearest kindred was a practitioner of these arts; till his conscience troubled him'.[10]

Pepys, as Clerk of the Acts to the Navy Board, involved with the provisioning and equipping of the Fleet, came into contact with more than one 'she-merchant' in the course of his official duties, with pleasanter consequences. Mrs Elizabeth Russell had been the wife of a respected ship's chandler named Robert

Russell. After his death in 1663, the widow took on the business – including the practice of sweetening those able to put business in her way. She sent Mrs Pepys a fine St George in alabaster, which the latter placed in her bedroom; Pepys himself received a case of knives with agate hafts, which he described as 'very pretty'.[11]

Far from showing any prejudice against the female in such a role, Pepys seems to have been both impressed and pleased by the phenomenon. Sarah Bland was the wife of a provision merchant named John Bland to whom Pepys went in December 1662 in order to discuss supplies for Tangier, a newly-acquired possession, part of the dowry of Queen Catherine. After the official business was over, Pepys stayed on to eat a dish of anchovies, and drink wine and cider: 'very merry', he commented, 'but above all, pleased to hear Mrs Bland talk like a merchant in her husband's business very well; and it seems she doth understand it and perform a great deal'. Two years later he was once again 'fain to admire the knowledge and experience of Mrs Bland, who I think as good a merchant as her husband'.[12]

Mrs Constance Pley was admired for her business sense and dealings not only by Samuel Pepys but by Colonel Bullen Reymes, a Dorset landowner and Member of Parliament, and a man with a reputation for financial acumen. He became Mrs Pley's business partner and – as a result of these transactions – intimate friend.[13]

Bullen Reymes, a Royalist, had been brought up in the service of the Duchess of Buckingham – Catherine Manners, widow of the first Duke and only surviving child of the sixth Earl of Rutland. Reymes married the co-heiress to extensive properties in Dorset and Somerset. After the Restoration, he was made Charles II's envoy to inspect Tangier after the Moorish invasion of 1664, and Surveyor of the Great Wardrobe (a financial post). At the time of the Dutch War he acted as the Portsmouth Commissioner for Sick and Wounded Seamen. A friend of John Evelyn, it was on the latter's nomination that in 1667 Reymes was made a Fellow of the Royal Society. A man of the world in every sense, charming, educated, well-travelled, Reymes paid no small compliment to Constance Pley at the end of his life; the first instruction which he left to his son, was to 'keep fair with Mrs Pley... he is sure she will not wrong him'. Yet by upbringing Mrs Pley seemed destined merely for the obscurity of her own household in a Dorset town.

Colonel Reymes's esteemed partner was born Constance Wise: a name of Bunyanesque appropriateness. In June 1635 Constance Wise married George Pley at Melcombe Church in Melcombe Regis, Dorset.[14] George Pley fought in the Civil War, reaching the rank of captain on the Parliamentary side; later he was to become Puritan Mayor of Weymouth. Under the Commonwealth he had already begun to supply Cromwell's fine new Navy with sailcloth, manufactured under his supervision in his cottages in and around Weymouth. Shortly after the Restoration Captain Pley was joined in business by Constance, their son George junior and Bullen Reymes. In the words of Bullen Reymes's biographer, Constance Pley now became 'the driving force of the enterprise', which was expanded to include the manufacture of hemp and cordage, and the import of canvas and other 'stuffs' from France.[15]

These were good times to live in for those involved in the out-fitting of ships – that is, until they came to present the bills for payment. The King himself, described by Bullen Reymes's friend Evelyn as 'a great lover of the sea', took an obsessional interest in all the details of shipbuilding and naval fortification.[16] English foreign policy after the Restoration, guided by hostility towards the Dutch and nervous rivalry with the French, demanded ships to implement it in either case, while the expanding empire – including the new jewel of Tangier – was sea-based. The Pleys, headed by Constance, were vigorous in their exploitation of this apparently favourable situation. In March 1664, and later in December, Constance Pley's name features in a contract with the Navy Commissioners for different kinds of canvas – the only woman's name to appear. Correspondence was however almost as much a feature of the business as supervision of the work and importation.

Between June 1660 and August 1672 nearly 100 letters were written on behalf of the joint enterprise to correspondents who included the Navy Commissioners such as Sir William Coventry and Thomas Middleton at Portsmouth, Sir John Mennes, the Comptroller of the Navy, and Sir George Carteret, the Navy Treasurer, as well as Pepys. Constance Pley herself wrote most of the letters – fourteen to Pepys alone are recorded, although only one of his has survived.[17] Bullen Reymes wrote of Mrs Pley's style; 'her oil will be better than my vinegar'. But if Mrs Pley's tone was never vinegary, it was sometimes highly charged. Most of the letters are pleas of varying degrees of urgency for payment, in order that the Pleys and Bullen Reymes should be able to pay their own workmen and suppliers.

In September 1664 Bullen Reymes himself fired off a furious letter to the Navy Commissioners, having discovered some patterns of canvas known as Noyals (for sails) at the docks supplied by Mr Browne and Le Texer, said to be the same as that used by the French King. It was, he pointed out bitterly, not a jot better than their own – and in any case the partners were owed £20,000! Under the circumstances, Parliament should at least see that they continued to buy the Pleys's sailcloth and cordage; whose business 'would have been aground long since but for his woman partner'.

The precarious finances of the King's administration were not improved by the prospect of war with the Dutch; this war itself, which broke out in March 1665, plunged the Government's credit downwards while elevating its expenses. The result was catastrophic, at least in financial terms (at the Battle of Lowestoft in June a naval defeat was inflicted on the Dutch by a fleet headed by the Duke of York). Everyone involved in the war, who depended in some way upon payment from a depleted Exchequer, suffered.

The sufferings of the seamen and their dependants, denied their promised pay and given 'tickets' or IOUs, were so acute that in July the following year a maddened mob of women demonstrators – over 300 of them – surged into the yard of the Navy Office, and stayed there, in Pepys's words 'clamouring and swearing, and cursing us'. Then the women broke into the garden which gave them access to Pepys's closet window 'and tormented me'. Many were demonstrating on behalf of their husbands, who had been taken prisoner and were lying penniless and starving in foreign prisons.[18] The extent to which those complaints were justified can be seen by the fact that this was one female mob from which officialdom did not shrink in disgust. Pepys himself felt sorry for the women and called one back to give her extra money as they were departing; she blessed him. When the Navy Board ordered the relief of the prisoners, it was to be done 'without any trouble to be given to any of their relations in attendance here (demonstrating) for the same'.[19]

In 1665 the plight of the sail-makers, desperate for payment for work done for which the Pleys had no money to give them, was not much better; then there was the question of paying for goods imported from France (George Pley junior was now at St Malo supervising that end of the business). Mrs Pley bombarded Sir George Carteret with requests for payment, couched in language which would surely have brought forth recompense, had any recompense been available. At one point she worked out that the Navy Board owed her well over £8,000 and she invoked God himself to move Sir George Carteret's hard heart.[20]

Young George Pley's position at St Malo also concerned her as the 'breach' with France was seen to be approaching: Constance Pley wrote to Pepys demanding a convoy home for £10,000's worth of hemp and other goods, lest they become the object of 'nefarious plundering'. But when the precious cargo did arrive, still Constance Pley was not paid for it – as she told Sir John Mennes on 3 August, this was a poor requital for all her tedious waitings, the great risk she had taken, and the care. In the absence of payment, she had to draw £500 upon her son's credit, something she was loath to do, but 'necessity hath no law'.[21]

The twentieth of August brought an anguished letter from Constance Pley to Pepys; £15,000's worth of goods delivered, and still no payment! From this she 'can apprehend nothing but an approaching ruin, unless speedy relief be granted; £6,000 owing is wanted this month and next'. She 'must end her days in sorrow for meddling in this affair, and bringing in Colonel Reymes and other friends to suffer with her'.[22]

The summer of 1665 was one of gathering crisis, and not only for the Government's many creditors. The first ominous signs of plague were seen in London in June; by August the capital was paralysed. Pepys, making his will, wrote on the tenth that the town was so 'unhealthy' that a man could not reckon on surviving more than two days. The King and the court had already gone to Oxford; even more to the point the Exchequer had moved to the old palace of Nonsuch in Surrey. The King's minister, Arlington, engaged in finding funds for a spring campaign, complained of the difficulty of raising money at that distance.[23] For Mrs Pley it was the difficulty of getting paid.

Trade was of course as adversely affected as everything else dependent on the busy working hum of a capital city. The rich merchants and their families, like the courtiers, fled. Many of them took refuge on ships moored on the river Thames from Greenwich to Limehouse.[24] Mrs Pley heard from one of her correspondents, Richard Fuller, that every day was like Sunday in the City of London; not one merchant in 100 was left. She enclosed Fuller's letter with her own, since Fuller was one of those who protested that health and rest were being 'snatched from him' because Mrs Pley could not meet her obligations, and that she was 'going about to murder him'. At all points Mrs Pley took the responsibility for the business upon herself; payment *must* be forthcoming, so that 'the reputation of her husband and Colonel Reymes, who were drawn into the business by her advice, were not shipwrecked'.

In the meantime George Pley at St Malo, animated by something of his mother's determined spirit, seized every opportunity to trade despite the French 'vapour' or threat of impending war. A small English ship which had sailed on to the French rocks in error, and thus had the right to ask for help to get on its way, was used to send canvas, yarn and hemp back to England. But as Constance Pley told Pepys in December, things brought in by 'stealth' inevitably cost most; she must be paid something out of the Prize Office, for that at least was enriched by the proceeds of wartime capture at sea.[25]

At last some payment came. Mrs Pley's immediate ambition, after she had recovered from her abundance of joy, was 'once more to fill the King's storehouse which is very empty'. But the new year brought with it no halcyon period either for England or the Pleys. In January 1666 Mrs Pley was once more begging on her knees for £500 out of £2,000 owed for goods manufactured in the West Country, to 'stop the mouths of the poor people in her employ'. By late February she described herself as so short both in purse and credit, that she 'scarce dares show her face'. She suffered from a conviction that her appeals were being neglected just because they were so perpetual, but necessity left her no choice. As she told Pepys, if only a special clerk could deal with her on business matters, she could avoid these endless personal applications. Her ultimate threat was that she would come up to London herself and sort matters out.[26]

All the time the people at the centre were not without sympathy for Mrs Pley's case: in the middle of April Thomas Middleton wrote to Pepys, 'Madam Pley complains much for want of money; it would be a pity to let so good a manufacture of English canvas fail for want of encouragement.' The trouble was that the King's financial situation, and that of the country as a whole, was parlous; the Fire of London, coming in high summer to cleanse away the dreaded plague, was in a financial sense a further disaster. In the summer of 1667 the Dutch successfully raided the Medway. Mrs Pley was given 'assignments', i.e. first call, on the Navy tallies at the Guildhall; but in March 1668 Sir William Coventry was telling Pepys that Mrs Pley had written in despair that she could not even secure these payments. Surely 'the burning of London cannot go so deep in the Royal aid … as to hazard her money', Coventry commented. In 1669 there appear to have been some orders to pay.

The business intimacy between Colonel Reymes and Constance Pley, the respect which he felt for his 'woman partner', led to another venture being arranged between them. In the spring of 1666, a marriage was brought about between Tabitha Reymes and George Pley junior, the girl receiving a portion of £1,000. Public prosperity came to the Pley family following Colonel Reymes's elevation as Vice-Admiral of Dorset. Captain Pley was made his deputy; George Pley junior Collector of Customs at Lyme.

The name of the son born to George and Tabitha, Reymes Pley, commemorated the unusual – for its time – business association between the boy's paternal grandmother and his maternal grandfather. Was there another more romantic aspect – more usual for the time – to this association? Colonel Reymes, left a widower while still a vigorous man, was both attractive to women and susceptible to their charms; for example there was a neighbouring Widow Rodney whose 'fair hands' he wished to kiss, having had much delight from her 'sweet and pleasant conversation' in the course of a journey by stagecoach from London to Salisbury.

The Colonel never remarried, and at his death he instructed his son via his faithful maid Hester Clinch to 'burn all Woman's letters' that he found among his papers. The directive to his son to 'keep fair with Mrs Pley' was however the first and therefore most important instruction in this document; the letter-burning directive comes two paragraphs lower and is not connected to it.[27] The Colonel's attitude and language to Constance Pley was not that of a lover: she was formally and gratefully addressed as his 'sister'. In his will he wrote; 'I give to my sister Constance Pley (my very intimate dear friend and one whom I greatly value and do acknowledge to have been highly obliged by and as having received many obligations from her ever since I knew her) my great Diamond Ring already in her possession, desiring her to accept of it in Testimony of my thankfulness and constant owning her as such to my very last.'[28]

Constance Pley was a 'sister' who was in a position to help Colonel Reymes with a series of loans when times were hard, such as at the beginning of the Dutch War; he borrowed as much as £400 at a time from her, although the amounts were always repaid. When Reymes wrote to Captain Cocke, Receiver for the Sick and Wounded, urging payment for Mrs Pley, he pleaded: 'Pray be punctual with her, she being as famous a she merchant as you have met with in England, one who turns and winds thirty thousand pounds a year, and that even with ... Sir George Carteret.' He added: 'She is also my friend.' There is surely no need to doubt the truth or deny the strength of that description.

And what of the she-merchant herself, what was her motivation? Beyond the particular family circumstances in which she found herself at the Restoration, part of the unusually small family unit, so that every member was needed to act, if the family business was to expand. Fortunately the inimitable and inquisitive Pepys was on hand to ask her. On 16 January 1666 Mrs Pley replied to one of his letters, which does not survive, but clearly contained an inquiry. She explained that several of her family had died years before – 'being formerly deprived of her children' – and more recently her surviving daughter 'within the space of four months was married and buried'. Since then, Mrs Pley wrote, business had been her 'sole delight in this world ... It is a charity to keep her in full employment.'[29]

William Hazlitt reported a conversation among his friends in which all agreed that Oliver Cromwell 'with his fine, frank, rough, pimply face, and wily policy' was the only statesman in history they would wish to have seen.[30] In any similar discussion concerning women born in the seventeenth century, Cromwell's granddaughter Bridget Bendish must certainly have a strong claim to be selected on curiosity value alone. By general consent she bore an alarming – or exciting, depending on your point of view – physical resemblance to her grandfather.

It was one pleasing aspect of the Restoration that no vengeance was exacted from the Protector's large tribe of relatives (although they had all, like putative princes and princesses, benefited from his supremacy). The Lady Protectress ended her days in peace in Northamptonshire with her son-in-law John Claypole; in general this particular Cromwell family sank back into the ranks of the gentry from which it had suddenly and so blazingly emerged. By 1670 King Charles II, in his genial way, was accepting the hospitality of Oliver's second son Henry at his house near Newmarket. Mary Cromwell, who married the

Yorkshire magnate Viscount Fauconberg towards the end of the Commonwealth period, went on superbly to enjoy the life of a great lady at court.

Nevertheless the baleful image of Old Noll, warts – or pimples – and all, continued to fascinate the post-Restoration society which had survived him; the 1660s saw a number of plays in which Cromwell featured as tyrant, usurper and so forth, but always as the central character. After 1670 there were still plenty of people alive who could not only testify to Bridget Bendish's physical likeness to her infamous progenitor – 'if their imaginations can add a female dress, a few years in age, and a very little softening of the features' – but also found in this resemblance a subject of cosy fascination.[31] It was an added titillation that in her nature too, as well as her appearance, Bridget Bendish seemed to derive much from her grandfather, and some of the wilder, stranger elements in it; all this in the person of a married woman, later widow, living in Yarmouth and running a salt-works.

Bridget Bendish, born Bridget Ireton in 1649 or 1650, was the fourth child of Cromwell's eldest daughter Bridget, his anxious scrupulous 'dear Biddy', always worrying over the state of her own soul. Her father was Henry Ireton, Cromwell's brilliant dedicated right-hand man. Ireton was left behind by Cromwell to rule over conquered Ireland, a career cut short by his death in 1651 at the age of forty. Young Bridget, who would have been eight or nine when her grandfather died in 1658, was thus quite old enough to remember him. In addition, Bridget was largely brought up by her grandmother the Protectress during the absence of her mother in Ireland; for Bridget Cromwell's second husband Charles Fleetwood, another of her father's associates, was also given command there.

Bridget's childhood memories then consisted of life in the protectoral palace of Whitehall (where incidentally something approaching royal state was kept, at least where the position and prestige of the Protector himself was concerned). At the age of six, she sat between her grandfather's knees during a session of the Council of State. When one of those present objected, the Protector loftily replied: 'There is nothing I would discuss with any one of you which I would not equally confide to that child.'[32]

After the Restoration, Bridget lived for a while with her mother and step-father Fleetwood at Stoke Newington. In 1670 she married Thomas Bendish, a leading member of the Independent Church at Yarmouth on the Norfolk coast (a connection of that Sir Thomas Bendish, the Ambassador at Constantinople who had wearily ejected the Quaker Mary Fisher). Her grandfather, such a prominent supporter of the Independents during the Civil War period, would surely have been gratified by Bridget's choice of bridegroom. In any case, Bridget Bendish, helped on by her early memories and fortified no doubt by a physical resemblance which grew stronger with the passing years, now constituted herself the unofficial guardian of her grandfather's memory. 'Ah, that was what I learned from my grandfather' was a favourite observation[33] – a good or at least impressive remark to be able to make, if your grandfather happened to be Oliver Cromwell.

There was a famous incident when one of her fellow passengers in a stagecoach made some slighting remark about Cromwell, unwitting of the identity of his neighbour. On arrival in London Mrs Bendish challenged him – unsuccessfully – to a duel with a sword. Her aunt Mary Viscountess Fauconberg was, as has been mentioned, a great lady at the court of Charles II, her husband leading a distinguished diplomatic career under his auspices; although aunt would subsequently leave niece a substantial legacy, there was a moment when Bridget Bendish flew into a fury with Mary Fauconberg, on hearing her grandfather (and Mary's father) disparaged under the Fauconberg roof. Bridget, with her usual passion, declared that if her grandmother had not been the most virtuous woman in the world, she would have believed Mary to have been a bastard. As to Oliver Cromwell 'next to the twelve apostles, he was the first saint in heaven'.[34]

It must be said that few, even among his most perfervid admirers, would have agreed with such a remark at any period in Cromwell's lifetime. As to Oliver himself, his quizzical reception of the ecstatically reverential Lady Eleanor Davies ('But we are not all Saints,' – see p.305) shows that he would certainly have dismissed his granddaughter's overweening championship with a smile and a shake of his head.

The Bendishes settled down in South Town (once known as Little Yarmouth) on the outskirts of Great Yarmouth. There, on a marshy tract known as Cobham Island, for several centuries the property of the corporation and sold by it in 1657, lay the old-established salt-pans and refineries. The importance of the North Sea herring trade in the seventeenth century led to an equivalent emphasis being placed on salt. The 'good red herring' which abounded off the east coast of England (for which English and Dutch fishing-fleets competed) was either smoked or salted at the ports; salted fish was both a necessity in winter in the absence of fresh meat, and a profitable export to Catholic (Friday-fish-eating) Europe.[35]

Salt-works being good business – indeed, the fishermen complained of the stranglehold which the shorebound salt-providers exerted upon their trade – the Bendishes lived in a handsome mansion nearby. Thomas Bendish owned farms as well as salt-works; until his death in 1707, Mrs Bendish worked alongside him in the conduct of his two businesses (including actual physical labour) as well as running her own household and raising three children. Her incessant love of drudgery, as it was seen by observers, reminded some of her grandmother the Protectress who had not allowed protectoral state to rob her of the pleasures of her own kitchen and household work. On Thomas Bendish's death, his widow inherited an income of £2,000 or £3,000 a year and the handsome mansion, as well as the farms and salt-works with whose management she was already closely concerned.[36]

For all the drudgery, there was something scintillating, even charismatic about the personality of Mrs Bendish, when she chose to exhibit that facet of herself. One who had known her described how she would be among her workmen 'from the earliest morning to the decline of day; insensible to all the necessities and calls of nature, and in a habit and appearance beneath the meanest of them and neither suiting her character or sex'. After that, 'having eaten and drunk almost to excess' of whatever was put before her 'without choice or distinction', Mrs Bendish would throw herself down on to the nearest couch or bed and fall into a deep sleep. Then she would rise 'with new life and vigour', and proceed to dress herself 'in all the riches and grandeur of appearance' with a view to attending the assembly at Yarmouth. Here she would regularly appear, 'one of the most brilliant there', sparkling in the company 'as a lady who once expected ... to have been one of the first persons in Europe'.[37]

In later life Mrs Bendish was remembered in company as a striking presence attired in black, what was by now being termed 'the Quaker's colour'; her dress would be of silk, with a scarf or hood (not then fashionable) of the same material. But among her workmen she was seen 'stumping about with an old straw hat on her head, her hair about her ears, without stays, and when it was cold an old blanket about her shoulders and a staff in her hands – in a word, exactly accoutred to mount the stage as a witch in Macbeth'.[38]

Politics continued to interest Mrs Bendish under the Stuarts, provided it was possible to strike out for the ideals she imagined her grandfather would have approved. She was involved to a small degree in that murky tangle, the Rye House Plot of 1683 (which led to the execution of William Lord Russell) and is said to have lobbied for the accession of William III. Queen Mary allowed Mrs Bendish to be presented to her by Archbishop Tillotson and there was some talk of a pension, although the Queen's death put an end to the project.[39]

In religion, she was an extreme Calvinist, some of her religious habits certainly bearing a strong resemblance to those of her grandfather in his early days: 'she would retire to her closet, where, by fasting, meditation and prayer, she would work up her spirit to a degree of rapture, and then inflexibly determine her conduct by some text of Scripture that occurred to her, which she regarded as a divine revelation'. It was said that once 'the vapours' were raised by this method and 'the animal spirits brought up to an unusual ferment', no one could sway Mrs Bendish from her course, not even the 'plainest evidence of the same Scripture against it.'[40]

Was there a streak of the same depression in her nature which had caused Oliver as a young man to be categorized as *valde melancholicus* by Sir Theodore Mayerne? Dr Isaac Watts, a friend to Mrs Bendish, dedicated an ode to her entitled 'Against tears'. If so, Mrs Bendish certainly possessed in full measure the other side of Cromwell's complex character, the upswing which led Richard Baxter in *Reliquiae Baxterianae* to describe him as 'naturally of such a vivacity, hilarity and alacrity as another man is when he hath drunken a cup too much'.[41] As Mrs Bendish grew older, she developed a tendency to call on her friends at nine or ten at night (if the house was not shut up) and would often stay on till one in the morning; 'she would on her visits drink wine in great plenty', wrote a young man who remembered them. Hewling Luson was connected to the Cromwell family because his aunt Hannah Hewling (the brave Baptist maid of the West Country) had married one of Henry Cromwell's sons. 'The wine used to put her tongue into brisk motion, though', he added quickly, 'I do not remember that she was ever disgracefully exposed by it.'

Hewling Luson thought Bridget Bendish was like the Protector in her 'restless unabated spirit'; the difference was that in him this spirit 'by the coincidence of a thousand favourable circumstances' brought him to the summit of power and fame; in Mrs Bendish, the same spirit generally entangled her in disasters.

It was true that Mrs Bendish was no Constance Pley when it came to business. Her profuse, even wild, generosity whatever her financial circumstances got her into trouble with her business creditors, who took the line that their claims should precede those of the poor. We owe our original knowledge of Mrs Bendish to the character sketch by the Rev. Samuel Say, a Dissenting minister in Ipswich who was inspired to take up his pen by the publication of Clarendon's *History*, including his epitaph on Cromwell: 'a brave bad man'. The sketch is however hostile in tone; it has been suggested that Mr Say quarrelled with Mrs Bendish over her disposition of her aunt Fauconberg's legacy, which she wanted to distribute among the poor and he thought should be used to reimburse her equally deserving creditors.[42] He certainly reproached her for her behaviour on this occasion (without, it seems, swaying her) and admits that he felt by turns 'her friendship and resentment'. Subsequent chroniclers of the Cromwell family history dug out other witnesses who were kinder and more sympathetic towards her manifest eccentricities.

Dr Jeremy Brooke, paying tribute to her courage in helping Dissenters in a period of persecution, believed that this extraordinary woman born into another sphere, would have been 'among the most admirable heroines'; another Zenobia, she would have supported an empire or defended a capital. He praised her charitable endeavours (with less thought to her creditors than Mr Say).[43] Hewling Luson suggested by implication that it was difficult for a mere woman to accommodate the Cromwellian character. He wrote that she had as much of Cromwell's courage 'as a female constitution could receive, which was often expressed with more ardour than the rules of female decorum could excuse'.[44]

It cannot be denied that Bridget Bendish's behaviour was often bizarre. Hewling Luson describes her leaving these late-night sessions of drink and talk on the back of her old mare, known locally as 'the old lady'. On these occasions Mrs Bendish often raised her voice in one of Watt's versions of the Psalms: thus 'the two old souls, the mare and her mistress, one gently trotting and the other loudly singing' jogged home to Yarmouth in the small hours of the morning.

As the years passed, the mare was employed to pull Mrs Bendish's chaise. Still avid in the cause of business, Mrs Bendish took a particular interest in the subject of cattle-grazing. She would travel overnight in her chaise to attend the fairs, expeditions which 'afforded exercises at once for her courage and enthusiasm'. Night to her, she said, was like day; surrounded by the most frightful storm, she would feel a particular happiness, sing this or that Psalm 'and doubted not that angels surrounded her chaise'.[45]

So the odd combination of a sacred monster as a grandfather and a prosperous businessman as a husband produced a way of life which, however strange it appeared to outsiders, was satisfying to the lady herself in its independence.

CHAPTER TWENTY

Wanton and Free

~~~

'Some Men are of that Humour, as they hate Honest,
Chaste Women...they love the Company and
Conversation of Wanton and free Women.'

MARGARET DUCHESS OF NEWCASTLE,
CCXI Sociable Letters, 1664

In the late seventeenth century what is sometimes described
(on no particular evidence) as the oldest profession was not
necessarily the most disagreeable one for a woman to adopt
– provided she was able to adopt it at an economically high level.
The King – Charles II followed by his brother James II, equally
lecherous but more neurotic about it – constituted the apex of
the social pyramid; it was a pyramid which any audacious pretty
woman might aspire to scale if she caught the monarch's eye.

A handsome upstanding young man in the reign of Elizabeth
with a taste for poetry and adventure might dream of catching
the old Queen's eye; the same young man's son might dream of
catching the eye of old King James twenty years later. Let us
imagine this cavalier's granddaughter, the fortune culled from the
immoral earnings of her ancestors lost in the Civil Wars. In her
turn she might dream of catching the eye not only of the King
himself but of any of the rich and famous protectors who aped
his behaviour; she might become what a character in one of
Aphra Behn's plays described as 'that glorious insolent Thing,
That makes Mankind such Slaves, almighty Curtezan'. When
Richard Allestree in *The Ladies Calling* of 1673 expatiated on the
unhappy lot of harlots ('Their most exquisite deckings are but

like the garlands on a beast designed for sacrifice; their richest gowns are but the chains, not of their ornament but of slavery') he was protesting against the luxury in which such women so evidently lived.[1]

There was a universal truth expressed by Margaret Duchess of Newcastle: 'Some Men are of that Humour, as they hate Honest. Chaste Women ... they love the Company and Conversation of Wanton and free Women.'[2] This truth was a positive advantage at this period to the women concerned if the men were powerful enough, and the women sufficiently bold, cynical or just plain desperate.

After all, it was not as if the economic alternatives for women of all classes who had to provide for themselves were really so very enticing. Not everyone was as high-minded as the poet Jane Barker, who described herself in 1688 as indifferent to the charge of being an 'Old Maid'. (The phrase was probably first used in the pejorative sense in *The Ladies Calling*: 'An Old Maid is now thought such a curse.') She was content to lead the existence of a good (single) woman:

> Suffer me not to fall into the Pow'rs
> Of Mens almost Omnipotent Amours;
> But in this happy Life let me remain
> Fearless of Twenty five and all its train.

More than one gentlewoman without a portion found herself able to sacrifice the much-vaunted respectability of being a waiting-woman or housekeeper for the pleasanter if less moral life of being a kept woman – a 'Miss' or mistress. The exquisite Jane Roberts, mistress to Rochester amongst others, was a clergyman's daughter. She died young (in 1679) with 'a great sense of her former ill life', but there is no suggestion that this was anything more than a deathbed repentance;[3] if Jane Roberts, to whom Aphra Behn dedicated *The Feign'd Curtezans*, had lived, she would undoubtedly have continued to pursue her career among the other 'insolent Things'.

If there was a shortage of husbands, it appears there was no shortage of protectors. Mary Evelyn in *Mundus Muliebris*, laying down the rules by which a gallant should conduct his courtship, took it for granted that he had a choice 'whether his Expedition be for Marriage or Mistress'. *The Womens Complaint against their Bad Husbands*, a satiric piece of 1676, complained that in 'this frivolous Age' many preferred the novelty of the mistress however painted her face, to the established wife, although the writer (unlike the more worldly Margaret Duchess of Newcastle) could not see what 'temptations or allurements' were couched in 'the Monosyllable Miss' which were not also to be found in the word 'wife'. Palamede, in Dryden's play of 1672, *Marriage-à-la-Mode*, complained that 'all Mankind' was setting up with mistresses, so that the demand was beginning to exceed the supply; as a result 'poor little creatures, without beauty, birth or breeding, but only impudence, go off at unreasonable rates: and a man, in these hard times, snaps at 'em'.[4]

It was not a purely literary conceit. Francis North, Lord Guilford, was seriously advised to 'keep a Whore' because he was being frowned upon 'for want of doing so'. The playwright Mrs Mary Manley used the form of a novel *Rivella*, to give a true account of her own early romantic life. At the age of fourteen she was 'Married [bigamously], possessed and ruined' by her perfidious guardian. He finally abandoned her. Mrs Manley then went into the service of Charles II's erstwhile paramour Barbara Duchess of Cleveland; here a former admirer surfaced with the proposition that she should live in the country as his mistress, an offer which 'could no longer do her an Injury in the Opinion of the World' because of her disgrace.[5] In rejecting the offer on the grounds that she needed to feel herself in love with the protector (she subsequently lived for love as the mistress of another much less well-off man, a lawyer named John Tilly), Mrs Manley showed herself for the first, but not the last time, to be a highly eccentric woman by the standards of her time.

The characters in Aphra Behn's play of 1676 *The Town-Fop* included Betty Flauntit, a kept woman or 'a Person of Pleasure' as she was termed. While Betty Flauntit complained that 'a Miss has as painful a life as a Wife; our Men drink, stay out late, and whore, like any Husbands', for those who could not find husbands the conditions of life, like those of marriage, were not disagreeable unless the protector chose to make them so.[6] The children of such unions were often mentioned quite openly and publicly in the father's will, and in general provision was made for them.

Henry Sidney, always said to be the handsomest man at the Restoration court, was exceptional in that when he died unmarried in 1704 he left numerous illegitimate children for whom he refused to provide. The brother of Dorothy Countess of Sunderland (but born almost a generation later), he showed none of her charm of character, especially when dealing with Grace Worthley, his mistress of twenty years' standing. Mrs Worthley was a widow, but a poor one, her husband having been killed at sea in 1665 during the second Dutch War. She was gently born, living originally at Stoke Hall in Cheshire. The role of kept mistress to Henry Sidney was therefore an opportunity for support for one who might not otherwise have found it easy to survive; she bore Sidney a son. But it is clear that Mrs Worthley also adored her debonair protector for his own sake. Writing to him in 1689 she referred to herself as 'a poor, deluded woman, that hath loved you above myself, nay, above heaven or honour'.[7]

The trouble was that Sidney had acquired a new mistress at the beginning of the 1680s: Diana Countess of Oxford, wickedly attractive, one of the almighty courtesans of the court. By 1682 Grace Worthley was lamenting her dismissal after so many years, at the orders of one whom she described as 'the common Countess of Oxford' with 'her adulterous bastards'. Her son by Sidney was no longer acknowledged: 'all this to please his great Mistress'. Desperate for lack of money, Grace Worthley threatened to shoot Sidney.

Sidney's reaction was to depute his servant to pay Mrs Worthley £12. 10s a quarter. If there was any more fuss, he threatened her with a warrant for arrest, which as a Privy Councillor he assured her he would be able to secure.

A few years later the discarded mistress heard that Sidney might be visiting her old neighbourhood in company with the new King William III. The news provoked a pathetic letter of nostalgia for country innocence: 'That I might once before I die make a visit to the good old wooden house at Stoke...where I was born and bred...I wish your Lordship would do what is reasonable by me, that I might go into Cheshire and there end my days. I should enjoy more happiness in one month in Cheshire than I have done in all the twenty-five years I have mis-spent in London.' Two years later Grace Worthley was still pleading for money to return to Stoke Hall, having in the meantime been escorted away from her lover's door by a constable and a beadle. Part of this petition of 1694 consisted of a pathetic list of Grace Worthley's relatives to prove that she had originally come of a respectable family.

While a measure of such tragedies was inherent in the insecurity of the situation (although wives as well as mistresses were deserted) Henry Sidney was rated at the time to be specially hard-hearted as well as handsome. Betty Becke, the mistress of Lord Sandwich, had an altogether jollier time, either because her own nature was more resilient or because his was more susceptible. In the spring of 1663 Lord Sandwich, Pepys's patron, while recovering from a serious illness, lodged at the house of a merchant's wife named Mrs Becke in Chelsea. Mr Becke was a merchant who had come down in the world; Mrs Becke, acting as a landlady, had the reputation of being a good and gracious manager, with her food well dressed and presented. Other comforts were provided by her daughters.

By the August of 1663, Pepys heard that his patron doted on one of the Becke girls; his days were spent at court but he passed all his evenings with her, as well as dispensing a great deal of money. Lord Sandwich was at this point a man approaching forty, in a powerful official position; although Pepys was in a sense not surprised that Lord Sandwich should show himself 'amorous' when everyone else at court was busy doing so, in another way he was deeply shocked to see his patron 'grossly play the beast and fool'. Lord Sandwich's 'folly', he was horrified to discover, included taking Betty Becke out in public, playing on his lute under her window 'and forty other poor sordid things'.[8]

At this point Pepys was convinced that Lord Sandwich was dabbling with one who was 'a Common Strumpet'. Another report spoke of Betty Becke as 'a woman of very bad fame and very impudent'. In November therefore Pepys was moved to write his patron a magisterial letter of reproof on the subject: how the world took a grave view of Lord Sandwich's continued sojourn in a house of 'bad report' when his health was clearly mended; Betty Becke was charged with being 'a common Courtesan' there being places and persons to whom she was all too well known; the notorious wantonness of 'that slut at Chelsea', as Pepys assured his patron Betty Becke was commonly known, was causing scandal to adhere to the name of Lord Sandwich.[9]

The following June Lord Sandwich did try the well-known adulterous expedient of using his daughters as a cover for visiting Mrs Becke; unfortunately the girls in question were well able to 'perceive all'. In consequence they hated the place, and complained that their father's one aim was to 'pack them out of doors to the park'; while he stayed behind with Betty Becke.[10]

The next move – on the part of Lord Sandwich's wife – was an equally time-honoured one in the great game of adultery. Lady Sandwich was suddenly inspired to go down to Chelsea herself in order to pay a call upon Mrs Becke the landlady. As Lady Sandwich told Pepys: 'And by and by the daughter came in …'. By some extraordinary chance – 'for she never knew they had a daughter', let alone more than one – Lady Sandwich found herself feeling very troubled, and 'her heart did rise as soon as she appeared…' As for Betty Becke, by another surprising coincidence, she seemed 'the most ugly woman' that Lady Sandwich had ever seen. As Pepys commented tersely, all this, if it was true, was very strange; 'but I believe it is not'.[11]

However when the Becke family – invited by Lady Sandwich – came to call upon the Sandwiches in London, Pepys found that his own view of Betty was radically altered. She was neither 'a Common Strumpet' nor remarkably ugly. Although she did not have one good feature, Betty was nevertheless 'a fine lady', with a good figure, altogether 'very well carriaged and mighty discreet'.

Pepys made a point of trying to draw her out in the company of Lord Sandwich's hostile young daughters. When she did contribute to the conversation, as she did from time to time, she spoke 'mighty finely'. Pepys reversed his verdict. Betty Becke was now 'a woman of such an air, as I wonder the less at my Lord's favour to her'; he saw that Betty's true charm lay in her intelligence – 'she hath brains enough to entangle him'. Two or three hours were spent in her company, Pepys and the rest of the ladies adjourning to Kensington where, in the famous garden with its fountain where Anne Conway had played as a little girl, now belonging to her elder step-brother, they all enjoyed some 'brave music' and singing. All in all, Pepys was delighted with the day's work: 'Above all I have seen my Lord's Mistress.'[12]

Five years later, as the intimate record provided by the diary draws to a close, Pepys reported that one of Lord Sandwich's daughters was recovering from sickness in her turn in the Becke house in Chelsea. Lord Sandwich intended to visit her; but Pepys still suspected that it was 'more for young Mrs Becke's sake than for hers'.[13]

Economics apart, there was the subtler question of independence for the mistress. When the Duchess of Newcastle referred to the allurements of women who were wanton and free, she had in mind their conduct rather than their status. Nevertheless it was true of the seventeenth century as people imagined it had been in ancient Rome: it was possible in theory at least for a courtesan to enjoy a measure of independence denied to her married sister, for whom security and adherence to the social norm were accompanied by the need for absolute subordination to her husband, legally and in every other way. Courtesans were sympathetically and even admirably treated in Restoration plays: Otway's Aquilina in *Venice Preserv'd* – 'Nicky Nacky' scornfully trouncing her elderly admirer at his own request – or Aphra Behn's much courted Angelica Bianca in *The Rover* who vowed that 'nothing but Gold shall charm my Heart'. (Although even the spirited courtesan Aquilina received a sharp put-down from her lover Pierre when she attempted to discuss politics: 'How! A woman ask Questions out of Bed!)[14]

In 1695 Rachel Lady Russell wrote a long letter of maternal advice to her nineteen-year-old daughter Katherine Lady Roos, interesting because it reveals such a very low expectation of female happiness even for a nice young lady married to a highly eligible young man. 'Believe me, child,' wrote Lady Russell, 'life is a continual labour, checkered with care and pleasure, therefore rejoice in your portion, take the world as you find it, and you will I trust find heaviness may endure for a night, but joy comes in the morning.'[15] (Admittedly Lady Russell had endured an exceptional sorrow, but then she had also been granted an exceptionally happy marriage.) For most women of this time life was indeed a continual labour – literally as well as metaphorically so. Even so, there were deep springs of strength and independence within the nature of certain females in this as in every other age, which would continue to bubble inextinguishably forth whenever the circumstances were propitious. For some of these, taking the world as they found it meant something a good deal more high-spirited, if less moral than the noble but essentially passive course advocated by Lady Russell. For such a woman, the life of 'that glorious insolent thing ... almighty Curtezan' brought rewards beyond the merely financial.

For this reason Catherine Sedley is the most personally fascinating among the numerous royal mistresses because as an heiress, the alternative of a good marriage was open to her in youth. Instead of the 'dull manage of a servile house' in Anne Countess of Winchilsea's phrase, she chose the more testing career of mistress to James II, when Duke of York. Moreover the weapons at her disposal included neither beauty nor any other form of attraction evident to the outward eye; even in youth Catherine Sedley was not reckoned to be pretty. She had a long nose and an unfashionably big mouth at a time when the ideal was a delicate rosebud; her complexion was too pale, lacking the carmine tint which made the approved beauties a contrast of 'white and red'; a cast in her eye enabled her enemies to describe her gleefully as squinting. Above all, she was considered much too thin at a time when the contemporary taste ran to the luscious: 'Fubbs' – for chubby – was Charles II's tender nickname for Louise de la Kéroualle, Duchess of Portsmouth. '*D'une extrême maigreur*', wrote the French envoy Barillon of Catherine, although he admired her vivacity.[16] Skinny as a girl Catherine Sedley became positively gaunt as the years passed.

Catherine Sedley conducted her campaign for a place – and a high place too – in society through her wits. In an age when both sexes combined to praise the dulcet female voice expressing softly modest feminine sentiments, Catherine Sedley triumphantly made herself feared by an exceptionally sharp tongue.

This strong vessel was born on 21 December 1657, the only child of the poet, playwright and Restoration Wit Sir Charles Sedley and Lady Catherine Savage, the heiress daughter of Earl Rivers. The mother was wealthy but she was also unstable; a few years after Catherine's birth she was mad enough to be placed under the care of a doctor – a Catholic because she herself, unlike her husband and daughter, was a Catholic. Catherine's mother began to suffer from delusions that she was the Queen, having to be addressed by those who attended her as 'Your Majesty'. She was finally confined in a Catholic convent abroad.[17]

What was to become of Catherine, her father's sole legitimate heiress and, in the conditions which made divorce and remarriage virtually impossible, likely to remain so? It was decided to place the girl at court as a Maid of Honour; after an unsuccessful attempt to enter the Queen's household, Catherine was placed in that of Mary of Modena, then Duchess of York. Catherine seems to have made her mark early on along the path on which she intended to travel; in June 1673, when she was still only fifteen, Evelyn described her when she visited him at home as 'none of the most virtuous but a wit'.[18]

Still, the witty Catherine did have a portion of £6,000, according to popular repute, and a further £4,000 at her father's death; there would have been more but for her father's liaison with Ann Ayscough. Catherine Sedley's arms when she reached the age of twenty-one described her as 'sole daughter and heir' of her father.[19] Yet after a series of affairs Sir Charles had formed a

permanent liaison with Ann, the penniless daughter of a
Yorkshire gentleman, which resulted in the birth of an illegitimate son. Catherine's mother outlived her husband but Sir
Charles firmly termed his relationship with Ann Ayscough a
'marriage' and called the boy his heir. In his own words:

> What a priest says moves not the mind
> Souls are by love, not words, combined.

All the same £10,000 was no small sum as a portion. In 1677, for
example, Sir Winston and Lady Churchill were interested in the
prospect of Catherine as a bride for their son John (later first
Duke of Marlborough), to the disgust of his sweetheart and
eventual wife Sarah Jennings. Barillon described Catherine then
as very rich and very ugly; but Sarah, after Marlborough's death,
called her a 'shocking creature'.[20] This however being eminently
an age when cash counted more than scandal, such a wealthy
young woman, however provocative, could easily have secured a
husband had she so wished.

Instead, Catherine Sedley remained unmarried. When she did
eventually take a husband nearly twenty years later, it was as a
mature woman approaching forty with a remarkable past behind
her; she also had a further sizeable fortune to accompany her, as
a souvenir of that past. As an unmarried girl she was entitled to
keep her post as Maid of Honour to the Duchess of York and
that was certainly a position of which Catherine Sedley, unlike
those other more sensitive plants in the same household, Anne
Killigrew and Anne Countess of Winchilsea, made full worldly
use. By the time she was twenty 'Dorinda', as she was nicknamed
in satiric verse, was a celebrated if not popular character at court.

> Dorinda's sparkling Wit, and Eyes
> United, cast too fierce a Light,
> Which blazes high but quickly dies
> Pains not the Heart but hurts the Sight . . .

wrote the poet and Wit Lord Dorset, playing on her alleged

squint. Dorinda's personal Cupid was said to be no 'wingéd God' but 'a Black-Guard Boy' – one of the troop of insolent urchins loosely attached to the lower ranks of the royal household.[21]

Most important of all, at the beginning of 1678, Catherine Sedley became the mistress of the Duke of York, supplanting Arabella, the sister of her proposed suitor, John Churchill. The mistresses of the Duke became a legend for their ugliness, once King Charles II had ventured the sly opinion that they must have been prescribed for his brother by his confessors. In fact several of those favoured by the Duke gave the lie to the joke: Susan Lady Belasyse was an acknowledged beauty, while the doe-eyed Elizabeth Countess of Chesterfield (she whom her jealous husband carried off to The Peak) was one of the loveliest women ever to be painted by Lely. It was a combination of the King's wit with Catherine Sedley's own which gave rise to the legend. For Catherine was one of those clever women who created a style out of her own lack of conventional attractions. Dorset hammered the point of her plainness in verse (Dorset's especial venom towards Catherine Sedley was probably due to the fact that she rejected his advances, hell having no fury like a satirist scorned):

> For tho' we all allow you Wit
> We can't a handsome face.
> Then where's the pleasure, where's the Good,
> Of spending Time and Cost?
> For if your Wit be'ent Understood
> Your Keeper's Bliss is lost.

But Catherine made the same joke herself with more economy: 'We are none of us handsome,' she declared of the Duke's harem, 'and if we had wit, he has not enough to discover it.'[22]

The crudity of some of the Wits' printed attacks on women of the court who had incurred their displeasure make them literally unprintable: Sir Carr Scroope, merely describing Catherine as being 'as mad as her mother and as vicious as her father', was using language which under the circumstances was comparatively mild.[23] A vein of morose dislike for womankind – 'the silliest part of God's Creation' in Rochester's words – except during the act of sexual congress, runs through their works, including poetry as well as lampoons. And if it can be argued that the maddening feminine silliness referred to earlier (see p.401) provoked some of it, it is noticeable that Catherine Sedley, an undeniably intelligent woman, provoked even more.

None of this prevented James Duke of York from falling passionately in love with his wife's Maid of Honour. Sir Charles Sedley once inquired of a new arrival at court whether she would turn out to be 'a Beauty, a Miss, a Wit, or a Politician'. Catherine Sedley triumphantly combined the activities of a Miss and a Wit without the helpful attribute of being a Beauty. Sometime before March 1679 she was known to have borne a daughter, known as Lady Catherine Darnley, whose paternity was officially ascribed to the Duke. Mary of Modena, Duchess of York, was said to be 'very melancholy' at this news, especially as the Duke was presently being obliged by the course of Exclusionist politics to leave England. The satirists too marked the event: 'little Sid, She who lately slipped her Kid'.[24]

Catherine was to bear several other children to the Duke, including a son, James Darnley; none of them survived infancy. There seems however some doubt as to whether the Duchess's melancholy over the arrival of little Catherine Darnley was fully justified. To Colonel James Grahame, another member of the Duke of York's household – he was Keeper of the Privy Purse – was also ascribed the honour of her paternity; in later years Lady Catherine Darnley bore a strong physical resemblance to his legitimate daughter. As the wife of John Sheffield, Earl of Mulgrave and in 1703 created Duke of Buckingham, Lady Catherine Darnley was so haughty as to be nicknamed 'Princess Buckingham' but according to Walpole there were still those who muttered that she was nothing but old Grahame's daughter.[25] Grahame, who was Catherine Sedley's confidant in her intrigues and remained so, was almost certainly also her lover. However, Mary of Modena never displayed any of that kindly tolerance towards her husband's mistresses which so signally marked the wise character of Charles II's wife Catherine of Braganza.

Perhaps it was because she was so much younger than her husband – nearly twenty-five years – or perhaps it was because Mary of Modena was herself a very pretty young woman. By the summer of 1680 she was declared to be once more 'very melancholy' on the subject of Mrs Sedley by her women: 'She prays all day almost.'[26]

Alas, piety was not necessarily the best way for an 'Honest, Chaste' woman to combat the attractions of a 'Wanton and free' one. It was said of Catherine Sedley that 'there was no restraint in what she said of or to anybody'.[27] Like Nell Gwynn, she was a licensed jester, wit in their mistresses being one taste the two Stuart brothers had in common. As a Protestant herself, she regularly made jokes about the Duke's Catholic priests which one suspects secretly delighted the middle-aged royal roué, torn between guilt and concupiscence.

The death of Charles II in early February 1685 transformed the lives of James and Mary of Modena, now King and Queen of England. A few days later a message to Catherine from the new monarch broke the news that her life too was to be transformed: warned by his brother's example, King James had decided to lead another kind of life. It was to be a life without Catherine Sedley. She should therefore either go abroad or depart for the country; he would provide for her 'but he would see her no more'.[28]

Catherine however refused to go. Her emaciation at this point struck all observers; there was nothing else frail about her. In the end a compromise was reached by which Catherine was installed in a house which had belonged to the King's former mistress Arabella Churchill, and for which he now paid £10,000: No. 21 St James's Square. (The locality was considered sufficiently removed from the royal palace at Whitehall.) She also received a pension of £4,000 from the Privy Purse. Armed with this, Catherine, who had a taste both for music and the arts, proceeded to employ the finest sculptors and painters to adorn her new residence.[29]

It is not known precisely how long the King's good resolution lasted. Little James Darnley, born the previous September, died on the eve of the King's coronation. One story connected the

King's resumption of the affair with his remorse at the child's death. James Darnley was certainly given a royal burial. He was placed in the vault at Westminster Abbey created for Mary Queen of Scots, where the King's many legitimate dead infants were already buried, along with such august personages as Elizabeth of Bohemia and Rupert of the Rhine; the plate on his coffin described him as 'natural son to King James the second… Aged about eight months.'[30] At any rate before very long Catherine Sedley was being conducted up that notorious Privy Staircase leading to the King's apartments in Whitehall which had more than justified its existence during the previous reign.

Was Catherine Sedley also 'a Politician' as well as 'a Wit' and 'a Miss'? At one point the Protestant faction were accused by Lord Sunderland of using her to forward their interests with the King just because Catherine was a 'Protestant whore', as Nell Gwynn had once insouciantly termed herself. But the allegation was unfounded, according to James II's biographer, John Miller.[31] The next real drama in Catherine's life concerned rank rather than politics. In mid-January the King took the decision to make his mistress Countess of Dorchester and Baroness Darlington in her own right. (Henry Pierrepont, the irascible Marquess of Dorchester who was the father of Lady Anne Roos, had died in 1680 without male heirs – his second wife, Katherine Stanley, daughter of the heroic Countess of Derby, had no children – and the title was extinct.)

There was uproar at the court. The rumour that Catherine would also be granted the convenient apartments which had once belonged to Louise Duchess of Portsmouth, *maîtresse en titre* of Charles II in his last years, did nothing to allay the Queen's fury. On 19 January, shortly after 'Mrs Sedley (concubine to—)', as Evelyn discreetly called her in his diary, was officially created a Countess, the diarist noticed that Mary of Modena neither spoke nor ate during the course of two dinners.[32] King James was weakly astonished when his wife threatened to enter a convent if Catherine was not compelled to quit the court.

Catherine for her part had very different plans for herself. She was determined to be received by the Queen in her new rank as a countess. She was in fact already dressed to attend the formal royal reception known as the Drawing-room, when a message came saying that she was refused admittance. 'The hearts of all virtuous ladies and honest wives were filled with inexpressible joy,' wrote a contemporary. The King's act generously attested 'their matrimonial privileges'.[33] The King had once more bowed his head to the pressures of his wife and his priests; he indicated that Catherine should go, and did not even grant her that final interview which she had once made him promise would precede any final parting.

Passivity under stress was as alien to Catherine's nature as discretion in triumph. Once more she declined point-blank to move, posing as a martyr to the machinations of the Jesuits because she was a Protestant. A joke went the rounds that Catherine was taking her stand on her rights under Magna Carta and was refusing to be deported without her consent. Meanwhile '*L'Affaire de Mademoiselle Sidley*' as the French envoy called it, continued to preoccupy not only the court Wits, but also the King's various advisers who, even if Catherine had played no political role, saw in her departure 'a trial of their interest with their great Master'.[34]

At one point Catherine either suffered or pretended to suffer a miscarriage to delay matters. She also clamoured loudly against the prospect of being exiled to any Catholic country, saying that Hortense Duchesse de Mazarin had warned her against all convents, and she feared to spend the rest of her life among nuns. (Her mother's fate must have played some part in heating up her imagination on this subject.) Lastly she discovered a neat way of circumventing another proposal to send her to Holland: if she went there, Catherine said, she would insist on being received there at court by James's married daughter, Mary Princess of Orange.[35]

In the end the lot fell upon Ireland. Here Catherine did have some friends and she also had some lands granted to her by the King. This made Ireland in her opinion 'the less invidious as well as the more obscure part of the world'. Catherine left on 17

February in a retinue of four coaches-and-six; by March she was installed in Dublin, posing a problem for English officials. They feared to receive her too courteously lest they incur the Queen's displeasure (as it was, even their sketchy greetings offended Mary of Modena).[36]

It was not long, however, before rumours of the volatile Countess's imminent return, fuelled by the refurbishment of her St James's Square house, were causing the Queen's 'pious mind' to be thoroughly 'discomposed'. Catherine wondered aloud in letters to her English friends why the Queen worried so much over her supposed powers of fascination: 'She thinks much better of me than I deserve.' All the same Catherine pined for England and good English gossip: 'Send the news true or false, I care not. I love an English lie ...' As for Ireland: 'The English have generally a humour I do not approve of, which is affecting to like nothing but their own country; so were it possible, I would commend this place.' Unfortunately she found it intolerable. 'I find them not only senseless, but a melancholy sort of people,' she wrote tartly, 'and speak all in the tone of the cripples of London.'[37] (Many of whom were of Irish origin and thus begged in an Irish accent.)

November 1686 saw the Countess back at court once more, taking her place unchallenged and with her usual aplomb. She also bought Ham House near Weybridge from the widow of the sixth Duke of Norfolk. Although her influence with James was considered to have declined, Mary of Modena at Windsor could still be relied upon to weep if the King was late returning, convinced that he had been with the Countess of Dorchester.

The revolutionary events of 1688 and 1689 which resulted in the displacement of King James by his son-in-law William and daughter Mary placed Catherine, at least in theory, in an extremely awkward position. Catherine herself was certainly frank enough about it: 'Nothing curbs me in wishing well to the present king [William] but the fear his success may turn to my rueing.' It was true. On the one hand her royal protector had vanished; on the other hand the new Queen Mary was liable to look but coldly on her father's erstwhile mistress. Meanwhile the fact that Sir Charles Sedley was a prominent supporter of William of Orange gave a joyous opportunity to the Wits:

> But Sidley has some colour for his Treason
> A daughter Ravished without any Reason…
> And she to keep her Father's honour up
> Drinks to the Dutch with Orange in her Cup.[38]

'Never anybody, sure, was so unfortunately misunderstood as me,' wrote Catherine. The trouble was that Catherine's letters to King James abroad, asking for money for herself and her daughter, *were* liable to be misunderstood as Jacobite plotting; especially as she was obliged to use the Jacobite conduits to dispatch them, including the network headed by Lord Preston, brother of her confidant Colonel Grahame. No evidence has been found that she took a more active part in the Jacobite conspiracies than seeking money; and the counter-suggestion that she was placed among the conspirators as a Williamite spy is equally unproven.[39] What is clear is that Catherine's prime instinct was for survival, that instinct which had already carried her along successfully on her somewhat perilous course for fifteen years. 'My lord,' she wrote to the Williamite Earl of Nottingham in September 1689, whose aid she implored, 'I can't travel with a bundle under my arm tho' the King [William] is pleased to use me like a woman of that rank.' By December 1689 she was desperately refuting any suggestion that she had meddled in politics: 'knowing myself very unfit for it'.[40]

Admission to court in view of Queen Mary's hostility was once more the problem, as it had been during the previous reign, with the previous Queen Mary (of Modena). 'I believe the Queen thinks legion [i.e. the devil] is my name,' wrote Catherine. She was indignant to hear that every day ladies were being admitted whom Catherine 'would be very sorry to be compared to'. She instanced Hortense Duchesse de Mazarin, Barbara Duchess of Cleveland, Diana Countess of Oxford (Mrs Worthley's successful rival) and Susan Lady Belasyse. Full of injured innocence, Catherine told Lord Nottingham that 'the jury might possibly acquit me that would whip [for being whores] every one of the ladies afore mentioned'.[41] In the end Catherine Countess of Dorchester did secure admission.

Where the Queen's icy looks were concerned, Catherine proved herself equal to the occasion. Queen Mary's Regan-like indifference to her ageing father's sufferings was the talk of London at the time; even those who had supported King James's ousting were taken aback by her lightheartedness, her lack of filial honour for her father as prescribed in the Ten Commandments. Catherine told Queen Mary blandly that she was much surprised at her disapproving demeanour towards her adulterous self. 'For,' she said, 'if I have broke one commandment, you have another; and what I did was more natural.' It was left to King William to give her a more sympathetic audience, not out of passion but because he 'feared the lash of her tongue'. He also granted her a pension of £1,500 a year. That left Catherine unable to decide where her political sympathies lay: 'for both the queens us'd her badly, and both kings, she said, were civil to her'.[42]

As well as the wit, the spirit was also undiminished in Catherine. Some of Catherine's lands in the reclaimed Fens, granted to her in 1683 by the Duke of York, were granted after the Revolution by King William to the Earl of Torrington, more out of confusion than malice. Catherine took the case to the High Court of Chancery and won, but Torrington brought in a Bill by leave of the House of Commons to confirm his grant. At which Catherine 'prayed' the House of Commons in her turn, appearing on her own behalf at the Bar of the House. She was, however, not successful. Although the House added a clause to Torrington's Bill granting the Countess of Dorchester £4,000 arrears in rents, and an annuity of £600, the bill was in the end 'passed in the negative'; so Catherine never got her rents.[43]

Finally in August 1696, when she was thirty-eight years old, Catherine married Sir David Colyear, a veteran Scots soldier who had served under William III in Flanders. The Wits had a field-day: 'Proud with the Spoils of Royal Cully', they called her, adding: 'The Devil and Sir David take her.' The thick paint now applied to the appearance of the 'Wither'd Countess' was also the subject of much comment, nor did Catherine's sharp tongue escape censure:

> Too old for lust and proof against all Shame
> Her only business now is to defame.

Sixteen years before, Dorset had already gloated over her decline:

> Tell me, Dorinda, why so gay …
> Wilt thou still sparkle in the box,
> Still ogle in the ring?
> Canst thou forget thy age and pox?
> Can all that shines on shells and rocks
> Make thee a fine young thing?

But Dorset was premature in his rejoicing. Sir David was later created Earl of Portmore; Catherine bore him two sons, one of whom inherited the title. It seems that her style as a mother was no more hypocritical than her style as a mistress had been, for she told the boys: 'If any body call either of you the son of a whore you must bear it for you are so: but if they call you bastards, fight till you die; for you are an honest man's sons.' At the court of Queen Anne, Dorinda was still to be seen sparkling away in 'great splendour', covered in diamonds. At the coronation of George I, when the Archbishop of Canterbury, according to custom, went round the throne formally demanding the consent of the people, it was Catherine who was heard to say: 'Does the old Fool think that Anybody here will say no to his Question when there are so many drawn Swords?'[44]

Catherine was still tottering round Bath in her finery in 1717, and finally died in the October of that year. If a mis-spent life by most standards, hers could hardly be termed a wasted one.

The life of Mrs Jane Myddelton, like that of Catherine Sedley, was founded on masculine support in return for sexual favours, although of Sir Charles Sedley's categories Jane Myddelton was regarded as 'a Beauty' rather than 'a Miss'. She performed the functions of a mistress, it was true, to a variety of eligible men – men eligible to keep a 'great Mistress', that is. But the role of a beauty, which Jane Myddelton was so admirably fitted by nature to play, somehow elevated her beyond anything contemptible in the popular esteem; her affairs were seen more as a tribute paid to her great beauty, as the affairs of certain very beautiful and essentially passive women have been seen all through history.

The daughter of Sir Robert Needham, Jane married Charles Myddelton of Ruabon in June 1660 when she was fifteen. He was ten years her senior and a widower, a man of good family but small fortune, being the sixth son of Sir Thomas Myddelton Kt. Jane bore her husband two daughters: another Jane, born the following year, and Althamia. At first the newly-married pair lived with Sir Robert Needham in Lambeth. There seems to have been some plan for settling in Plas Newydd or New Hall in the parish of Ruabon with the help of Sir Thomas Myddelton; in 1664 Charles Myddelton wrote to his father: 'I long for nothing more than to be with you.' But at Easter 1668 the Myddeltons settled in Charles Street, in the parish of St Martin-in-the-Fields, where they were still living nearly twenty years later.[43]

It was the court which was the centre of the Myddeltons' life. Jane soon won a reputation as 'the most beautiful woman in England – and the most amiable', one which she preserved for the rest of her life: in 1683 when she was approaching forty, Evelyn was still able to write of her, the 'famous and indeed incomparable beauty, Mrs Myddelton'.[46] Jane never amassed a great fortune as did some of the avaricious royal mistresses, but the indisputable asset of the wife's dazzling appearance enabled both Myddeltons to enjoy an agreeable life at the court, without any official position, quite beyond their normal financial expectations.

In Jane Myddelton's features, in total contrast to those of Catherine Sedley, were to be found the ideal of seventeenth-century beauty as laid down in the rules of the time. Here was the perfect oval face with the lofty smooth forehead – 'the high temples' of *The Ladies Dictionary* – completed by a neat little chin. Here was the nose neither too big nor too small, the little mouth with its cupid's bow upper lip, the well-marked arched brows. Here too was the well-rounded figure, the milky white *décolletage* above the plump round high breasts – 'two little worlds of beauty' – which caused Pepys, admiring her from afar at the theatre, to rate her as having 'a very excellent face and body, I think'.[47] Above all Jane Myddelton was blonde.

Although men of course continued to fall passionately in love with dark women as they had always done, there was no doubt that the spectacle of a blonde beauty aroused a particular poetical reverence in observers, as though some extraterrestrial being, the Venus of the *Aeneid* perhaps, was passing that way: 'a tint of rose glowed on her neck and a scent of Heaven breathed from the divine hair of her head'. This was the language used about the lovely blonde Maid of Honour Frances Jennings (sister of Sarah Duchess of Marlborough) by Anthony Hamilton: 'To sum up in a few words – her face reminded one of the dawn, or of some Goddess of the Spring…'[48] Dark ladies had to contend with the conviction that saturnine looks concealed a saturnine temperament: Sir Henry Cholmley of Scarborough was proud that his blonde mother had brought about 'the whitening of black shadows' in his family's physical inheritance, while of Henry Oxinden of Deane's intended bride Elizabeth Meredith it was written that her outward fairness was 'a fair ambassador of a most fair mind.'[49]

Equally Hamilton wrote of Jane Myddelton that she was all 'white and golden', and that she was magnificently made. Her thick blonde ringlets surrounded a face which Lely loved to paint. 'Fair and foolish', wrote Margaret Duchess of Newcastle angrily of blondes in general (she was not one); Henrietta Maria Blagge, Margaret Godolphin's sister, another blonde Maid of Honour, was accused of being 'whey-faced' and 'yellower than a quince' by the Comte de Gramont, who reserved praise for those ladies who accepted his advances. For all these jealous carpings, contemporary handbooks were full of recipes for dyeing the hair blonde as well as whitening the complexion. And from the point of view of Jane Myddelton's lovers, the warning of *The Ladies Dictionary* that yellow hair had been since the time of the Danes a sign of lustfulness – 'golden Flames' sparkling without might indicate similar flames burning within – was no doubt enticing rather than the reverse.[50]

All the same it must be said that a look of cow-like complacency stamps Jane Myddelton's fair face, even at the deft hands of Lely. Despite her famous amiability, her air of redolent languor was not to everyone's taste. Her refinement and her pretensions to intelligence irritated everyone not madly in love with her, and even a few who were – 'she was the most tiresome when she wished to be most brilliant' – being one of those who larded her talk with French expressions. A rival beauty also told Pepys (who was always fascinated to hear such details about the belles of the court) that Jane Myddelton gave off 'a continued sour base smell', especially if she was a little hot. Nevertheless her protectors included Ralph Montagu, that notable ladies' man, who finally married another blonde beauty, but a wealthy one, Elizabeth Countess of Northumberland; Richard Jones, later Viscount Ranelagh, reprobate son of the esteemed Katherine Viscountess Ranelagh; and Francis Russell, brother of William, fifth Earl of Bedford, who took her to visit Evelyn at Sayes Court. She was after all, as Saint-Evremond's epitaph declared of her, '*illustre entre les belles*'. She died in 1692 at the age of forty-seven. It was said of her decease that she died gracefully, as though she had studied how to do it; and so in a sense the 'incomparable' beauty had.[51]

For the women of the poor, the career of the common prostitute certainly promised the possibility of what the great Irish historian Lecky in his sonorous passage on her suffering figure – 'the most mournful, and in some respects the most awful, upon which the eye of the moralist can dwell' – described as 'disease and abject wretchedness and an early death'. Compared to this, the style of Mrs Myddelton – all white and gold – was shimmering and luxurious indeed. Yet to be realistic the lives of 'your common jilts who will oblige everybody' should be contrasted not with that of Mrs Myddelton but with the daily round of their social equals. Women who supported themselves as manure-gatherers, salt-spreaders and the like[52] (not the pleasantest of jobs) might well envy the financial rewards of prostitution, even if their superior morals prevented them from turning to it.

The figures for these financial rewards are of course so infinitely variable, and also obtained in such a random fashion from the records and literature of the time, that it is difficult to be precise. At the beginning of the seventeenth century, 6d a 'bout' – Pepys's word – was quoted in the country, and up to 20d in the city. In 1649 Ann Morgan of Wells was overheard being offered 1s by a client to 'lie with thee'; she proceeded to demand 18d because he had torn her coat and 'hindered me the knitting of half a hose'. But Ann Morgan was known to charge 2s 6d, double the usual fee, to soldiers. Robert Hooke, picking up a 'call girl' as he termed her, at a coffee-house in Change Alley, Cornhill, in the 1670s, paid her 5s. If an average rate for a female weeder or spinner of between 2d and 4d a day is borne in mind, or for a domestic servant between £2 and £4 a year, it will be seen that under certain circumstances prostitution was at least financially tempting. Most tempting of all economically was the prospect of trade in the New World: when conditions were bad (the Fire of London, for example, had a most depressing effect on the market and the whores had to lower their prices) enterprising ladies set off for Barbados or Virginia where the general shortage of women aided business.[53]

Returning to Lecky's picture, it must be said that disease and abject wretchedness and an early death at this level were not solely the fate of the prostitute, nor indeed of the female sex as a whole. Venereal disease was so widespread – having been spreading since the late fifteenth century – that the dreaded 'pox' received a certain amount of social tolerance. After the Restoration the poet and courtier Dorset wrote a good-humoured letter on the subject to one of his 'Misses' – probably a well-known prostitute called Moll Hinton – enclosing a small sum of money: 'a Little Advice', he wrote, 'and a great deal of

Physick may in time restore you to that health I wish you had enjoyed a Sunday night instead of – your humble suffering servant'. Remedies and recipes against the pox would be given where in the same publication measures against conception were not mentioned.[54]

Furthermore, for the harlot there was always the possibility of upward social mobility, another prerogative following her traditional one of power without responsibility. Nell Gwynn, for example, was the daughter of old Madam Gwynn, who kept something very close to a bawdy-house. Her original profession, that of an orange-girl at the theatre, was one distinguished from prostitution more by its additional duties of fruit-selling than anything else; but her son by Charles II was created a duke. (And from pretty witty Nelly, who towards the end of her life could barely manage the two letters E.G. as a signature,[55] an English ducal house descends today.) This was an encouraging story, if not to the chaste.

In 1660 a list of common whores in London mentioned Orange Nan and Mrs Watson an orange-seller, as well as Betty Orange, prepared to do business at home at Dung Wharf. Where Nell was concerned, it was relevant that the orange-girls at the theatre needed a good deal of natural wit and spirit to ply their trade. There was considerable competition: from the women known as 'vizard masks' for example, from the accoutrement which became the badge of their calling, who also used the pit to pick up their clients; to say nothing of the actors on the stage, whose spectacle generally took place in competition with, rather than as an alternative to the activities of the orange-girls. Disease apart, the profession was not without its dangers: in 1679 the playwright Thomas Otway challenged the young John Churchill to a duel for 'beating an orange wench' in the Dorset Garden Theatre; 'and both were wounded, but Churchill most' (we do not learn the fate of the orange wench). At the Theatre Royal, however, few would have ventured to tackle the regular orange-girl, 'Orange Betty' Mackarel, alluded to as 'the Giantess Betty Mackarela' and a byword not only for her strength and her promiscuity but also for her impudence: the Wits jostling with her in the pit would be 'hot at repartee with Orange Betty'.[56]

In the 1660s Frances Jennings, she whose face reminded one of the dawn, and another Maid of Honour, Goditha Price, decided to disguise themselves as orange-girls in order to consult a fortune-teller anonymously.[37] It was easy to disguise the rather swarthy and distinctly stumpy Mrs Price; but Frances, just because of 'her brilliant fairness' and her particular grace of manner, was rather more difficult. All the same the two girls purchased some oranges, and thus equipped hired a hackney-coach. It was a night on which their mistress the Duchess of York had gone to the theatre (Frances pleading illness) and somehow it was irresistible for the two girls to stop there and begin to sell their oranges under the very noses of the court. Mrs Price accosted Henry Sidney, looking more of an Adonis than ever and even more splendidly dressed than usual; Frances tackled the famous libertine Harry Killigrew (Anne Killigrew's cousin).

Seeing two women together, one older and rather plain and the other very pretty, Killigrew made the assumption, natural to the time and place, that one was the other's bawd or manager. Asked if he would like to buy some oranges, Killigrew replied. 'Not just now but if you like to bring me this little girl tomorrow, it shall be worth all the oranges in the shops to you.' His hand, which he had kept under Frances's chin, began to stray downwards towards her bosom. Frances furiously rebuked him.

'Ha! Ha!,' exclaimed Killigrew, 'but this is strange upon my honour! A little whore who tries to raise her fee by being ladylike and unwilling!'

Only one man present recognized them and that was Henry Brounckner, known as the best chess-player in England, who combined this hobby with that of keeping a house of pleasure near London, stocked with 'several working-girls'. Brounckner's attention was caught by the good quality of the girls' shoes, as well as Frances's 'prettiest imaginable leg' (which originally he fancied would merit her inclusion in his harem). Brounckner however kept his peace, hoping to have material with which to twit Frances Jennings's fiancé later.

Prostitutes in an infinite variety of forms were omnipresent in seventeenth-century England, something taken for granted even by a Puritan counsellor like William Gouge, who suggested that a husband might be driven to visit them if a wife did not perform her marital duties. Cases of prostitution and scandalous lewdness, having been in the control of the church, gradually developed into indictable offences under the common law as the century progressed. It was felt that the church's administration was inefficient and corrupt, while the punishments meted out by the ecclesiastical courts to those presented to them were inadequate. Local ordinances for the suppression of brothels were founded in the doctrine that such places constituted a breach of the peace, a view promulgated by Coke, who described bawdy-houses as 'the cause of many mischiefs'.[58]

Whores – and whorehouses – being a fact of life, from the customer's point of view it was a case of striking some kind of balance between what his purse could afford and what his sensibilities could stand. The opportunities were infinite, ranging from Oxford Kate's in Bow Street, a public eating-place as well as a covert bawdy-house (Sir Ralph Verney visited it under the Commonwealth because they dressed meat so well) down to the drabs on the mean streets 'like Copper Farthings in the Way of Trade, only used for the convenience of readier Change'.[59]

An Act of Charles I for their suppression described how wayfarers in Cowcross, Turmil Street, Charterhouse Lane, Saffronhill, Bloomsbury, Petticoat Lane, Wapping, Ratcliff and divers other places were 'pestered with many immodest, lascivious, and shameless women generally reputed for notorious common and professed whores'. Sitting at the doors of their houses, sometimes at the doors of sack-houses, these women were 'exposing and offering themselves to passengers'.[60] Others acted with butchers and poulterers, selling themselves in markets on Sabbath days. Others still were involved in robberies, and thus entered the criminal records as a thief as well as a whore.

The Wandering Whore was a publication, probably written as well as published by John Garfield, of which five numbers appeared between 1660 and 1661, taking advantage of the newly permissive atmosphere following the Restoration. It used as its form a favourite device in this particular literary market, a conversation between a young whore and old bawd, and included what has been taken to be a comprehensive list of streets noted for prostitution and for brothels, such as Fleet Lane, Long Acre and Lincoln's Inn Fields. Other favourable districts for this kind of enterprise in London were Lewkenor's Lane, Whetstone's Park, Cheapside or Moorfields.[61]

Outside London, organized prostitution was mainly concentrated in the bigger towns, to which visits could be paid. Cambridge for example in 1676 had no fewer than thirteen bawdy-houses. It should not for this reason be seen as an unchecked centre of disrepute. Elizabeth Aynsworth had kept a loose house at Cambridge in the 1660s, but was banished thence at the instigation of the university proctors. She settled down again at the Reindeer Inn at Bishop's Stortford, to which 'all the goodfellows' of the county speedily repaired. She once served the very proctor responsible for her dismissal 'a most elegant supper' on silver plate. His party dared not touch the meal for fear they would have 'a lord's reckoning' to pay, but Mrs Aynsworth then appeared and observed with some style that it was a gift, since she was so grateful to the proctor for contributing to her advancement. Ale-houses and inns generally provided a natural network for such needs, knowing what local talent could be called upon.[62]

Then there were the looser arrangements. Thomas Heath of Thame, a maltster, was presented before the ecclesiastical court for having 'bought' the wife of George Fuller of Chinner for three weeks; he paid 2d per pound of her weight, which, after Mrs Fuller had been weighed in, resulted in 29s and one farthing changing hands. (In court the maltster admitted the sale, but denied that intercourse had taken place as a result.)[63]

Pepy's relationship with Betty Lane, later Martin, was certainly not a straightforward one of client and prostitute: Betty Lane and her sister Doll, with whom Pepys also dallied, were linendrapers in Westminster Hall, from whom Pepys purchased his linen 'bands'; they were distinguished sharply in Pepys's canon from the 'sluts' at the Black Spread Eagle in Bride Lane, who turned his stomach. On the other hand Betty granted Pepys the most intimate sexual favours over a long period of time, more or less whenever he demanded them; neither her marriage to the Exchequer clerk Samuel Martin nor pregnancy proving any impediment. In return she received entertainment of wine and chicken and cake when that was her prime need, and Pepys's patronage when Samuel Martin wanted a post. Pepys in his diary consistently criticized Betty for her lack of 'modesty' in what she permitted him to do to her and equally consistently resolved not to see her again. 'I perceive she is come to be very bad and offers anything', he wrote piously in February 1666. By June however Pepys was recording that he had had Betty 'both devante and backwards which is also muy bon plazer'. His utilitarian attitude to Betty Martin was not to be equated with his romantic feeling for the banished 'companion', poor little Deb Willet. When Pepys encountered Deb by chance years after her dismissal, he took her into an alley-way and forced her to touch him intimately. Deb's reluctance to do this happily convinced Pepys that she was still 'honest and modest'.[64] For Betty Martin's part, sex was simply one of a number of ways in which she tried to keep afloat. She too used or attempted to use Pepys; although he seems to have had rather the best of the bargain, at least according to the diary.

Famous madams included Mistress Damaris Page, given by Pepys the honorific title of 'the great bawd of the seamen'. Then there was Madam Cresswell, who had her house pulled down by the London apprentices in the riots of 1668. (Why did the apprentices frequent the bawdy-houses, if they were to pull them down? inquired Charles II, sensibly enough.) There were frequent references to Madam Cresswell in the literature of the time, from the high of Otway's *Venice Preserv'd* ('To lewdness every night the lecher ran ... Match him at Mothers Creswold's if you can') to the low of the satires. The apprentices' attitude to the bawdy-houses was indeed ambivalent. *The Whore's Rhetorick* was another fictional dialogue of 1683 in which the old bawd 'Madam Cresswell' instructed the young whore 'Dorothea' in her duties; these included keeping herself free for the apprentices on Sundays, when their masters gave them the day off.[65]

The real Madam Cresswell lived to be convicted in 1681 of 'above thirty years' practice of bawdry'. By the time she died towards the end of the century, she had turned optimistically to a public parade of piety. Madam Cresswell bequeathed £10 for an Anglican clergyman to preach her funeral sermon, but with that caution inculcated by the thirty years of business in her particular profession, she made it a condition that he spoke 'nothing but well of her'. The clergyman solved the problem by mentioning her name only briefly in the course of his oration, and in these terms: 'She was born well, she lived well, and she died well; for she was born with the name Cresswell, she lived in Clerkenwell and Camberwell, and she died in Bridewell.'[66]

The fictional Madam Cresswell of *The Whore's Rhetorick* was described as 'livid' in appearance, with hoary eyebrows, yellow gummy eyes, sagging breasts and a beard: in short the prototype of the menacing witch-like female, frightening because she was ugly and ugly because she was old. Dorothea, on the other hand, as a virginal gentlewoman, represented someone for whom a more hopeful future was proposed. She was described as one whose father 'had much more Nobility in his Veins than Money in his Purse', her dowry having been sacrificed in the Civil Wars. Unable to go out to work like her brothers, Dorothea was advised by Madam Cresswell to put her beauty up for sale and become 'a Woman of the Town'.[67]

The ancient bawd pointed out to Dorothea that 'Liberty was the first and the greatest benefit of nature', and that in consequence she should look on it as 'the great business' of her life to please others and enrich herself. That way Dorothea could look forward to retirement in the country, or even contemplate marriage, so long as she secured a third of her husband's estate as a dower: 'the most precious Jewel, next to life and liberty'. A rich merchant or some other honest citizen was probably the best hope for setting her up: 'these are the golden lovers', better than 'a score of ranting Blades'.[68]

Where her work with old men was concerned, Dorothea was adjured to bear in mind England's historic past: 'It is odds if sometimes in a rapture a-Bed, he do not get astride of thy Back, to demonstrate how he managed his horse at Naseby fight' (some forty years earlier). With all her lovers, it was essential for Dorothea to add to her lover's pleasure by simulating her own: 'You must not forget to use the natural accents of dying persons ... You must add to these ejaculations, aspirations, sighs, intermissions of words, and such like gallantries, whereby you may give your Mate to believe, that you are melted, dissolved and wholly consumed in pleasure, though Ladies of large business are generally no more moved by an embrace, than if they were made of Wood or stone.' Blushing was also a useful accomplishment: 'it is a token of modesty, and yet an amorous sign'.[69]

It is not suggested that all whores enjoyed the rich standard of life suggested by Madam Cresswell for Dorothea, or that they were equally salubrious. 'A trading lady', said the old bawd, needed 'a small convenient house of her own', with one or two maids, otherwise she would not be content; everything within had to be exceptionally neat and clean (including Dorothea's own person). Jenny Cromwell, Jenny Middleton, Moll Hinton, Sue Willis and Doll Chamberlain, the celebrated women of the town to be found at the New Exchange, were likely to lead a more rackety life. *The Wandering Whore*, listing the well-known prostitutes of 1660, gave exotic names such as the Queen of Morocco as well as some more homely: Welsh Nan Peg the Seaman's Wife, Long-Haired Mrs Spencer in Spitalfields, Mrs Osbridge's Scolding Daughter (catering clearly for some special masochistic taste) and Mrs Osbridge herself, who practised within Bedlam.[70]

In 1671 the Earl of Dorset announced that he was bored by the constant sentimental addresses to ladies of the court under pastoral names. Instead he proposed to serenade 'Black Bess' – the notorious prostitute Bess Morris:

> Methinks the poor town has been troubled too long
> With Phillis and Chloris in every song
> By fools, who at once can both love and despair,
> And will never leave calling 'em cruel and fair;
> Which justly provokes me in rhyme to express
> The truth that I know of bonny Black Bess.

The ploughman and squire, the arranter clown,
At home she subdued in her paragon gown;
But now she adorns both the boxes and pit,
And the proudest town gallants are forc'd to submit;
All hearts fall a-leaping, wherever she comes
And beat day and night, like my Lord Craven's drums.

In Restoration society Bess Morris had her place as well as Phillis and Chloris, and was well aware of it. When 'a great woman' named Bess to her face as Dorset's whore, Bess Morris answered that she was proud of the fact that she pleased at least 'one man of wit'; let 'all the coxcombs dance to bed with you!' she retorted.[71]

CHAPTER TWENTY-ONE

Actress as Honey-Pot

'Tis as hard a matter for a pretty Woman to keep herself honest in a Theatre, as 'tis for an Apothecary to keep his Treacle from the Flies in Hot Weather; for every Libertine in the Audience will be buzzing about her Honey-Pot…'

TOM BROWN, 'From worthy Mrs Behn the Poetress to the famous Virgin Actress'

According to John Evelyn, Margaret Godolphin was so mortified to find herself 'an Actoress' in 1674, in the court masque *Calisto*, that she spent all her time off stage reading a book of devotion; she could hardly wait for the performance to end before rushing to her oratory to pray. This distaste was recorded with ecstatic approval by Evelyn: in her dress worth nearly £300, and £20,000's worth of borrowed jewels his favourite looked like 'a Saint in Glory'; even when on the stage, she had the air of abstracting herself from it.[1]

The behaviour of the rest of the cast did not live up to this high standard. The 'tiring-room' was crowded with gallants, with whom the lady performers passed the time agreeably between entrances. The celebrated singer Mrs Knight, whose services had been called upon to supplement the somewhat weak voices of the amateurs, was an ex-mistress of the King. Renowned for the range of her voice, she had recently been 'roaming' in Italy, as a result of which her range was still further extended. Mrs Knight sang 'incomparably' on this occasion; nevertheless she was not a particularly welcome sight at court to the royal ladies. Another professional invited, Moll Davis – 'Dear Miss, delight of all the nobler sort' – had cast such enchantment over the King with the sweetness of her singing on stage that he had made her his mistress on the strength of it; she had recently borne him a child.

Although Evelyn was carrying prudery a little far in suggesting that Margaret Godolphin condemned a masque – the real cause of her pique lay elsewhere[2] – nevertheless it was true that in the 1670s a respectable woman could not give her profession as that of 'Actress' and expect to keep either her reputation or her person intact.

It was a royal warrant of 21 August 1660 which brought Englishwomen on to the English stage for the first time, so that plays should become 'useful and instructive representations of human life', from being merely 'harmless delights'. Before that, women had been seen on stage – but they had been foreigners, and as such highly suspect. Some of these were more travelling performers, mountebanks in the original sense of the word (*monta in banco* – mount on the bench), than actresses: in the time of Queen Elizabeth for example the honest town of Lyme had felt both thrilled and threatened by the 'unchaste, shameless, and unnatural tumbling of Italian women'. In 1629 a troupe of genuine actresses had arrived from France and had performed at Blackfriars, in the Red Bull and Fortune Theatres; they had been hissed off the stage by the English as being immoral. Later William Prynne in *Histriomastix* denounced them as 'notorious whores'.[3]

Under the Protectorate, when Sir William Davenant performed the brilliant conjuring trick of persuading the music-loving Cromwell that the new dramatic form of opera bore absolutely no relation to the scandalous theatre, a woman, Mrs Edward Coleman, had sung the part of Ianthe in the 'opera' *The Siege of Rhodes*. (Later, conveniently, *The Siege of Rhodes* turned out to be a play, and a very popular one too. Mrs Betterton made the part of Ianthe so much hers that she was generally referred to under that name rather than her own.) The conception of the court masque, so beloved of Queen Henrietta Maria and King Charles I, was also preserved during the Protectorate, because in that too music played its soothing part. At the wedding of Mary Cromwell a masque, with pastorals by Marvell, graced the protectoral court in which the young bride appeared; Cromwell himself may have played a non-speaking part.[4] However, a masque – for all Margaret Godolphin's megrims – was not a professional theatrical performance and nor was an opera – by protectoral decision.

It was a few months after the warrant – sometime in November or December 1660 – that one young Englishwoman actually stepped on to the London stage as the first swallow to signify the long hot summer of the English actress. We do not and shall presumably never know her name, although we know the play – *The Moor of Venice* – and the part – Desdemona. (Before that, as it was wittily said, with men of forty or fifty playing wenches of fifteen, when you called Desdemona: 'enter Giant'.)[5] Two companies had been given the monopoly of the London stage by the King's warrant, following the Restoration: The King's Company under Thomas Killigrew and The Duke's Company under Davenant. Although on balance of probability the claim of The King's Company to provide the first actress has been allowed, both companies actually claimed it; which means that the honour lies between Anne Marshall, Mary Saunderson (Mrs Betterton) and Katherine Corey, who became a specialist in old women's roles, famously creating that of the Widow Blackacre in Congreve's *The Double Dealer*. If Katherine Corey is ruled out as an unlikely Desdemona for this reason, the choice lies between Anne Marshall and Mary Saunderson.[6]

Mary Saunderson, who married the great actor-manager Thomas Betterton in 1662 when she was about twenty-five, would be a worthy founder of her profession; since she was the famous exception to the rule that all actresses of this period were to be considered potential prostitutes. 'Having, by nature, all the accomplishments required to make a perfect actress,' wrote Betterton's biographer Charles Gildon, 'she added to them the distinguishing characteristic of a virtuous life.' So wondrous was her virtue that she was actually engaged to coach the young Princesses Mary and Anne in *Calisto*, a task for which those participants Mrs Knight and Moll Davis would certainly not have been held suitable. Shortly before Mrs Betterton's marriage

Pepys was ravished by her performance in the title role of *The Duchess of Malfi* (Betterton played Bosola), the play itself being one of the most popular tragedies in the repertory of The Duke's Company. A long career in the theatre at her husband's side ended with the admirable Mrs Betterton training up other younger actresses, including Anne Bracegirdle.[7]

Most of her colleagues presented a very different image to the public. By 1666 Evelyn was finding the professional theatre increasingly distasteful, because audiences were abused by an 'atheistical liberty', to wit, 'foul and indecent women, now (and never till now) permitted to appear and act'; he much preferred the special court performances. In the 1680s the word actress was virtually synonymous with that of 'Miss' or kept woman, at least in the expectations of the public.[8] The burden of proof otherwise fell upon the individual actress, but there were very few who essayed to make the point. The trouble was that those 'useful and instructive representations of human life', the kind of new plays inspired by the opportunity of putting women on the stage, might be brilliant comedies of manners or turgid tragedies of emotion or some combination of the two, but in general they were extremely frank in their depiction of promiscuity. Inevitably and excitedly, the public merged the personality of the actress with that of her character on stage.

As a result, the convenient identification of actress and 'Miss' led to young ladies becoming actresses precisely in order to secure a rich admirer. Now contemporaries pitied the 'little playhouse creatures', as Mrs Squeamish termed them in *The Country Wife*, only if they did not manage to pick up a protector. The casting-couch made its first appearance in our social history when a young woman was sometimes obliged to sacrifice her virtue in order to obtain a coveted place in the theatre from one of its patrons. It was an investment she expected to recoup in the shape of the desired wealthy keeper, once she could display her pretty face to advantage on the stage itself. The beaux of the court expected in their turn to keep a pretty actress; it figured along with all their other expenses in the cause of public display, such as gaudy clothes and fine horses. In this way George Porter kept Mrs Jane Long, Sir Robert Howard (the nephew of his namesake, the lover of Lady Purbeck) Mrs Uphill, Sir Philip Howard Mrs Betty Hall, and the Earl of Peterborough Mrs Johnson.[9]

The *louche* atmosphere of the times is well caught by a joyful letter of 1677 from Harry Savile to Lord Rochester, then ill in the country. Savile tried to tempt Rochester to London with the prospect of a sweet new French *comédienne* called Françoise Pitel: 'a young wench of fifteen'. Savile declared 'it were a shame she should carry away a maidenhead she pretends to have brought', but unfortunately the price was so steep that no one currently in London could afford it.[10]

This two-way traffic called forth many references in the plays of the time. Some of these took the rueful side of management: 'our Women who adorn each Play, Bred at our cost, become at length your prey'. Others pointed to the actress herself as predator, since she intended:

> With open blandishments and secret art
> To glide into some keeping cullies heart
> Who neither sense nor manhood understands
> And jilt him of his patrimonial lands.[11]

Be that as it may, by the 1670s the word actress had secured in England that raffish connotation which would linger round it, for better or for worse, in fiction as well as fact, for the next 250 years.

It had not always been so. The first actresses often concealed their origins, while the honorific appellation 'Mrs' pronounced mistress, which they were granted – as opposed to the opprobrious 'Miss' – sometimes makes their marital status hard to unravel. Yet it is clear that they were neither 'Misses' nor the daughters of 'Misses'. Some, like Peg Hughes, came from actors' families. Others were drawn from that same penurious segment of society which supplied waiting-women and the like, where the daughters were likely to go husbandless if they had no dowry. Singing and dancing being the prerequisites of a ladylike education such as that provided by the Chelsea girls' schools, there were plenty of pupils in the early days from which to choose; some of whom later came to form part of what Anthony Hamilton called 'the whole joyous troop of singers and dancers who ministered to His Majesty's slighter pleasures'.[12]

Hannah Woolley, advocating the role of gentlewoman in *The Queen-like Closet* as being the best option available to the unendowed girl, drew attention to the alternatives: 'Some who have apt Wits and that Dame Nature hath been favourable to, they are courted to be Players.' The fact was those who had been favoured by Dame Nature did not necessarily share Hannah Woolley's particular sense of priorities. Mrs Pepys's gentlewoman, Gosnell, was one of these. Finding the post of gentlewoman too restrictive, she left to find her freedom (see p.386). A few months later, in May 1663 'Who should we see come upon the stage', wrote Pepys, 'but Gosnell, my wife's maid'. Unfortunately Gosnell 'neither spoke, danced nor sung; which I was sorry for. But she becomes the stage very well.' The following year Pepys saw Gosnell again, singing and dancing finely at first, but finally falling out of tune. Poor Gosnell! Her career never amounted to much more than being an understudy and an occasional singer. Four years later she was singing the performance 'meanly' throughout, and had lost her looks: Sir Carr Scroope characterized her as 'that old hag'. Finally Gosnell was discharged and vanished from view.[13]

Gosnell had been the daughter of a widow with very little money but genteel connections. Among the first actresses there were plenty of Gosnells, who preferred the liberty and adventure of the stage to a life of doing shell-work with Mrs Pepys, only they turned out to be more talented. Anne and Rebecca Marshall were the daughters of a country parson, who as chaplain to Lord Gerard had been married off to the illegitimate daughter of a Cheshire squire. Mrs Shadwell's father was either a Norwich public notary or 'a decayed knight'; Charlotte Butler was the daughter of a widowed shopkeeper. Accounts of Mrs Barry's origins varied: she was either an orphan brought up by Lady Davenant to be her 'woman' in Norfolk, or the daughter of a barrister called Robert Barry who ruined himself fighting for the King.[14]

Wherever they began, the first actresses – and their managers – were not slow to take advantage of their unique opportunities for display, and profit from that display. Inheriting the famous pre-Restoration female 'breeches' parts from the men who had previously played them, they made of them something yet more titillating. Actresses with pretty legs, like Peg Hughes and Nell Gwynn, welcomed this legitimate opportunity for showing them off in public, not otherwise granted to them by the costume of the time; then there were the infinite enjoyable possibilities of the *double entendre*. New plays were rapidly written employing the old device for a new reason: it has been estimated that nearly a third of all the plays first produced after 1660 and before 1700 contained one or more breeches roles.[15] Audiences, unused to such bonanzas, were enchanted when Betty Boutel, playing Fidelia disguised as a boy in Wycherly's *The Plain Dealer*, had her peruke pulled off and her breasts felt by the actor playing Vernish.

The costumes for the more straightforward women's parts offered opportunities for self-advertisement too.[16] The actress would first don a loose smock of Holland linen falling below the knees, with short sleeves and a very low-cut draw-string neck (it was in these smocks that they spent their hours resting off stage; a convenient costume it might be thought for receiving the gallants who pestered the tiring-rooms with their attentions, including during the performances, to judge from the frequent prohibitions issued against such behaviour). After the smock came wood or whalebone stays. Holland drawers followed for those who intended to dance: Nell Gwynn had a habit of wearing 'Rhinegraves' for the King's delectation, special short wide divided skirts which flew up as she danced.[17] Thread or silk stockings, gartered above and below the knee, were worn with high-heeled shoes and buckles. Two or three petticoats, a tight bodice and an over-skirt completed the outfit; this left the bosom more or less bare (so that actresses generally wore a scarf – 'a whisk' – out of doors).

What with the Holland smocks and the low-cut dresses, the

opportunities for actors on stage – in the course of plays which made frequent use of such gestures – and the gallants off stage, to 'towse and mowse' with a willing actress were virtually unlimited. Pepys was shocked by the backstage incidents he witnessed, including the bad language of the actresses.[18] Only the leading actress had a room to herself.

Nor were the financial rewards of being an actress such as to make additional income unnecessary. For one thing actresses had to supply their own petticoats, shoes, stockings, gloves and scarves as well as other living expenses; the introduction of liveries paid for by the King was thus a welcome economy, not a humiliation. (When the King, the Duke of York and the Earl of Oxford lent their coronation robes for Orrery's *Henry V*, in which Betterton played Owen Tudor and Mrs Betterton the Princess of France, it was as much to do with economy as with the close informal relationship which existed between the court and the theatre; the court supplying the Lord Chamberlain, whose duty it was to license the players.) Runs of plays were often as short as two or three days and it has been estimated that no one worked for much more than thirty or thirty-five weeks in the year.[19] The shutting of the London theatres for eighteen months at the time of the Great Plague brought about further hardship.

A young actress would receive 10s to 15s a week and would be expected to work for nothing at the beginning of her career. Even the great Mrs Barry only received 30s at the height of her fame, although she also received much larger sums from benefit performances. Mrs Betterton, paid the enormous sum of 50s a week in 1691, was the wife of the principal actor, who was also incidentally the man who ran the company. There were rules which prevented actresses (and actors) from moving between the two companies without permission; the amalgamation of The King's Company and The Duke's Company between 1682 and 1695 as The United Company increased the problems of actors by setting up a monopoly.

Unmarried actresses lived as close as possible to the theatre, the Fleet Street and Covent Garden area for The Duke's

Company and Drury Lane for The King's Company; Davenant originally boarded some of his leading actresses, including Moll Davis, in his own apartments. As against these conditions, the life of the kept woman with her own house, best of all her own settlement from her protector, offered innumerable advantages unknown to the virtuous. It is hardly surprising that a large number of actresses succumbed to the temptation.

It was not the talentless who adopted this code of behaviour, rather the reverse. Of the eighty women, who appeared on the Restoration stage, listed by name by J.H. Wilson in his comprehensive study of the subject,[20] twelve who enjoyed an enduring reputation as courtesans or 'Misses' included the most celebrated performers such as Elizabeth Barry and Betty Boutel, an innocent-looking Fidelia, but off stage known as 'Chestnut-maned Boutel, whom all the Town F–ks'. The ladies, it should be said, thrived on this combination of public and private acclaim: Betty Boutel spent twenty-six years on the stage and Elizabeth Barry thirty-five. As for Mrs Bracegirdle, who made a special parade of her virtue, she was described as one that had got 'more Money out of dissembling her Lewdness than others by professing it'; and it seems that she was kept at different times by both Congreve and Lord Scarsdale.[21]

At least another twelve, either lazier, unluckier or less successful, are known to have left the theatre to become straightforward kept women or prostitutes. Another thirty are mentioned so briefly as being on the stage, that it is likely that many of them also vanished into prostitution. 'Mistaken Drab, back to thy Mother's stall'; with these cruel words the pretensions of Sarah Cooke, Rochester's protégée, to be an actress were dismissed by a satirist in the 1680s. In fact 'Miss Sarah's' origins were not so low as indicated; nor was she quite devoid of talent, since she was wanted by Dryden to play Octavia in *All For Love*.[22] Nevertheless the supposition that an unsuccessful actress, having come from the stews, would return to them, was a characteristic one of the period.

Roughly a quarter of these actresses lived respectable lives, so far as we know, and most of these, like Mrs Betterton, were married to fellow-actors; it seems that in the seventeenth century show-business marriages reversed the modern trend and were more stable than otherwise. In general, as the jovial satirist Tom Brown wrote in *Letters from the Dead to the Living* (this letter was headed: 'From worthy Mrs Behn the Poetress, to the famous Virgin Actress'): "Tis as hard a matter for a pretty Woman to keep herself honest in a Theatre, as 'tis for an Apothecary to keep his Treacle from the Flies in Hot Weather; for every Libertine in the Audience will be buzzing about her Honey-Pot…'[23]

Hester Davenport, widely known as 'Roxalana' after her performance in that part in *The Siege of Rhodes* in 1661, was 'a charming, graceful creature and one that acted to perfection'. She was about twenty at the time of her first fame. With her exceptional looks – a beauty that made men 'take ill courses' wrote Anthony à Wood – she captured the heart of the Earl of Oxford, then a childless widower of forty-four. He was a Knight of the Garter, handsome, famously rich, notoriously proud; he was also a lover of the theatre (as his loan of his coronation robes would evince). However, these were the early years before the identification of actress and 'Miss' had thoroughly set in, and there is reason to believe that Roxalana herself attached as much importance to her talent as to her looks; she was after all in proper employment and as the darling of the stage able to support herself.[24] She therefore began by refusing Lord Oxford's tender of protection.

Offers of services and presents were of no avail, nor were insults, nor, in the last resort, were 'spells' and incantations. Lord Oxford could neither smoke nor gamble as a result of his obsession. Various contemporary accounts agree that Hester Davenport only finally succumbed because Lord Oxford made it seem lawful for her to do so (an elaborate process which neither of them would probably have thought necessary ten years later). In Anthony Hamilton's words, where Love had failed, he 'invoked the aid of Hymen'.[25] First Lord Oxford displayed to his Roxalana a signed contract of marriage. He then enacted that scene which was to become a commonplace of Restoration drama, the fake wedding ceremony, with the minister played by his own trumpeter and the witness by his kettle-drummer. A fellow-actress, who was not in the plot, stood witness for Roxalana.

The next morning, according to the most colourful description of the episode (by the Baroness d'Aulnoy), Lord Oxford aroused his 'bride' with the surprising words: 'Wake up, Roxalana, it is time for you to go.' At which the betrayed woman burst out screaming and wounded her husband-lover with his own sword. The trumpeter and the kettle-drummer vanished; the actress-witness was told Roxalana had merely been playing a part in a play. Whatever her initial revulsion, Roxalana did continue the relationship; she left the stage and bore Lord Oxford a son, Aubrey de Vere, a couple of years – not nine months – later.

Nevertheless Anthony à Wood wrote of Roxalana as having married 'the Earl of Oxon', and another account criticized Lord Oxford for 'marrying his whore' as well as 'spending his estate'. Roxalana complained to the King that she had been deceived and secured a large pension of 1,000 crowns per annum. She also continued to term herself the Countess of Oxford for the rest of her life: at the time of her second – or first – marriage, which occurred after Lord Oxford's death in 1703, she was termed Dame Hester, Dowager Countess of Oxford; she signed her will Hester Oxford.[26] None of this prevented Lord Oxford himself from marrying, in 1673, that fascinating if promiscuous beauty Diana Kirke, successful rival to Mrs Grace Worthley for the affections of Henry Sidney (see p.483).

The solution may lie in the loose nature of marriage at the time. Given that Roxalana was joined together with Lord Oxford in some kind of union in some kind of ceremony, perhaps she herself did not inquire too closely into its validity. 'You may think she was but an actress...' observed Mrs Hobart to her fellow Maid of Honour Mrs Temple, telling this cautionary story about the evil intentions of the opposite sex;[27] yet in the early sixties, this mere actress might put up considerable resistance before sinking into the role of 'Miss'.

Peg Hughes, on the other hand, arrived on the stage five years later 'a mighty pretty woman' but not a modest one, for she had a reputation already for being Sir Charles Sedley's mistress.[28] She proceeded to capture the heart of that old warhorse, the King's cousin, Prince Rupert. Peg Hughes's brother was a minor comedian (later killed in a brawl at Windsor over the relative claims of his sister and Nell Gwynn to be 'handsomer'). Her first appearance may have been as Desdemona in an *Othello* seen by Pepys in February 1669; she probably replaced another actress called Davenport, Frances, no relation to Hester, who had vanished 'to be kept by somebody' a few weeks earlier. Peg Hughes was certainly acting by the summer – in May Pepys was granted a backstage kiss – although her first recorded performance was as Panura in Fletcher's *The Island Princess*.

Like Roxalana, Peg Hughes resisted her elderly royal admirer in the first place, although unlike Roxalana, she was hardly concerned to preserve her virtue. The fatal encounter took place at the fashionable spa of Tunbridge Wells; Queen Catherine had sent for the players from London to divert the court. To the ribald glee of the younger gallants and the open pleasure of the King, Prince Rupert became quickly obsessed by the 'mighty pretty' actress, deserting all his habitual scientific pastimes. It was 'farewell to alembics, crucibles, furnaces and the black tools of alchemy; farewell to mathematical instruments and speculations! Powder and perfume now filled his whole mind...'[29] At first Peg seems to have been reluctant to leave the fun of the stage and to have regarded the Prince's passion as rather ridiculous (perhaps he was one of those who, as in Madam Cresswell's advice to Dorothea, recalled 'Naseby fight' in moments of amorous excitement).

The following year more worldly counsels prevailed. Peg Hughes became the Prince's mistress, being installed by him in a substantial house at Hammersmith (George IV's spurned Queen, Caroline, later lived there). She bore him a daughter named Ruperta in 1673, at which point she quitted the stage for three years. It should be said that Peg Hughes, whose acting had been widely praised by her contemporaries, also proved an admirable concubine. At first there were local difficulties: in 1674 Peg

Hughes was suspected of acquiring some of the jewels which had once belonged to Prince Rupert's mother, Elizabeth of Bohemia. But as the years wore on, Prince Rupert's sister, the Electress Sophia, grew to appreciate the good care which Peg took of her elderly protector. The Electress described Mrs Hughes as '*très modeste*', or at least the most modest of that not conspicuously modest English court; she wished 'Mistress Hus' (or sometimes Hews) had produced a son for her brother, but in any case wished to embrace 'pretty Ruperta'.[30]

In 1682 Prince Rupert's health began to give way. He praised Peg Hughes's solicitude in a letter to the Electress which also conveyed a picture of the happy family life enjoyed in Hammersmith: 'She [Peg] took great care of me during my illness', he told his sister, 'and I am obliged to her for many things … As for the little one [Ruperta] she cannot resemble me, she is turning into the prettiest creature. She already rules the whole house and sometimes argues with her mother, which makes us all laugh.' Prince Rupert died at the end of November. In his will, for which the Earl of Craven was trustee, he divided his property between 'Margaret Hewes' and 'Ruperta my natural daughter begotten on the body of the said Margaret Hewes'. In addition Ruperta was charged to be a good obedient daughter and not to marry without her mother's consent.[31]

Ruperta carried out her father's dying commands. She made a suitable match to Lieutenant-General Emmanuel Scroope of Norfolk, and had children.† Peg Hughes was the giddy one, and in the end Ruperta had to look after her mother (Peg lived till 1719). Despite receiving the huge sum of £6,000 from the will of Prince Rupert, Peg Hughes gambled it all away. Another of Tom Brown's fictional dialogues in *Letters from the Dead to the Living* took place between Peg and Nell Gwynn, her rival for 'handsomeness'. Nell Gwynn's sentiments were probably based on truth. Nell was made to reproach Peg for losing by gambling what she had acquired by whoredom: 'for a woman who has

---

†Today Sir Rupert Bromley Bt represents the direct line of descent from Ruperta, Prince Rupert and of course Peg Hughes.

enriched herself by one, to impoverish herself by the other, is so great a fault, that a harlot deserves correction for it'.[32]

Anne Marshall, who shares with Mary Betterton the claim to be the first professional English actress, was one of a pair of striking dark-haired sisters; later in her career she acted under her married name of Mrs Anne Quin, leaving the title of 'Mrs Marshall' to her younger sister Rebecca or 'Beck'.[33] The equation of dark tints with tragic grandeur marked both women out for the proud and passionate female roles created pre-eminently by Dryden, in the new type of 'heroic drama', the opposite pole to the brightness and lightness (and lewdness) of Restoration comedy. Rebecca Marshall had the additional advantage for queenly roles – of which there was a plentiful supply – of being very tall. 'Behold how night sits lovely on her Eye-brows While day breaks from her eyes!', or 'Her quick black eye does wander with desire', or 'Her long black locks, on her fair shoulders flow'; these contemporary allusions commemorate the saturnine beauty of the Marshall sisters.

Anne Marshall, as a founder member of The King's Company and a leading lady there from 1661 onwards, played Zempoalla in *The Indian Queen* which Dryden co-wrote with Sir Robert Howard, and then Almeria in Dryden's *The Indian Emperor*. Pepys praised her Zempoalla and thought it done 'excellently well, as ever I heard woman in my life', even if Anne Marshall's voice was not quite so sweet as Mrs Betterton's.[34] But in depicting the character of Zempoalla, 'the usurping Indian Queen' of Mexico who fell in love with her enemy Montezuma, a little stridency would not have come amiss, for she habitually expressed herself in lines like these:

> Great God of vengeance, here I firmly vow,
> Make but my Mexicans successful now,
> And with a thousand feasts thy flames I'll feed;
> And that I take, shall on the altars bleed ...[35]

At the end of the play, defeated and her love scorned, Zempoalla killed herself. Almeria in the sequel was Zempoalla's daughter, equally beautiful, equally tempestuous, equally proud. Catching the eye of the new Emperor of Mexico, Montezuma, who proposed to take her as his wife, Almeria vowed to use his passion to avenge her mother:

> If news be carried to the shades below
> The Indian queen will be more pleased, to know
> That I his scorns on him, who scorned her, pay.[36]

At the end of *The Indian Emperor* however it was Almeria's destiny, like that of her mother, to die. She killed herself at the feet of the Spanish conqueror Cortez, the object of her unrequited love, as Montezuma had been that of Zempoalla.

Rebecca Marshall joined her sister at The King's Company sometime in the summer of 1663 but seems to have been a mere apprentice up until the closure of the theatres in June 1665. Besides being always plagued with debt she had a stormy character: in real life her adventures, if not on such a lofty level, were at least as tempestuous as those of Dryden's 'barbarian Princesses'. In 1665 she complained about the attentions of a certain Mark Trevor of the Temple to the Lord Chamberlain (considered the protector as well as the licenser of the theatrical profession); Mark Trevor responded by assaulting her. This brought a second complaint from Rebecca Marshall: that Mark Trevor had 'affronted her both on and off the stage, attacked her in a coach with his sword etc., and threatens vengeance for her complaining of him to the Lord Chamberlain'.[37]

Two years later there was further trouble with Sir Hugh Middleton. Having insulted the women of The King's Company as a whole, he had the temerity to come round to their tiring-room at the Theatre Royal. Beck Marshall forthwith and roundly denounced him. Sir Hugh Middleton denounced *her*, calling her 'a jade'. Beck then went to the King and secured his promise of protection. Unfortunately she proceeded to boast of this moral victory. Whereupon Sir Hugh Middleton hired some ruffians who waylaid the actress on her way home and rubbed the most disgusting filth all over her. In general Beck Marshall could look after herself: in a further row with Orange Moll, plying her wares at the theatre, both sides gave as good as they got in language and blows.

Naturally her morals were not elevated. She had for example a liaison with the famous fop Sir George Hewell, to whom she bore a daughter. A satire of 1683 suggested that the daughter was no more virtuous than the mother:

> Proud Curtizan Marshall, 'Tis the time to give o'er
> Since now your Daughter, she is turned whore.

Beck Marshall also acted as go-between or procuress to Barbara Duchess of Cleveland, who conceived a passion for the well-known actor Charles Hart.

At the reopening of the theatres in November 1666, the position between the sisters was reversed. The interregnum had given an opportunity to the younger actresses to come to the fore, prominent among them the ex-orange-girl Nell Gwynn with her pretty legs and her talent for comedy, and the 'mighty pretty and fine and noble' Beck Marshall: 'very handsome near-hand' wrote Pepys, sitting close to her at the theatre. In December 1666 Beck Marshall played the part of Evadne, the corrupted heroine of Beaumont and Fletcher's *The Maid's Tragedy*, a part hitherto considered the prerogative of her sister. Pepys noted that 'the younger Marshall' had become 'a pretty good actor'. Early the next year it was Rebecca Marshall who played the lead part of the Queen of Sicily in Dryden's *Secret Love or The Maiden Queen* – 'very good and passionate' – while Anne, having been transformed into Mrs Quin by marriage at some unknown date in between, was condemned to play the secondary part of Candiope, Princess of the Blood; Nell Gwynn incidentally scored a great success in the 'comical' part of Florimel, the Maid of Honour.[38]

The situation was not to be borne, at least from the elder sister's point of view. Nor did Anne Marshall Quin attempt to bear it. She left the theatre once more shortly afterwards and petitioned the Lord Chamberlain to restore her to her old roles – and her old stature as a leading lady. This included the privilege of a dressing-room for her own private use. As a result on 4 May 1667 the Lord Chamberlain instructed The King's Company to admit Mrs Anne Quin 'to Act again at Theatre Royall and that you assign her all her own parts which she formerly had and that none other be permitted to act any of her parts without her consent. And that you assign her a dressing room with a chimney in it to be only for her use and whom she shall admit.'[39]

The petition worked. In a performance of Boyle's *The Black Prince* in October 1667, elder sisters will be relieved to learn that Anne Quin played the romantic part of Alizia Pierce, while younger sisters will burn to hear that Rebecca Marshall played the dull part of Plantagenet. The important part of Donna Aurelia in Dryden's *An Evening's Love* followed for Anne Quin in 1668, with Rebecca Marshall uncast. Anne Quin also re-created her famous part of Zempoalla in June 1668; if Pepys no longer doted upon her quite so much, the rest of the world was full of praise.[40]

However, by October 1669 Mrs Quin had left The King's Company once more, to reappear some years later in The Duke's Company, where she played the part of the courtesan Angelica Bianca in Aphra Behn's *The Rover* and a whole list of other important parts in the late seventies and early eighties (she is last heard of in 1682). These included Lady Knowall, Aphra Behn's caricature of Mary Astell, in *Sir Patient Fancy*; Lady Squeamish in Otway's *Friendship in Fashion*, and Queen Elizabeth in Banks's *The Unhappy Favourite* (a role to which her regal appearance and manner were especially well suited).

The departure of her sister left Rebecca Marshall in full command at The King's Company. She took over the part of Donna Aurelia, and continued as a leading actress there until 1677 when she briefly caught up with her sister again at The Duke's Company for a few months before leaving the stage for good.

It has to be borne in mind that for all the worldly advancement of a Roxalana, a Peg Hughes, and the busy Marshall sisters there were many actresses who fell through the net, were not fought over at court, or ended their lives as 'Dame Hester, Countess of Oxford', but like Gosnell, faltered and disappeared. Elizabeth Farley, generally known as Mrs Weaver, was one of these. She was born about 1640, and as a member of The King's Company from 1660 to 1665, played secondary roles at the Theatre Royal.

According to Pepys's actress friend Mrs Knepp, Elizabeth Farley was 'first spoiled' i.e. seduced, by the King himself. If true, the relationship did not last very long, for by the winter of 1660 Elizabeth Farley was living with James Weaver, a gentleman of Gray's Inn.[41] Although she was never married to Weaver, Elizabeth Farley ran up bills of credit as his wife, and was also generally listed as Mrs Weaver in the cast lists of the theatre. Weaver not only cast off his mistress but also sought permission of the Lord Chamberlain to sue her for the return of £30; and she had other debts. Furthermore Elizabeth Farley was by now pregnant, although she continued desperately to act, since so long as she was a member of The King's Company, she was immune from arrest.

The visible signs of her pregnancy could not be concealed for ever. 'Mrs Weaver' was finally discharged. Carefully misrepresenting the cause of her dismissal, Elizabeth Farley appealed to the King for reinstatement. Sir Henry Bennet, on behalf of the King, was ordered to see to it. At this point Sir Robert Howard, the principal shareholder in The King's Company, issued an indignant protest. Mrs Weaver, he said, had been dismissed because she was 'big with child' and 'shamefully so' since she was not married. Women of quality were declaring that they could not possibly come to the theatre to watch an actress in such a condition. 'Truly, Sir, we are willing to bring the Stage to be a place of some Credit, and not an infamous place for all persons of Honour to avoid', protested Howard.[42] (This was at a moment, incidentally, when the King's *maîtresse en titre*, Barbara, future Duchess of Cleveland, was just recovering from the birth of the second of the five bastards she bore to the King; admittedly she was legally married to Roger Palmer at the time;

nevertheless the genteel protest was striking evidence of the double standard which operated.)

Elizabeth Farley did return to the stage, and played the part of 'fair Alibech', Almeria's sympathetic younger sister, in *The Indian Emperor* of 1665, a secondary but not unimportant role. Debts continued to pursue her. When the theatres closed in the summer of 1665 owing to the plague she effectively vanished from view. It is possible she returned to the stage from time to time in the 1670s, under her own name; but if she is the 'Mrs Farley' named in a poem of Rochester's she became a prostitute.

Elizabeth Barry – 'famous Madam Barry' – was by acclaim the greatest actress of the Restoration period and beyond, her reign extending from the 1670s until 1710, when she made her last appearance on the stage. Yet the beginnings of her story are such as to encourage any first-time failure on the stage to persevere. What was more, she might never have pursued her career further had not the most notorious libertine of the age, the Earl of Rochester, come 'buzzing about her Honey-Pot'.

No one ever pretended Mrs Barry numbered beauty among her gifts: 'middle-sized' with 'darkish Hair, light eyes, dark Eyebrows ... indifferently plump', was one unenthusiastic description.[43] She also had a mouth which was slightly drawn up on one side, which she used to try to conceal by composing her face as though about to be painted. Her portrait by Kneller shows a face which is distinctly plain, with a Roman nose and thick lips; even if there is an air of intelligence about it, and more than a hint of determination.

It is easy to believe from such a picture that Mrs Barry at the height of her fame was held to be 'the Finest Woman in the World upon the Stage, and the ugliest woman off on't'.[44] Nevertheless it was not likely that the homely creature she represented as a girl would have caught Rochester's eye had Mrs Barry not belonged to the traditionally promiscuous profession of actress. It can be argued therefore that this aura of promiscuity, while it ruined some young women, helped to advance Mrs Barry.

The story of Mrs Barry, like her origins, has to be pieced together from various (often conflicting) accounts.[45] It seems that she first appeared on the stage in 1674 when she was sixteen. Mrs Barry was thus some twenty years younger than Mrs Betterton and Hester Davenport, the founders of her profession. She played Isabella Queen of Hungary in *Mustapha*, by Roger Boyle, Earl of Orrery (brother of Mary Countess of Warwick and Katherine Viscountess Ranelagh). This début was a disaster. According to Colley Cibber, Mrs Barry was considered so feeble that she was discharged from the company at the end of her first year. Anthony Aston wrote: 'for some time they could make nothing of her; she could neither sing nor dance', not even in a country dance. Mrs Barry was not the only actress-goose whom Rochester determined to turn into a swan. Had he not attempted the same transformation on Sarah Cooke – 'Miss Sarah' – that 'Mistaken Drab' so utterly unable even after Rochester's tuition to impress the critical Wits, that she was ordered back to her 'Mother's stall'? It would therefore not be right to credit Rochester with an unerring eye in this respect: he struck unlucky with 'Miss Sarah' for all her ravishing looks; with Mrs Barry, much less easy on the eye, he struck very lucky indeed.

What should be credited to him without reservation is the manner of his tutorage. This, which might be described as an early form of method-acting, in the hands of the amazing Mrs Barry enabled her to give a proper reality, something rare indeed at the time, to the whole range of female parts in Restoration drama: 'solemn and august' in tragedy, 'alert, easy and genteel' in comedy.[46] As we have seen, the first generation of actresses (with the exception of Mrs Betterton) tended to be admired in one or the other.

The original failing of Mrs Barry was that while she had 'an excellent understanding' she lacked a musical ear: thus she could not catch 'the sounds or emphases taught her; but fell into a disagreeable tone, the fault of most young stage-adventurers'. Lord Rochester's solution was 'to enter into the meaning of every sentiment; he taught her not only the proper cadence or sounding of the voice, but to seize also the passions, and adapt her whole behaviour to the situations of the characters'. He would rehearse her in a part more than thirty times. As a result Betterton said that she could transform a play that would disgust the most patient reader, calling her 'incomparable': 'her action was always just, and produced naturally by the sentiments of the part'. At a time when artificial heroics were considered an inevitable concomitant of such heroines as those created by Dryden, Mrs Barry could wipe away real tears when acting out a tragic death scene.[47]

Rochester had taken over Mrs Barry's career in the first place for a bet: after the disastrous début, he vowed he would make her the most accomplished performer at the Dorset Garden Theatre (the new home of The Duke's Company) within six months. He certainly won his bet. *Alcibiades*, the first tragedy by Thomas Otway, performed in September 1675, featured Thomas Betterton in the title role, with Mrs Betterton as his betrothed Timandra; it was in the small part of Alcibiades' sister Draxilla that Mrs Barry reappeared on the London stage. It was probably after this and before her appearance as Leonora in *Abdelazar* by Aphra Behn the following July that Rochester coached her, although the precise sequence is uncertain.[48] At all events, the new improved Mrs Barry captured more than critical attention: she also won the heart of Thomas Otway. As a result, he laid at her feet the type of bouquet which only a playwright can bestow upon an actress – a series of plays. Mrs Barry dazzled in such varied parts as Monimia, the pathetic eponymous heroine of *The Orphan*, and Lavinia (Juliet) in Otway's adaptation of *Romeo and Juliet*. This was an unpopular play, at least in Shakespeare's version, after the Restoration. Otway's adaptation, which also drew on Plutarch, was entitled *The History and Fall of Caius Marius*; which led to Mrs Barry as Lavinia pronouncing (to her lover, known as Marius junior) the interesting line: 'O Marius, Marius, wherefore art thou Marius.'[49] Most striking of all Mrs Barry's creations in the first flush of her success was that of 'beauteous Belvidera', the plangent heroine of *Venice Preserv'd*.

In all however Mrs Barry created over 100 roles, at The Duke's Company, as the leading lady of The United Company after 1682, and at the breakaway Lincoln's Inn Fields Company after 1695; although by now she was surrendering the juvenile leading parts to a rising young actress called Anne Bracegirdle. Her parts included that of Hellena in Aphra Behn's *The Rover* (a 'breeches' part), Arabella in Ravenscroft's *The London Cuckolds*, Lady Brute in Vanbrugh's *The Provok'd Wife* and Cordelia in another of those bastard versions of Shakespeare which audiences so much preferred to the glorious originals, Nahum Tate's *Lear* (Cordelia finally married Edgar and lived happily ever after). In 1694 Thomas Southerne, author of *The Fatal Marriage*, paid a graceful tribute to her handling of Isabella, his ill-fated heroine: 'I made the play for her part, and her part has made the play for me.'[50]

In *Venice Preserv'd*, Thomas Betterton as Jaffeir gave Mrs Barry as Belvidera, on her first entrance, this lyrical salutation which sums up the romantic view of the female in the late seventeenth century:

> Sure all ill-stories of thy sex are false:
> O woman! lovely woman! Nature made thee
> To temper man: we had been brutes without you:
> Angels are painted fair, to look like you;
> There's in you all that we believe of heaven,
> Amazing brightness, purity and truth![51]

It was ironic under the circumstances that Mrs Barry herself, angel painted fair on stage as she might be, was the focus of so many 'ill-stories' off it, which if only half of them were true, more than justified the opposing cynical view of the female sex. Mrs Barry was dissolute ('She has been a Rioter in her time', wrote Gildon): that in itself was not unusual. She was bad-tempered and at times even violent. Although her good breeding – more or less – was said to make her on stage 'Mistress of that Behaviour which sets off the well-bred Gentlewoman', Mrs Barry was capable of exhibiting quite another side to her character, stage or no stage. In a famous incident, Mrs Barry and 'Chestnut-maned [Betty] Boutel', acting in Lee's *The Rival Queens*, quarrelled over a scarf as the play was about to begin. On the all-too appropriate line:

> Die, sorceress, die and all my wrongs die with thee!

Mrs Barry as Roxana struck Mrs Boutel playing the rival queen Statira with such force that her blunted stage dagger managed to penetrate Mrs Boutel's stays, and pierce the flesh beneath.[52]

Furthermore Mrs Barry was mercenary. Where her professional life was concerned, that was understandable, in view of the low salaries paid to actresses at the time: for example, she insisted on receiving the proceeds of a benefit at the theatre, hitherto generally reserved for writers. But she was also mercenary where her affections were concerned, to an extent that amazed even this worldly age. It was not so much the settlement she was supposed to have secured from the playwright Sir George Etherege (Mrs Barry could see for herself what happened to the unendowed actress), but Tom Brown wrote: 'Should you lie with her all night, she would not know you next morning, unless you had another five pounds at your service.' The lampoons which blasted the private lives of all the famous actresses and courtesans of the time (with the ever-glowing exception of Mrs Betterton) showed in later years a particular bitterness towards the 'slattern Betty Barry'.

> At thirty eight a very hopeful whore,
> The only one o'th' trade that's not profuse,
> (A policy was taught her by the Jews),
> Tho' still the highest bidder she will choose.

At the same time it had to be admitted that Mrs Barry was one whom 'every fop upon the stage admires'.[53] It was as though her defiant combination of talent and calculation was especially exacerbating.

Thomas Otway despaired of Mrs Barry's treatment of him: while accepting the parts, it is said that she would not even requite his besotted love with a kiss. Otway referred to himself as being fobbed off 'with gross, thick, homespun friendship, the common Coin that passes betwixt Worldly Interests'. He addressed a series of agonized letters to his beloved, confessing that since the first day he saw her, 'I have hardly enjoy'd one Hour of perfect Quiet'; and yet he could not break loose: 'though I have languished for seven long tedious Years of Desire, jealously and despairingly; yet, every Minute I see you, I still discover something new and bewitching'.[54]

Otway was bitter in the knowledge that Rochester had succeeded where he had failed: 'I have consulted my Pride, whether after a Rival's Possession I ought to ruin all my Peace for a Woman that another has been more blest in, though no Man ever loved as I did: But Love, victorious Love, o'er throws all that, and tells me, it is his Nature never to remember; he still looks forward from the present hour, expecting new Dawns, new rising Happiness, never looks back, never regards what is past, left behind him, but buries and forgets it quite in the hot fierce pursuit of Joy before him.' On the other hand Rochester, on the evidence of his own letters (thirty-four survive, although they are undated and the originals have vanished), suffered equally from jealousy where Mrs Barry was concerned, for all the consummation of his desire. It was thought by contemporaries that Mrs Barry was the great love of Rochester's life: she was 'his passion', wrote one, and another claimed that he never loved anyone else 'so sincerely' as Mrs Barry.[55]

In poetry Rochester could serenade 'The Mistress' with elegance:

> An age in her embraces past
> Would seem a winter's day,
> Where life and light with envious haste
> Are torn and snatch'd away.
>
> But, oh! how slowly minutes roll
> When absent from her eyes,
> That fed my love, which is my soul,
> It languishes and dies.

The letters were less controlled: 'Madam, There is now no minute of my life that does not afford me some new argument how much I love you; the little joy I take in every thing wherein you are not concern'd, the pleasing perplexity of endless thought, which I fall into, wherever you are brought to my remembrance; and lastly, the continual disquiet I am in, during your absence, convince me sufficiently that I do you justice in loving you, so as woman was never loved before.' And again: 'Seeing you is as necessary to my life as breathing; so that I must see you, or be yours no more; for that's the image I have of dying…' Writing to Mrs Barry at three in the morning, a letter of furious expostulation, Rochester ended: 'I thank God I can distinguish, I can see very woman in you… 'Tis impossible for me to curse you; but give me leave to pity myself, which is more than ever you will do for me.'[56]

Rochester's relationship with Mrs Barry lasted for about four years; towards the end of it, in 1677, she bore him a daughter. Rochester was by this time immured in the country, crippled and virtually blind from disease, moving towards that classic reprobate's deathbed in which he would abandon his wicked ways for the consolations of religion. Savile broke the news to him: 'Your Lordship has a daughter born by the body of Mrs Barry of which I give your honour joy.' Savile added that the mother's lying-in was not being held in 'much state' since Mrs Barry was living in great poverty in the Mall. The woman who had taken her in was 'not without some gentle reflections on your Lordship's want either of generosity or bowels [compassion] towards a lady who had not refused you the full enjoyment of her charms'.[57]

Rochester was however at this point pursued by his creditors as well as cut off from London by his physical condition, so that it is difficult to see how he could in fact have helped his mistress financially. He contented himself with writing to her: 'Madam, Your safe delivery has deliver'd me too from fears for your sake, which were, I'll promise you, as burthensome to me, as your great belly could be to you. Every thing has fallen out to my wish, for you are out of danger, and the child is of the soft sex I love…' The child, mentioned in Rochester's will under the name of Elizabeth Clarke, where she was left £40, died in 1689 at the age of twelve. At some point before Rochester's death in 1682 little Elizabeth Clarke was taken away briefly from her mother's care because of her want of 'discretion' in bringing her up. Rochester wrote firmly but kindly on the subject: 'Madam, I am far from delighting in the grief I have given you, by taking away the child: and you, who made it so absolutely necessary for me to do so, must take that excuse from me, for all the ill nature of it …! I hope very shortly to restore to you a finer girl than ever.'[58]

Doubtless Mrs Barry did show lack of discretion in her way of life: 'You have a character, and you maintain it', wrote Rochester in one of the anguished letters.[59] Yet her legendary rapacity and even her coldness and severity towards her admirers are at least explicable when one bears in mind the alternative: the wretched downfall experienced by an actress like Elizabeth Farley. Famous as Mrs Barry was, she had no alternative but to give birth to her child in poverty, without support from husband or lover, and only the help of a 'protectress'; that was the predictable fate of an actress who became pregnant. A little rapacity may be pardoned under the circumstances.

Mrs Barry retired to Acton – then pleasant countryside – when she finally left the stage in her fifties after her long reign. She died there in 1713. She is said to have been the victim of a bite from a pet lap-dog, which she did not know had been 'seized with madness'.[60] If the story is true, it was an appropriately bizarre and tragic end for the first of the great English dramatic actresses, a line of descent leading down to Mrs Siddons in the next century.

Although her plain memorial stone is still to be seen in the church at Acton where she lies buried, the words of Colley Cibber himself constitute her best epitaph: 'Mrs Barry, in Characters of Greatness, had a Presence of elevated dignity, her Mien and Motion superb and gracefully majestick; her Voice full, clear, and strong, so that no Violence of Passion could be too much for her: And when Distress or Tenderness possess'd her, she subsided into the most affecting Melody and Softness. In the Art of exciting Pity She had a Power beyond all the Actresses I have yet seen, or what your Imagination can conceive.'[61]

CHAPTER TWENTY-TWO

The Modest Midwife

~~~~~~~

> 'It is observable that in all the ages of the world and throughout all countries in the world, the help of grave and modest women (with us termed Midwives) hath ever been useful for release and succour of all the daughters of Evah, whom God hath appointed to bear children into this world.'
>
> JACOB RUEFF, *The Expert Midwife*, 1637

I n the seventeenth century every woman who had the opportunity to conceive was likely to give birth at least once during her lifetime: the heiress, the Quaker, the prostitute and the actress were all equal in this respect. And if a woman did not actually give birth, she had some other form of obstetrical experience. In the absence of any form of birth control (even coitus interruptus being notoriously uncertain) it was celibacy not marriage which was the relevant fact. Under the circumstances there were few women of the time from the idealistic Margaret Fell to the exotic Elizabeth Barry who did not fall at some point into the hands of those 'grave and modest women (with us termed Midwives)' in the words of Jacob Rueff's textbook of obstetrics.[1] The midwives could also be the agents of drama beyond the mere expedition of birth. It was the midwives' brutal 'search' of Frances Lady Purbeck, to prove her adultery with Sir Robert Howard, which caused her to flee her mother-in-law's roof. Witches were also subject to a routine search by the local midwives to discover the devil's marks; as were those women who sought to escape punishment on the grounds that they were pregnant.

The all-pervasive presence of the midwife in women's lives

may be illustrated by the indignant sentiments of *The Midwives Just Petition* of January 1643: let war cease, men return again to their wives so as to 'bring them yearly under the delivering power of the midwife'. *The Midwives Just Complaint* of 22 September 1646 echoed the thought: to the midwives, 'whereas many miseries do attend upon civil wars', nothing was worse than the gross interruption to their trade: 'For many men, hopeful to have begot a race of soldiers, were there killed on a sudden, before they had performed anything to the benefit of midwives.' Such a development was to be lamented: 'We were formerly well paid and highly respected in our parishes for our great skill and midnight industry; but now our art doth fail us, and little getting have we in this age, barren of all natural joys, and only fruitful of bloody calamities.'[2]

At first sight there is something wonderfully solipsistic about this interpretation of recent military events in England as being aimed at the overthrow of the midwives' 'midnight industry' rather than more political changes. Yet to most women of the time, caught up in their cycle of perpetual parturition, the complaint would have been perfectly comprehensible. For they too were caught up in the 'midnight industry' which touched most females far more closely than politics.

It could be said that nothing was more crucial to the life of the average woman than the character and skills of her midwife. Doctors were rarely in attendance at births, and when they were, concentrated on the rich, for obvious reasons. The rise of the so-called 'Man-Midwife' in the course of the seventeenth century, once again affected only the tiny percentage of people who could afford his services.[3] For most women, lying-in meant the attendance of a female whom it was devoutly hoped would be skilled enough to bring about an easy birth and leave behind a live mother and live child when she left.

There were thus a vast range of professional helps available, from the grand midwives who attended the royal *accouchements* down to the humble helpmates of the poor. Where the latter were concerned a shilling or two was a normal fee at the beginning of the seventeenth century; whereas towards the end of it the anonymous business diary of a midwife shows a prosperous trade with some form of sliding scale.[4] In 1696 this midwife recorded about two deliveries a month, for payments varying from 5s to 10s. On 24 August 1698 Mrs Rowell paid her 12s 6d for the delivery of a daughter at the awkward time of seven o'clock on a Sunday morning – but since the midwife was also able to record that she 'laid Mrs Clarke next door' in the course of the same visit, she only charged the latter 2s 6d. By 1719, this midwife was attending approximately three confinements a month and charging an average of £1 a visit; all of which amounted to a handsome income. The midwife had a large practice in the Old Bailey area of the City of London, but a connection with the Barnardiston family – she attended to a number of their confinements – took her as far as Cornwall where she 'laid Madam Barnardiston'. All the same, the midwife was also aware of her social duty: when she 'laid a woman in the market' no payment was recorded, presumably because the mother was of the poor.

Then there were the payments traditionally made by the godparents to the midwife as well as the nurse (for this, if for no other reason, the midwife had a vested interest in delivering a live infant, for no baby meant no baptism, no 'gossip', and thus no present). In 1661 Pepys as godfather made a payment of 10s to the midwife. At the end of the century Sir Walter Calverley Bt was in the habit of giving a guinea or 20s regularly to the midwives of his godchildren.[5]

Attendance at a royal birth brought heavy responsibilities, a fact acknowledged by the handsome rewards which followed. James I's Queen, Anne of Denmark, gave birth to a number of children both before and after her arrival in England from Scotland: Alice Dennis, an English midwife, was paid £100 on two occasions. Another English midwife, Margaret Mercer, set off for Heidelberg in 1616 with a train of attendants in order to deliver the baby of Elizabeth of Bohemia, the Queen's daughter; for this she received a total of £84 4s.[6]

On the other hand Charles I's Queen, Henrietta Maria, as a French Princess, preferred a French midwife. In May 1629,

Henrietta Maria was confined with her first child ten weeks prematurely; this was unfortunately far too early for the attendance of the famous French midwife Madame Péronne, who was much in demand – the baby died. The royal doctor Sir Theodore Mayerne hastened to send a message to France that Madame Péronne's services were now no longer needed in England; she should be directed instead to the bedside of the Princess of Piedmont. The next year the Queen was pregnant again. This time Madame Péronne arrived well in advance, dispatched by Henrietta Maria's mother, Marie de Medici. The successful delivery of a healthy boy – the future King Charles II – after a labour of eight hours, was rewarded by the elated royal father with a payment to Madame Péronne of £1,000.[7]

Henrietta Maria had the advantage of her English in-laws because midwifery was in a more advanced state in France, with a noted school for midwives being established at the Hôtel-Dieu in Paris, including six weekly lectures on anatomy. The first midwife to enjoy an international reputation had indeed been a Frenchwoman named Louise Bourgeois, who published several books on obstetrics in the early seventeenth century.[8] One of England's most celebrated midwives in the first part of the seventeenth century was herself of foreign origin: Aurelia Florio, one of the midwives who examined the supposed witches of Lancashire, was the daughter of the scholar John Florio, Groom of the Privy Chamber and Reader in Italian to Anne of Denmark. She married the surgeon James Molins, member of a celebrated English medical family, and herself bore at least seven children, the majority of whom, no doubt as a result of their parents' abilities, grew to adulthood. Aurelia Florio died in 1641, but recent research in the registers of St Andrew, Holborn, has shown that her accomplished handling of her patients was commemorated by the unusual name Aurelia being bestowed on at least seven girls she had delivered, who were not apparently related to her.[9]

Alas, the very tribute indicated how few English midwives approached the standards and skill of an Aurelia Florio. The problem was partly one of language – as it so often was where women were concerned in this period. Only a handful of women could read Latin, the language of medical textbooks, and very few of the midwife class were to be counted among their number. But there was a remarkable scarcity of manuals written in English. The first one printed in England, entitled *The Byrth of Mankind*, had actually been translated from the Latin, which in turn had been translated from the German; after publication in 1540, it ran through thirteen editions, the last in 1654.[10] Such a long reign without medical updating demonstrated not only the desperate need for such sources, but also the primitive, virtually stationary nature of obstetrical knowledge at this time.

Jacob Rueff's textbook *The Expert Midwife* printed in an English translation in 1637, first appeared in Latin under the title *De Conceptu et Generatione Hominis* in 1554. Rueff, himself an expert surgeon, paid tribute in his introduction to the ancient origins of the midwives' profession: 'It is observable that in all the ages of the world and throughout all countries in the world...' such women had ever been useful 'for release and succour of all the daughters of Evah, whom God hath appointed to bear children into this world.' At the same time he pointed to the undeniable weakness of women as active obstetricians: the two methods of learning being the use of books or 'conference with the skilful', women were unhappily liable to fall behind in the former, since they were traditionally unable to understand anything except their native tongue.

Rueff's book, in its English translation, was intended to remedy this state of affairs. Nor did it approve in principle of the rise of the 'Man-Midwife'. On the contrary, it stated that some men had already gone far too far – 'perhaps for private profit' – in encroaching 'upon women's weaknesses and want of knowledge in these their peculiar businesses'.[11]

Rueff's argument that midwifery was the peculiar business of women (only sacrificed to men by default of learning) was certainly one with which the midwives themselves agreed. 'We knowing the cases of women better than any other', wrote a famous London midwife, Mrs Hester Shaw. Jane Sharp was another experienced midwife; in 1680 she either died or retired after forty years of active work. *The Midwives Book* of 1671, based on her experiences, was the first book of its sort written by an Englishwoman in English and as such is an interesting guide to women's own preoccupations on the subject. Like Rueff's book, that of Jane Sharp went through many editions, the last appearing in 1725 under the title of *The Compleat Midwife's Companion*, by popular demand, according to the printer. Jane Sharp was at pains to point out the range of her own studies: that she had had French, Dutch and Italian books on the subject translated in order to consult them. Like many others in her period, Jane Sharp took her stand on the Bible, and the fact that midwifery as a craft had been designed by God exclusively for the practice of women: 'Men-Midwives are forced to borrow the very name they practise by... The holy Scriptures hath recorded Midwives to the perpetual honour of the female Sex, there being not so much one word concerning Men-midwives mentioned there.'[12]

Jane Sharp then quoted the story of Shiphrah and Puah, the heroic midwives of the Israelites, in the first chapter of Exodus, who were instructed by the Egyptian King to get ready to kill any boy babies when they saw a Hebrew woman 'upon the [birthing] stools'. (It was this order which led to the concealment of the baby Moses in the bulrushes by his sister Miriam.) Shiphrah and Puah however 'feared God, and did not as the king of Egypt commanded them, but saved the men children alive'. They pretended to the Egyptian King that Hebrew women, unlike the women of the Egyptians, had a habit of giving birth before they could be reached by a midwife. The story ended: 'Therefore God dealt well with the midwives... he made them houses.'[13] (This text in the hands of women, was to the concept of exclusive female midwifery what the famous text of St Paul in the hands of men was to the concept of exclusive male preaching.)

According to Jane Sharp, the very fact that men enjoyed a superior education and could unlike women gain a knowledge of anatomy at university, demonstrated God's support for women as midwives. Without divine approval in the role, how should women have managed to preserve their reputation down the ages? 'It is not hard words that perform the work,' wrote Jane Sharp, 'as if none understood the Art of midwifery that cannot understand Greek.'[14] Like the heroism of Shiphrah and Puah, the innate and essentially natural skills of the midwives, handed down from generation to generation of women, were another cardinal point in the fierce discussions which broke out as to whether 'Men-Midwives' had any right to function at all.

This belief in the natural, inherited skill of a woman (as opposed to a man) to deliver a baby safely and healthily was implicitly supported by society; just as nursing in general was regarded as the prerogative of the weaker but tenderer vessel – 'woman's work' wrote Sir Ralph Verney (see p.244). At the beginning of the seventeenth century, the mistress of the household would count among her accomplishments not only cooking and the use of medicinal herbs, but also the ability to attend to her servants and neighbours in childbirth (Elizabeth Walker, for example, counted this among her good works). Lady Margaret Hoby was the pattern of the great lady ordering her servants and her estates, although unusual in that she kept a diary, half personal half spiritual, between 1599 and 1605 (the first known British woman's diary).[15] Of one particular Wednesday she wrote: 'In the morning at six o'clock I prayed privately: that done, I went to a wife in travail of child, about whom I was busy till one o'clock, about which time, she being delivered and I having praised God, returned home and betook myself to private prayer.' There are numerous other references to her attendances at the labours of local women; delivery being a basic female skill it was not considered relevant that Lady Margaret Hoby was herself childless. Mrs Pepys for example, who also had no children, was summoned to the bedside of Betty Mitchell in July 1668 'when she began to cry out'; she helped to deliver the child, and when it proved to be a girl, acted as her godmother.[16]

None of this emphasis on the archetypal role of women in the great drama of childbirth could however obliterate the unpleasant fact that all too many professional midwives were but ill-equipped to play it; since 'the business whereunto God hath ordained them [was] of so great and dangerous consequence as concerns the very lives of all such as come into the world', Reuff wrote, and numbers of mothers and infants died unnecessarily or were mutilated or otherwise injured as a result.[17] Jane Sharp was after all herself writing to remedy ignorance, while stoutly defending the exclusive right of her own sex to the work. As we shall see, a noted and independent-minded midwife of the time, Mrs Elizabeth Cellier, writing in the 1680s, ascribed an extraordinarily high figure of infant mortality to the mishandling of the midwives.

Horror stories of women and their babies being literally pulled apart, with fearful damage to both parties, abounded. Dr Percival Willughby, the son of Sir Percival Willughby of Wollaton in Cheshire, was a celebrated and skilful obstetrician He published an account of his cases, the *Country Midwife's Opusculum*:[18] in which he cited one incident which took place in Threadneedle Street, in the City of London, where the midwife tugged the mother one way and the other woman present tugged the emergent child the other. There were plenty of other tales of the protruding limbs of infants being cut off because they were holding up the process of birth.

Such stories fell into two main groups. In one the midwife accelerated the course of the labour unduly, instead of letting what Dr Willughby called 'Dame Nature, Eve's Friend' do her own work, with far more satisfactory results: for example Dr Willughby related how 'poor silly Mary Baker' produced a perfectly good child on the bare freezing ground, having avoided being 'miserably tortured' by the midwives. In the other group, the midwife or midwives proved incapable of helping forward a highly difficult birth. Alice Thornton described in her autobiography how her son died in 1657 because the midwife lacked the skill to 'turn' him. Mrs Elizabeth Freke was another diarist, who wrote from 1671 to 1714, her literacy being due to the solicitude of her father, a Fellow of All Souls, who educated all his four daughters.[19] She gave a chilling description of the birth of her son Ralph Freke in Wiltshire in June 1675: the labour lasted an agonizing five days, with four midwives in perpetual attendance, including a 'Man-Midwife' who half-way through the proceedings pronounced the baby dead. Mrs Freke's benevolent neighbour Lady Thynne was also in attendance as a charitable duty, and it was Lady Thynne who eventually secured the services of yet another midwife, Mrs Mills; she it was who successfully delivered a living child. (Little Ralph Freke even survived another seventeenth-century peril a few months later when a careless nurse broke his leg, and hid him in bed to conceal the fact, pretending he was teething.)

Expert practitioners were highly prized: Dr Willughby educated his two daughters so well – once again in the great seventeenth-century tradition of benevolent educative fathers – that they both enjoyed thriving careers as expert midwives. One 'Mrs' Willughby began by accompanying her father on his rounds, with the advantage of being able to call in her father in a particularly difficult case. One such dilemma occurred with the confinement of the 'wife of one of Oliver's creatures', under Cromwell's Protectorate; Mrs Willughby hastened to call in the senior doctor for fear of the political implications. By 1658 she was practising in London with great success. Her sister specialized in the delivery of twins, never forcing the pace of the second birth. (Both Willughbys, incidentally, married, like most midwives of the time. The antiquary George Ballard and his clever sister were the children of a midwife.)[20]

The fame of a Quaker midwife in Reading, Frances Kent, was sufficient for the Verney family after the Restoration to consider employing her despite her awkward beliefs (they were assured that Mrs Kent never discussed religious matters with her patients) and her price: she could command as much as £25. In 1684, however, when Sarah Fell was about to be delivered of her first child at the age of forty-two, Frances Kent's Quakerism was of course an added bonus. 'She is a fine woman', wrote Sarah, following her successful *accouchement*. 'It was the Lord sent her to me. It was the Lord's mercy that I had her, who is a very skilful and tender woman for that employment.'[21]

The overseeing of Quaker midwives was one of the responsibilities of the Women's Meetings: in February 1675 at Swarthmoor, a Meeting was informed that Mabel Brittaine had been so lacking in skill that the child was born dead. On examination, Mabel Brittaine was found sufficiently deficient in medical knowledge to be told to hire an assistant (if she did not, people who employed her did so at their own risk).[22]

The care of the Quakers was not matched in other sections of society. The midwife was by the nature of her profession a powerful social figure, but she was not necessarily a particularly edifying one. A traditional connection with drink – 'red-nosed midwives' – existed in the popular imagination, which was not unfounded. Dr Sermon in *The Ladies Companion*, or *The English Midwife* of 1671 suggested that midwives should be sober and discreet, 'not quarrelsome nor choleric', above all not 'rash and drunken women'. His picture of the ideal midwife – 'very cheerful, pleasant, and of good discourse, strong, not idle, but accustomed to exercise, that they may be the more able (if need requires) to watch' – makes it clear that the contrary was all too often to be found: that 'pitiful, old, ugly, ill-bred woman in a hat' for example, who married Pepys's Uncle Fenner in 1662 and was a midwife.[23]

A midwife's business, of its very nature, offered her the opportunity for certain murky sidelines, of which abortions were the most obvious; it was for fear of this that the authorities were zealous in their requirements that midwives were to report stillborn births. A practical woman who was not too particular might also most conveniently pursue the combined careers of midwife and procuress: several of the 'Crafty Bawds' mentioned in numbers of *The Wandering Whore*, such as Mrs Davies and Mrs Barber of Holborn, were also listed as midwives.[24]

Under the circumstances, the most important gynaecological advance of the seventeenth century was the invention of the forceps, by the beneficial use of which in a difficult and prolonged labour the infant could be skilfully delivered without damage to either mother or child. In the absence of the forceps, types of instruments available were as crude as the techniques by which they were employed. Richard Gough, in *The History of Myddle*, described how the village blacksmith made some 'iron hooks' at the direction of the local midwife; she was then able to draw forth a dead child from its mother successfully. The sensible Dr Willughby condemned the use of 'pothooks, pack-needles, silver spoons, thatcher's hooks and knives' to speed on 'Dame Nature' unnecessarily.[25] But of course where a birth was not straightforward, some form of instrument might have to be employed if mother and child were not to perish, immutably joined together (as so many did).

The man responsible for the invention of the forceps was a member of the Chamberlen family, probably Peter the Elder (so called to distinguish him from his brother and nephew, both also called Peter).[26] Unfortunately the character of Peter Chamberlen the Elder was that particular mixture of enlightenment and professional jealousy which has marked many inventors. On the one hand he called on King James I in 1616 to found a Society of Midwives: 'That some order may be settled by the State for [their] instruction and civil government.' On the other hand he deliberately and successfully guarded the secret of the forceps within the Chamberlen family: his motives being clearly financial, as were those of the Chamberlens who followed him and jealously kept up the tradition of secrecy. (Another member of the Chamberlen family, author of *Dr Chamberlen's Midwives practice* of 1665, which attacked other 'quacking' obstetrical textbooks, defended his refusal to give details of the forceps on the disingenuous grounds that they were by now 'a family secret' and not his to reveal.) As a result the forceps had to be reinvented quite separately in the eighteenth century.† In the seventeenth century much ammunition was given by this professional selfishness to those indignant midwives who protested that doctors and others tried to control and license them purely in order to restrict their activities and preserve their personal monopoly.

Many doctors were considered greedy and selfish, but many midwives were held to be ignorant, and there was something to be said for both points of view. Hitherto the licensing of the midwives had been performed by the bishops – Bishop Bonner is said to have been the first to do so[28] – a practice which had arisen

---

†In the nineteenth century Dr Peter Chamberlen's famous forceps were discovered, still tucked away in their box.[27]

in the previous century more for religious than for medical reasons. In an age of high infant mortality, it was very often left to the midwife, with mother and child *in extremis*, to perform the rite of baptism; it was her responsibility that the correct (Protestant) form should be used. At the same time, the ecclesiastical authorities were anxious that midwives should not invoke the darker powers of witchcraft to their aid; although the poor state of medical knowledge at the time, and the desperate sufferings of so many patients, must have made the invocation of supernatural aid where natural aid had failed irresistible to many caring midwives not otherwise connected with evil. (As early as 1486 *Malleus Maleficarum* had urged an oath upon midwives to eliminate the possibility of witchcraft being used.)[29]

The oath administered to Eleanor Pead, seeking a licence as a midwife from the Archbishop of Canterbury in 1567, is the earliest which has survived.[30] She promised among other things to help the poor as well as the rich, and not to allow a woman to name a man falsely as the father of her child; some significance being attached to these allegations of paternity, extracted as it were by the pangs of labour, which put a responsibility upon the midwife either to remember them or forget them. In addition she had to swear to use no sorcery or incantation, to employ a simple form of baptism if necessary and to register the child's birth with the curate, and not to use any cutting or dismembering in the course of the delivery.

The trouble with the bishops' licensing was that their interests were all in the supernatural: in the course of ecclesiastical visitations, it was customary to ask after the use of prohibited sorcery rather than the progress of deliveries. Dr Peter Chamberlen, son of Peter the Younger, cried out vigorously against a system whereby any woman 'with the testimony of two or three gossips' could pay a fee for her licence, and then hasten into practice. It was a system, he averred, which produced innumerable and 'uncontrolled female-arbiters of life and death'. In 1634 he attempted in his turn to form a Corporation of Midwives, with himself as governor; towards this end he seems to have held monthly meetings of midwives for the purpose of instruction at his home.[31]

This innovation aroused angry protests from the midwives at the interruption of their age-old business. Dr Chamberlen, it was asserted, had no greater skill than anyone else save for his 'iron instruments'. Chamberlen was also accused of bargaining with the rich for larger fees, and neglecting the care of the poor altogether. Among those midwives who petitioned was that Mrs Hester Shaw who may have been the violent midwife of Threadneedle Street criticized by Dr Percival Willughby.[32]

Hester Shaw, towards the end of her career, got into a dispute with Mr Thomas Clendon, the minister of Allhallows, Barking, over some stolen goods: her houses, and the other houses in her row, having been accidentally destroyed by gunpowder, a great deal of Hester Shaw's property had, according to her version, ended up in the minister's possession and stayed there.[33] The details of the case revealed incidentally how substantial could be the rewards of a lifetime of midwifery: two bags of silver, worth over £100 each, and quilted rolls of gold were mentioned as missing, as well as a quantity of silver plate. Hester Shaw was also described by the minister himself as of 'a good education, and volubility of tongue, and natural boldness, and confidence'. In herself therefore she also stood for the midwife as an independent female professional, secure (as she had hitherto always believed) in work which a man was quite unable to perform.

The midwives argued in front of Archbishop Laud and the Bishop of London at Lambeth Palace on 22 October 1634. Their case rested in essence on the importance of experience: 'it must be continual practise in this kind that will bring experience, and those women that desire to learn must be present at the delivery of many women and see the work and behaviour of such as be skilful midwives who will shew and direct them and resolve their doubts'. On the other hand there was a certain lack of logic in the way the midwives added that they also possessed books in English on anatomy, and 'most of them being able to read' (or so they claimed), these books would benefit them more than Dr Chamberlen's lectures on anatomy.[34]

After 1662, in the reversion to old ways brought about by the Restoration, the midwives proceeded as they had done formerly, taking an oath, paying their money, and returning home, in the words of a critical contemporary, 'as skilful as they went thither'. Parts of the oath still conveyed a chilling impression of contemporary abuses through ignorance: 'I will not destroy the child born of any woman, nor cut, nor pull off the head thereof, or otherwise dismember or hurt the same, or suffer it to be so hurt or dismembered.'[35]

The power struggle between the midwives and the doctors was finally resolved by the victory of the latter. Education, as ever in the seventeenth century, was the real key to woman's weakness. Members of the male sex were always likely by definition to have a far greater knowledge of medicine and anatomy than the average woman, if only for their ability to read Latin (as the midwife Jane Sharp herself admitted).[36] As for women doctors, some women did continue to practise medicine on a casual basis – in 1683 one Prudence Ludford of Little Barkhampton was presented at court for unlawful surgery – but the examinations required by the Faculties of Medicine and Surgery in the City of London excluded women.[37]

By the end of the century it had become customary to call in a 'Man-Midwife' for difficult cases. It has been suggested that the vogue for the 'Man-Midwife' among the upper classes may have spread from France (like other customs of an intimate nature as the use of the prophylactic sheath), after one of the mistresses of Louis XIV, Louise de la Vallière, had been attended by one. In 1780 the honouring of Sir David Hamilton by King George III, the first knighted obstetrician, indicated the course of the future in the medical profession. Those murmurs of feminine modesty at male examination which had persisted in the seventeenth century – Dr Willughby mentions cases where he was not permitted to gaze on the patient's face – and had been evinced by the vocal midwives as support for their traditional claims, died away in view of the superior need for truly skilled attention.[38] And that, it came to be agreed, could not be supplied by women.

Ironically enough there was far more substance to the

midwives' claims to represent the correct – because it was divinely-ordained and thus natural – approach to labour than many people, including the doctors, realized at the time. Recent research has come to criticize the 'meddling' male doctors who with their forceps intervened with the natural process of child-birth.[39] It is of course impossible (as was pointed out on p.92), to estimate with any certainty the figures for mortality in childbirth at this period; even the hazy figures available give no clue as to the relative responsibility of midwife, doctor, let alone that other important figure present at every childbed, 'Dame Nature' herself.

Obstetrics in any modern sense was in its infancy where doctors as well as midwives were concerned. This was an age when the Caesarean delivery was popularly – if not quite cor-rectly – believed to result in the inevitable death of the mother. The key work *De Generatione Animalium* by Dr William Harvey, described as 'the father of English midwifery',[40] was published in Latin in 1651 and, with a thirty-nine-page section 'Of the Birth' translated into English in 1653 (it had a strong influence, for example, on Dr Percival Willughby). But even Harvey was capable of harbouring such misconceptions as attributing to the foetus an active role in breaking out of the womb, in addition to the mother's contractions, on the analogy of the chicken breaking out of the egg.

While some of the notions cherished by the midwife Jane Sharp have a ludicrous sound to modern ears, others are sensible enough. On the one hand she believed the liver rather than the heart to be the fountain of the blood, that boys were begotten from the right 'stone' (testicle) and girls from the left, and that after conception boys lived in the right of the womb and girls on the left. On the other hand Jane Sharp believed in sustaining the strength of women during labour and in keeping them warm afterwards, both sound principles. She was much against hurry-ing on labour, warned against the difficulty of a breech presenta-tion, and she was aware of the threat of haemorrhage with the need to remove the 'after-burden' (placenta). Her chosen cover-ing for a recently delivered woman – the newly flayed skin of a sheep and a hare-skin on her belly – may sound bizarre, but William Sermon, a doctor, enunciated the same principle in 1671 in *The Ladies Companion* (though Dr Sermon preferred the skin of an ox).⁴¹

As for Dr Sermon, he too had his capricious notions: for example, he believed one flat breast to be a sign that one twin would be miscarried. Like many doctors and scientifically-minded people in the seventeenth century, he attached much importance to obtaining that popular talisman of the time, an eagle-stone, to aid an easy delivery. Lord Conway, husband of Anne Viscountess Conway and a Fellow of the Royal Society, took enormous trouble to find exactly the right size and shape of one before her delivery in December 1658; fabled to be found in the birds' nests, an eagle-stone was in fact merely an accidental configuration of an ordinary hollow pebble.⁴²

In such a primitive state of medicine, the midwives were not so far out in their emphasis on the importance of womanly experience. An accomplished sensible midwife like Jane Sharp would not really do much less well than a doctor like William Sermon, because in so many cases both of them were effectively helpless. Dr Sermon himself recognized this when he suggested that the 'discreet Midwife' should encourage her patient to call on the Almighty for help: 'and let them call to mind what God hath said with his own mouth; for it would be almost a miracle to see a woman delivered without pain'.

In another passage however, Dr Sermon did draw attention to a remarkable instance of childbirth without pain which he himself had witnessed by chance in 1644. The doctor was lurking in the hedgerows, hoping to shoot a hare, when he saw a woman on her way back from market 'delivered of a lusty Child in a Wood by herself'. Presently she encased the infant in some oak leaves and wrapped it in her apron. She then marched 'stoutly' for half a mile to what happened to be the doctor's uncle's house. Within two hours the woman felt well enough, having secured some proper linen for the child, to proceed on her way 'not in the least discouraged'. Dr Sermon knew of other examples in history of women delivered without pain. He also fondly believed that the contemporary women in America sprang out of a bed and ministered to their own husbands immediately after giving birth out of gratitude 'because they [the American husbands] take some pains to beget them with Child'. If only English women were equally unselfish, reflected Dr Sermon, their husbands would give up kissing their 'handsome Nurses' and generally misbehaving themselves with the neighbours in a similar situation.[43]

But such 'natural' childbeds were rare indeed in the conditions of seventeenth-century England. The real point about obstetrics and midwifery during this period (and for nearly 200 years to follow, until the invention of disinfectant by Joseph Lister in 1867 caused maternal mortality to decline sharply) was that the nature of bacterial infection itself was not understood. Here both doctors and midwives were alike in their ignorance.

Dr William Harvey called for cleanliness to prevent the onset of fever. Handbooks advocated common-sensical measures of hygiene for midwives. Jane Sharp called for pared nails, and Dr William Sermon for comely and neat midwives, hands small, fingers long not thick, 'nails pared, very close'. As for Jane Sharp's recipe for a herbal bath at the onset of labour, to include hollyhocks, bettony, mugwort, marjoram, mint, camomile, linseed and parsley boiled up together, that must at least have involved cleansing the patient; if her recommendation that the woman's 'privities' should be anointed with a compound of oil of sweet almonds, lilies, violets, duck's grease, hen's grease and wax, with butter, ground quince kernels and gum optional is less instantly appealing to modern sensibilities.[44] But none of the endless herbal remedies recommended in handbooks and household books alike for the inexorable female ordeal of childbirth had any real relevance to the problem of sepsis.

It was from septicaemia that the suffering patients died in their hundreds and thousands. This septicaemia was sometimes brought about by the unhygienic conditions of the home (although some immunity must have been established to those); more often it was brought about by that concomitant of most labours, 'the examining hand'.[45] Here both doctor and midwife were equally guilty. The doctor blithely and unknowingly brought with him infection from other cases which might include scarlet fever; the midwife from a daily round which might include the cow-byre and the farmyard generally as well as the lying-in of a neighbour.

It was a hideous truth that progress in this field could lead to greater not lesser mortality, as the examining hand of the doctor grew more skilful, and the importance of internal examination was increasingly stressed. The establishment of the first lying-in hospitals led to the first epidemics of puerperal fever, the first one accurately recorded being in the middle of the seventeenth century.[46]

It was in this sense that the least skilful midwives, lacking the knowledge to do much more than concentrate on their herbal remedies in the patient's own home, might actually do less harm, by not spreading infection, than the most practised of the doctors.

The ideal midwife (from the point of view of a masculine-dominated society, and no doubt from the point of view of most patients as well) might be 'modest and grave', but there was something about the intimate power of the position, the fact that most midwives acted throughout their careers as 'uncontrolled female arbiters' in the indignant phrase of Dr Peter Chamberlen, which could lead to the development of an altogether bolder type of woman. Mrs Elizabeth Cellier was that outspoken midwife who in 1687 announced that over 6,000 women had died in childbed within the last twenty years, more than 13,000 children had been abortive, and another 5,000 had died in the first month of their life; about two thirds of these had 'in all probability perished, for want of the due skill and care, in those women who practise the art of midwifery'.[47]

Her career previous to the initiation of her campaign for better training in midwifery had been equally bold, if not quite so judicious. For the details of her early life, we have to choose between the tales of her enemies – that she was born Elizabeth

Marshall, the daughter of a brazier or tinker living near Canterbury – and her own account in one of her self-justificatory pamphlets.[48] According to the latter, she was brought up by parents who were fervent Royalists – Protestants, but accused of papistry and idolatry on account of their Royalist sympathies. These perverse accusations led the young Elizabeth to inquire into the truths of the Catholic religion, as a result of which she herself became converted to it.

Elizabeth's first husband seems to have been an English merchant who went to Leghorn and died (the broadsheets had her indulging in a tripartite love affair the while with an Italian and his negro servant, as a result of which an illegitimate son was born). Her second husband vanished to Barbados leaving her with five children; whereupon Elizabeth moved to the City of London and set up as a midwife. Finally she married a French merchant named Pierre Cellier. At which point the dramatic part of her story began.

Clearly there were exciting opportunities for an expert Catholic midwife in London in the 1670s when so many great ladies, including the wife of the heir to the throne, were Catholics: Mrs Cellier ministered to Mary of Modena as well as other Catholic aristocrats. The autumn of 1678 however brought public tragedy into these domestic circles: the false accusations of Titus Oates and others concerning a 'Popish Plot' resulted in the arrest of five ancient Catholic noblemen, including the Earl of Powis and Lord Arundell of Wardour, on the highly unlikely charge that they had been conspiring to kill Charles II. Other Catholics, Jesuit priests, were also arrested on the same charge, possibly with slightly more substance. When witnesses for the defence of the Jesuits were brought from St Omer for their trial in the summer of 1679, it was natural that Mrs Cellier, with her intimate knowledge of the York household, and her continental connections through her husband's business, should lodge them. She also visited the prison and attempted to alleviate the lot of some of her humbler co-religionists there.

The details of the aftermath of the 'Popish Plot' are virtually impossible to disentangle.[49] First, plots had become good business, and any rascal was likely to invent them if he discerned profit in it. Second, both factions, that of Whig courtiers, headed by Shaftesbury, determined to exclude the Duke of York from the eventual succession, and that of the Catholics anxious to preserve him in it, were at the mercy of *agents provocateurs*. Unfortunately it was one of these, Thomas Dangerfield (although he masqueraded under a false name), that Mrs Cellier encountered in the course of one of her merciful visits to Newgate, where he lay in the debtors' prison.

When Dangerfield confided to Mrs Cellier the details of a plot that involved the Earl of Shaftesbury, he found a ready listener; not only was the Catholic York household under threat, but the husband of one of her patrons, the Earl of Powis, was actually in prison, for all of which Shaftesbury was to be blamed.

Mrs Cellier was kind to Dangerfield. She paid off his debts; she spent 16s redeeming his coat out of pawn. She took him into her employ. From this vantage point a plot was said to have been hatched, by which material, incriminating the Earl of Shaftesbury in a plot to kill the King, was planted in the rooms of Mansell, a leading Whig; other conspirators included the Countess of Powis. That at least was Dangerfield's story, for, being rearrested for debt once more, and carried back to Newgate, Dangerfield quickly turned his plot on its head, and made it a conspiracy of the Catholics against Shaftesbury.

Mrs Cellier, on the other hand, stuck stoutly to her original story. When incriminating documents were found concealed in 'a Meal-Tub' in her house (hence the appropriately ludicrous nickname given to this plot-that-never-was) she maintained that it was indeed information written by Dangerfield which had been found 'between the Pewter in my Kitchen', but this information contained details of a real conspiracy by the Whigs against the King: 'and as the Father of Lies did once tell the truth, so he hath inserted this one truth in his lying Narrative'. She added: 'from my part it was no motive but my Loyalty and Duty to his Majesty, and Love to Truth and Justice, that engaged me in this affair.'[50]

The Jesuit Father John Warner, who later gave a full account of these events from the Catholic point of view, described Mrs

Cellier as a woman of strong and 'almost' masculine temperament. It was a fatal caveat: 'Nature had endowed her with a lively, sharp and clean mind, but her powers of judgement were not of the same order; as was to be expected in the weaker sex.'[51] Certainly it is possible to see in Mrs Cellier's unwise championship of Dangerfield the rashness of one who was accustomed to trust her own decisions in one important if domestic sphere with success, and could not believe she would not be equally successful in the much wider world of politics and intrigue.

At all events she paid the penalty. The Meal-Tub Plot as a whole, with its alternative versions, was considered too fantastic even for this plot-hungry age. But Mrs Cellier was arrested and flung into Newgate, where of course she encountered her old protégé and new-found betrayer, Dangerfield. A prolonged pamphlet war subsequently broke out between Dangerfield and Mrs Cellier, when both were once more at liberty. Dangerfield in *The Grand Impostor Defeated* referred to Mrs Cellier as 'Mother Damnable' (the nickname of a notoriously foul-mouthed character who dispensed ale in Kentish Town).[52] Mrs Cellier for her part gave a superb version of the dialogue which ensued when she met Dangerfield in prison (even if it owed something to *esprit de l'escalier*, one hopes that she delivered at least a few of the following lines at the time):

DANGERFIELD: 'Madam, Madam, Pray speak to me, and tell me how you do.'

MRS CELLIER: 'I am sick, very sick of the Bloody Barbarous Villain.'

DANGERFIELD: 'Pray Madam speak low, and do not discompose yourself.'

MRS CELLIER: 'Nothing you do can discompose me: I Despise you so much, I am not Angry ...'

DANGERFIELD: 'I am very sorry for your Confinement, but I could not possibly help what I have done.'

MRS CELLIER: 'Bloody Villain, I am not confined, for *Stone Walls and Iron Bars, do not make a Prison, but a Guilty Conscience*: I am innocent ...'[53]

Dangerfield was pardoned by the King in response to political pressure. But despite constant petitions, it was not until June 1680 that Mrs Cellier was brought to trial at the King's Bench Court on a charge of high treason, having been a prisoner in Newgate for thirty-two weeks, for much of this in close confinement, unable to see her husband and children. Her conduct at her trial showed however that her spirit at least was unbowed. For example she demanded that Dissenters be excluded from the jury, on the grounds that the plot of which she was accused had been aimed against their interests. It was however in her vigorous attack upon the whole basis of Dangerfield's testimony that Mrs Cellier showed most courage – and enjoyed most success. She argued that Dangerfield might have been pardoned for his part, whatever it was, in the so-called Meal-Tub Plot, but he was still a convicted felon for other previous offences including burglary and perjury, which had brought upon him an unpardoned sentence of outlawry. 'The King cannot give an Act of Grace to one subject', argued Mrs Cellier, 'to the prejudice of another.'[34]

So Mrs Cellier was acquitted of high treason.

Before that, she had given good account of herself in the course of the trial, before the Lord Chief Justice and King Charles II, among others. A piece of broadsheet verse commemorated her courage:

> You taught the judges to interpret laws;
> Shewed Sergeant Maynard how to plead a cause;
> You turned and wound, and rough'd them at your will.[35]

Humour as well as courage was one of the weapons at her disposal, a weapon incidentally always likely to disarm King Charles II. At one point Mrs Cellier was accused of jesting about the alleged 'Presbyterian' plot in a tavern, in the course of which she told a bawdy story thought too immodest to repeat in court.

'What!' exclaimed the King, scenting some sudden possibility of distraction in this interminable and boring tangle; 'Can she speak Bawdy too?'

The King refused to lose sight of the subject. 'What did she say?' he repeated. 'Come, tell us the story'.

Mrs Cellier's official interlocutor began to stammer.

'She said – she said – she said – that so long as she did not lose her hands, she would get money as long as –'

It was Mrs Cellier who completed her own sentence: 'So long as Men kissed their Wives.'

At this the cross-examiner thought he perceived an opening. He swiftly added: 'By the oath I have taken, she said their Mistresses too.'

Mrs Cellier was more than equal to that. 'Did I so?' she inquired. 'Pray what else do they keep them for?'

'That was but witty', said the Lord Chancellor drily, in the presence of his philandering sovereign.

''Twas natural to her Practice', commented the kindly King.[56]

All would perhaps have been well for the triumphant Mrs Cellier following her acquittal, had not the temptation to be a petticoat-author, as well as an uncontrolled female arbiter, overcome her. She had already pushed her luck by refusing to pay the traditional guinea apiece to the jury upon her acquittal. (Had she been convicted the King would have been obliged to pay up.) Instead she wrote to the foreman with a gracious offer of payment in kind: 'Pray Sir accept of, and give my most humble Service to Your self, and all the Worthy Gentlemen of your Panel, and Yours and Their Several Ladies. And if You and They please, I will with no less Fidelity serve them in their Deliveries, than You have done me with Justice in mine …'[57]

Soon after the trial she had her own narrative in pamphlet form 'Printed for Elizabeth Cellier, and to be sold at her House in Arundel Street near St Clements Church.' Entitled *Malice Defeated*, it was said to be 'for the satisfaction of all Lovers of undisguised Truth'. *Malice Defeated* not only related all the circumstances of Mrs Cellier's acquaintance with Dangerfield, and the course of her trial, but it also included some trenchant criticisms of conditions within Newgate prison itself. She described hearing the groans of prisoners under torture, which so much resembled those of a woman in labour that Mrs Cellier innocently offered her services in relief. She wrote of a special chamber for prisoners whose crime consisted in adhering to the wrong religion, known sarcastically to the gaolers as 'The Chapel'; a grating permitted paying members of the public to witness their agonies. She wrote of instruments known as the shears, weighing forty to fifty pounds, affixed to the limbs of prisoners, which wore the flesh through to the bone. All of this made (and makes) *Malice Defeated* nothing if not a good read. As Sir Charles Lyttleton wrote to a friend in September: 'if you have not seen Mrs Cellier's narrative, 'tis well worth it'.[58]

Mrs Cellier concluded with an ingratiating acknowledgement of her own weaknesses: 'And as to my own Sex, I hope they will pardon the Errors of my story, as well as those bold Attempts of mine that occasioned it…though it may be thought too Masculine, yet was it the effects of my Loyal (more than Religious) Zeal to gain Proselites to his Service. And in all my defence, none can truly say but that I preserved the Modesty, though not the Timorousness common to my Sex.'[59]

This did not save her from a further trial, once more before the King's Bench – this time for libel. And this time Mrs Cellier was found guilty. She was fined £1,000, and sentenced to three sojourns in the pillory – from twelve to one at the Maypole in the Strand on market day, at Covent Garden and similarly at Charing Cross – while on each occasion a parcel of her publications was to be burnt by the common hangman. Even now Mrs Cellier was not quite vanquished. When the time came for her to take up her perilous position – the lot of a 'Popish' conspirator held at the mercy of the mob in the pillory in September 1680 was hardly enviable – Mrs Cellier began by feigning sickness. Unfortunately she was tricked into taking the emetic which she had procured for the purpose a day early. Then – at the age of fifty-odd – she declared that she was pregnant. Her groans and shrieks, as the women came to dress her for her fate, resulting in the calling of a physician; a pig's bladder full of blood, with which Mrs Cellier had intended to implement her imposture, was then discovered. (This pig's bladder proved an absolute boon to the writers of the broadsheets.)

Finally captive in the pillory, Mrs Cellier was greeted by a hail of stones. She carried a board, a piece of wood something like a battledore, with which to defend herself, otherwise she would surely have been brained. She also managed to keep her head one side of the board instead of poking it through as intended, so that she had some measure of protection. And as Rachel Lady Russell (no friend to this enemy of the Whigs) noted in a letter to her husband: 'All the stones that were thrown within reach, she took up and put in her pocket.'[60]

Mrs Cellier returned to publishing with renewed zest. As the anonymous author of *The Midwife Unmask'd* complained: 'This She-Champion and Midwife... now being cleared by the law', she 'rants and scratches like another Pucel d'Orleans or Joan of Arque; handling her Pen for the Papistical Cause, as the other did her Lance; and it is pity she has not likewise the Glory of her Martyrdom'.[61]

Nor was that the end of Mrs Cellier's public career. For all the hopeful 'searches' of other midwives, Queen Catherine of Braganza had never produced an heir for Charles II. Her own more successful midwifery had brought Mrs Cellier into that dangerous prominence where she had meddled, to her cost, with politics. Now with the succession of James II to his – officially – childless brother, Mrs Cellier was back in the centre of things again.

In June 1687 she took the opportunity of this newly favourable climate of opinion to float a scheme for a midwives' college.[62] By this she hoped to reduce those fearful casualties of unskilled carelessness on the part of midwives which had disquieted the Chamberlens and others since early in the century. Mrs Cellier's scheme was for a royal 'corporation' to be endowed to the tune of £5,000 or £6,000 a year 'by and for midwives', which in addition would serve as a hospital for foundling children.

Mrs Cellier's plan was on the surface well worked out. Women – to the limit of 1,000 – who were already skilled midwives were to be admitted on the payment of £5; they would then serve as matrons to twelve lesser houses or assistants to the governess. The next 1,000 would pay 50s on admission and 50s per year in fees; as their training proceeded, they would join the ranks of the matrons and assistants to the governess. The entire income of the first year (which according to these terms would be considerable) would be devoted to the building of the foundling hospital.

There were other provisions: no married person was to be admitted to the government of the hospital, in order to protect the interest of the foundlings. A woman sufficiently expert in writing would act as secretary to the governess of the hospital. The principal physician or male midwife would give a monthly lecture in public at which attendance would be compulsory; afterwards all the lectures would be entered in a book to which the midwives would have free recourse.

In a subsequent pamphlet the following year, Mrs Cellier showed herself capable of a humanitarian imagination where her foundlings were concerned.[63] Their surnames, she wrote, were to be chosen from the 'several Arts or Mysteries', or from 'Complexions and Shapes' or even on a more mundane level from the days of the week, but such children were not to be stigmatized by such opprobrious surnames as 'Bastard', so that in after life they would be capable of any employment, or even honour, without reference to the misfortune of their birth.

Combating the murmurs of the doctors in a pamphlet entitled *To Dr– An Answer to his Queries, concerning the Colledg* [sic] *of Midwives*, Mrs Cellier turned once more to the story of those enterprising Israelite midwives Shiphrah and Puah and expanded it. She argued that they could not have been merely midwives, for two women could not have coped with the whole tribe; therefore they were also teachers, and the scene of such consultations 'might well be called a College'. With that verve which the King's Bench Court would have recognized, Mrs Cellier said that since the Bible stated God had built these midwives 'houses', then the midwives' 'college' antedated the College of Physicians. For good measure, she threw in the fact that there had been colleges of women practising physic, coeval with the bards, before the arrival of the Romans; and that a college of women had centred round the Temple of Diana in London.[64]

The flaw in Mrs Cellier's scheme was the same flaw that had

vitiated the corporation, suggested half a century earlier by Dr Peter Chamberlen. Without being granted a monopoly, it would be impossible for this new foundation to impose higher standards, since too many midwives would simply continue in their same bad old ways. On the other hand Mrs Cellier's foundation was envisaged on far too small a scale to deal with the enormous number of midwives required by the female population of England, even if they had been willing and able to afford the fees.

For all this, and for all the queries raised by the doctors, King James II lent a sympathetic ear to Mrs Cellier's propositions. He evidently promised to enrol the midwives into a corporation by his Royal Charter.[65]

When Mrs Cellier published her second pamphlet on the subject of the foundation in January 1688, the Queen, Mary of Modena, was herself in the early stages of pregnancy. Her fruitful condition was a matter of some personal satisfaction to Mrs Cellier: had she not predicted that 'her Majesty was full of Children', and that therapeutic baths at a spa would assist her 'breeding'? Mrs Cellier's satisfaction was certainly shared by the royal parents-to-be, since Mary of Modena, who had lost a number of children at birth and in infancy, had not conceived for some years.

But this was a pregnancy of more than personal importance. Catholic subjects like Mrs Cellier viewed the prospect of the birth of a male heir – who would be Catholic – with enthusiasm, while Whigs and fanatical Protestants envisaged with equal dismay the blighting of the succession hopes of Mary and Anne, James's Protestant daughters by his first marriage.

Mrs Cellier ventured further prophecy concerning the many ways in which her corporation of midwives would bring benefits to the King their founder: 'And I doubt not but one way will be by giving him a Prince to his Royal consort, who like another Moses may become a mighty Captain to the Nation; and lead to Battle the Soldiers which the Hospital will preserve for him.'[66]

Alas, this time Mrs Cellier's prophesy was singularly wide of the mark. A prince *was* duly born to Mary of Modena – James Edward Stuart, born on 10 June 1688 – but he went into exile shortly after his birth; having by that birth precipitated the crisis which led to his father's downfall and flight. Known to history as the old Pretender, in no conceivable sense was this prince another Moses, and the soldiers whom he ordered to battle in his various unsuccessful attempts to recapture the throne of his father were greatly drawn from other sources and other nations than the foundlings of England. With the departure of her royal patron, Mrs Cellier's plans for a foundation collapsed.

So determined were King James's political enemies not to accept a Catholic succession – as represented by the baby prince born to Mary of Modena in June – that it was found convenient to believe that the baby himself was an imposter, smuggled into the palace in a warming-pan. Even Princess Anne (who should have known better) affected to credit this absurd story, because it conveniently supported her in her opposition to her father. At the time there were two midwives in attendance, Mrs De Labadie and Mrs Wilkins, both of whom received 500 guineas for what seemed to those within the royal chamber the joyful achievement of delivering the long-sought male heir (a daughter would have followed her Protestant step-sisters Mary and Anne in the succession and therefore would not have posed a threat). There were also doctors and a host of non-medical attendants, ladies of the court, many of them Protestants, amounting to a total of over sixty.[67]

But as luck would have it, one royal obstetrician, the latest member of the Chamberlen dynasty, Dr Hugh Chamberlen, was not actually present at the birth, being away attending a patient at Chatham. This simple chance, added to the fact that the doctor was himself a strong Whig, played into the hands of another strong Whig, Gilbert (later Bishop) Burnet: he spread the story that the Queen had deliberately sent away her doctor in order to facilitate the smuggling in of the changeling.

Years later Dr Chamberlen wrote to the Electress Sophia of Hanover about the events of that dramatic day, angry that he had been dragged into the scandal.[68] He explained that there was nothing sinister about the fact that the footman sent to St James's to fetch him when the Queen's birth pangs started had not found him there. The plain truth was that the Queen gave birth earlier than was expected; not the first woman to do so. Had the footman reached him, as he must certainly have expected to do, Dr Chamberlen would in fact have arrived just in time to interrupt the act of smuggling – supposing such a stratagem had actually been planned.

Dr Chamberlen's clinching argument was the presence of another vociferous Whig at the scene of the birth – the midwife, Mrs Wilkins. She, who was wont to cry out against the Jesuits who infested the place (finding a sympathetic ear in Dr Chamberlen), had been in no doubt about the circumstances of the baby prince's birth. To Dr Chamberlen now she expatiated indignantly on these rumours of substitution: 'Alas, will they not let the poor infant alone! I am certain no such thing as the bringing of a strange child in a warming-pan could be practised without my seeing it: attending constantly in and about all the avenues of the chamber.'

Lecky regarded the prostitute as 'the eternal priestess of humanity'. But in the seventeenth century it was the midwife who could best claim that title: grave if not always modest, pursuing her profession in and about all the avenues to every chamber, where history was made and where poverty was rampant, from the palace of St James (for 500 guineas) to the market-place where a busy midwife noted in her diary that she 'laid a woman' for nothing.

How Strong?

A prophetess observing the 'brave viragos' of the Leveller movement who petitioned outside the House of Commons in April 1649, despite the pained astonishment of its male inmates, might have predicted that women would be still 'stronger grown' half a century later.

The prophetess would have been wrong. By 1700 women were not in fact 'stronger grown'. In 1649 one Member of Parliament had exclaimed indignantly: 'it was not for women to Petition, they might stay at home and wash the dishes', an answer treated at the time with energetic disdain.[1] Fifty years later however women were staying at home and washing the dishes as they had always done, as though this eruption of an all-female body – thrilling or menacing depending on your point of view – had never taken place.

In fact where the status of the so-called weaker vessel was concerned, the seventeenth century saw very little improvement in real terms. On the contrary, since the general disturbance of society in the middle decades brought about a temporary unplanned elevation of certain women's authority, the graph of female progress, far from ascending in a straight line from the death of Queen Elizabeth to the accession of Queen Anne, rose during the middle decades to dip again with the restoration of the old order in 1660. (This cyclical pattern, whatever the special factors which brought it about in the seventeenth century, is perhaps worth bearing in mind; as with all forms of liberation, of which the liberation of women is only one example, it is easy to suppose in a time of freedom that the darker days of repression can never come again.)

It so happened that Anne, while still a princess, identified herself with the great Elizabeth; ill-educated and unhistorically-minded as she might be, the youthful Anne equated her own aggravation by her brother-in-law William III with that of Elizabeth by Mary Tudor: 'the Pr. discoursing her sufferings often made a parallel between herself and Qu. El.' wrote Abel Boyer, who tutored her son. Shortly after she ascended the throne, Queen Anne adopted the Latin motto *Semper Eadem* – Always the same – on the explicit grounds that it had been used by 'her predecessor of glorious memory'.[2] But in many ways *Semper Eadem* was a more appropriate motto for the fate of women in general in 1702, than for this one woman monarch in particular – not least because Queen Anne, unlike Queen Elizabeth, had been taught no Latin.

Of course there had been certain advances. But most of them, being shared equally with men, did not affect the relative standing of the sexes in respect to each other.

Literacy came into this category: there was an advance among women as a whole from the virtual illiteracy which prevailed (outside members of a tiny class) in 1600. But with progress came peril. The new differentiation between the types of education thought suitable for the respective sexes meant that male and female education, two ships sailing from the same harbour, now set very different courses, and it was only in rare instances in the future that they would catch sight of each other's sails.

The lack of Latin instruction in particular was a miserable handicap – remember the desperate plea of Basua Makin that 'tongues are learnt in order to [learn] things'. One historian has written of this period: 'Not to be able to read Latin was to go in blinkers.'[3] Such a lack could even affect those areas of traditional womanly skill such as midwifery and nursing: inevitably the woman (unskilled because she could not study in Latin, the language of medicine) lost out to the man (skilled because he could). As for those few females who did gamely surmount these obstacles, they also had to put up with 'those wise Jests and Scoffs that are put upon a Woman of Sense and Learning, a Philosophical Lady as she is call'd by way of Ridicule', in the words of Mary Astell in 1706;[4] these constituted a hazard undreamt of by the philosophical ladies of the late sixteenth century.

Women were no longer put to death for being witches in eighteenth-century England: although Jane Wenham, who was condemned to die in 1712 but subsequently reprieved, must have had some anxious moments, unless she was magically aware that to Alice Molland of Exeter in 1685 had already fallen the dubious honour of being the last witch to be killed in this country. Nevertheless the fact that the old women of the poor were able to relapse into their traditional practice of 'white' witchery, as 'cunning women' and healers, without fear of ugly reprisals based on primitive forces beyond their own control, certainly constituted an advance, albeit a somewhat negative one.

In general the war of words concerning the precise nature of woman's 'weakness' was being won by those who saw in this weakness something which entitled her to the special tenderness and protection of the male; there was no longer held to be something spiritually inferior about it. Indeed the notion of the 'softer sex', 'the gentle sex', which might actually be finer than its masculine opposite was growing in literature as the century grew to a close. A work of Cornelius Agrippa, *Female Pre-eminence or the Dignity and Excellency of that Sex, above the Male*, originally written in Latin in the early sixteenth century for the benefit of Margaret of Austria, daughter of the Emperor Maximillian I, appeared in an English version in 1670, adapted by Henry Care. Here it was boldly stated that where the soul was concerned there was 'the same innate worth and dignity' in both male and female, 'the Image of their Creator being stamped as fairly and shining as brightly in one, as 'tother'; but in all other respects 'the noble and delicate Feminine Race, doth almost to infinity excel that roughhewn boisterous kind, the Male'.⁵ Here was a line of reasoning which would lead eventually to the Victorian notion of woman as a creature too pure to be sullied by man's gross appetites.

When on 11 May 1699 the Rev. John Sprint preached a wedding sermon at Sherborne, *The Bride-Woman Counseller*, which trotted out all the old reproaches towards womankind, he was much attacked for it. He admitted himself that his views were by now largely old-fashioned, although he could wish to see them restored to currency. Sprint blamed women for all the faults of their husbands since Man's previously sweet nature had been soured by the Fall: 'You may thank your Mother Eve for it', he declared, 'who, when she had gotten a good Natur'd and Loving Husband, that was easy to be pleas'd, could not then be contented, but must try Practices with him.' Under these disgraceful circumstances, Sprint advocated the example of certain 'Persian Ladies who have the resemblance of a Foot worn on top of their Coronets' in order to indicate that 'the height of their Glory, Top-Knot and all, does stoop to their Husband's feet'.⁶

If few English ladies at the turn of the seventeenth century would have contemplated sporting 'the resemblance of a Foot' upon their Top-Knots, the lack of such an outward symbol of submission should not obscure the fact that their position at law with regard to their husbands was exactly the same in 1700 as it had been 100 years earlier: the authority of the husband remained, as it was then, absolute.

The Lawes Resolutions (probably written by lawyers in the late sixteenth century, but printed in 1632) had pointed out that a man might beat 'an outlaw, a traitor, a Pagan, his villein, or his wife because by the Law Common these persons can have no action'. In 1696 the author of *An Essay in Defense of the Female Sex* (anonymous except for her sex) evoked an even more piteous comparison: 'Women, like our Negroes in our western plantations, are born slaves, and live prisoners all their lives.'⁷ As against the lack of legal rights within marriage which applied to the vast majority of Englishwomen, the small amelioration brought about to heiresses by the development of Chancery, or

the increased choice of marriage partner (within socially prescribed limits) allowed to the young, were but limited advances.

Women remained weak at law, tied by what Samuel Hieron
had called 'this blessed knot of matrimony', something which did
not always live up to this enthusiastic description, but was nevertheless the binding which every girl was expected to accept if she
was to fulfil her role in society.[8] In this connection legal bewilder-
ment prevailed when any young woman who did not admit such
a state or something related to it encountered the authorities:
'Are you a maid, or a widow or a wife?' inquired the magistrate of
the Catholic nun, Mary Ward's colleague,[9] unable to accept the
concept of chosen celibacy in a female. It is significant that two
new types of woman which imposed themselves upon public
attention in the second half of the seventeenth century, the
Quaker and the actress, were both in their different ways outside
the law as it stood up till 1660.

In another area, even more crucial to their daily lives, women
were as weak (if not weaker) at the end of the century as at the
beginning. It was no one's fault that one of the consequences of
the development of gynaecology (before the nature of infection
was appreciated) meant that maternal mortality rose slightly by
the end of the century, with outbreaks of puerperal fever. The
fact remained that women's lot was 'a continual labour' in more
senses than one, as Rachel Lady Russell told her daughter
Katherine,[10] and with high maternal mortality, no proper means
of controlling conception, high infant mortality and high expectations of childbearing from their spouses, it was difficult to see
how it could be otherwise – with all the attendant family joys that
such persistent child-bearing also brought.

Men of course shared all the other physical miseries of women
induced by poverty and disease (having the additional privilege of
dying on the battlefield): life expectancy overall fell in certain
places in England after 1625 for a period,[11] another example of
the cyclical nature of progress. Then there were the emotional
sufferings equal for both sexes, including the deaths of infants; as
is made clear by the lamentations of such multi-fathers as
William Brownlow, with his twenty-two years of recorded grief.[12]

Nevertheless being Adam's sons rather than Eve's daughters, they could not and did not suffer what the poet Waller had once jocularly called down upon Dorothy Sidney when she chose another suitor: 'the first curse imposed on womankind – the pains of becoming a mother'.[13]

For all this, women in the seventeenth century were as they had always been, strong vessels where they had the opportunity: that is to say, where a particular combination of character and circumstance enabled them to be so. In this of course they were exactly like their male counterparts, no more no less. Who can tell what imponderable freak of character inspired the girl soldier Anne Dymoke to pursue such a courageous course after the death of her lover at sea, ending up in a Scottish garrison, when most other girls of her time and class would have remained quietly melancholic in the country in the first place? It was just that women, given the structure of society at the time, had vastly fewer opportunities to demonstrate their worth and resourcefulness.

It was the unexpected arrival of these opportunities which gave to the Civil War period its peculiar character for women; although even here one should note that the boldest she-soldier could not count on being free from 'the first curse'. Such heroines were often only detected by the unconcealable fact of pregnancy, as unavoidable a lot, it seemed, in uniform as out of it. The ballad of 'The Female Warrior', she who was 'at push of Pike ... As good as ever struck', commemorated this hazard:

> This valiant Amazon with courage fill'd
> For to Display her Colours was well skill'd
> Till pregnant nature did her Sex discover
> She fell a pieces, and was made a Mother.[14]

As for those women 'solicitors', they too lay under the first curse: from Mary Lady Verney, alone and gravid as she pleaded in vain with 'Old Men's Wife' to aid her husband's cause, to Elizabeth Lilburne, baptizing her baby Tower because he had been born in the Tower of London (John Lilburne's current prison).

It is however an almost universal fact of history that women have done well in wartime when they have been able or compelled to act as substitutes for men, showing themselves resourceful, courageous and strong in every sense of the words; in short displaying without much difficulty all those qualities generally described as masculine. It is another fact that the post-war period has generally seen a masculine retreat from this view of the female sex when the vacuum no longer needs to be filled. Post-Restoration England was no exception to this rule: indeed as early as 1657 Dr Jeremy Taylor, discoursing on friendship *In a Letter to the most Ingenious and Excellent Mrs Katherine Phillips* (the Matchless Orinda), attacked those morose cynics who would not admit women to this state: 'a man is the best friend in trouble', he wrote, 'but a woman may be equal to him in the days of joy … in peaceful Cities and times vertuous women are the beauties of society and the prettiness of friendship'.[15] His views were flattering enough considering the low opinion of women then prevalent, most men arguing against the mere possibility of friendship with the opposite sex, but the terms in which he couched them paid but scant attention to the realities of recent history.

On the other hand most women were undoubtedly pleased to see the return of peaceful conditions, the old order as it seemed, without analysing its social consequences for themselves. The fact that John Lilburne may (or may not) have included women in the natural order which endowed natural rights, and that John Locke thirty years later certainly did not, was of little importance to their 'continual labour'. While the fact that John Lilburne, revolutionary thinker concerning natural rights in public, was in private one of the most trying husbands a woman ever had to bear, goes perhaps some way to explaining the slow pace of the development of women's position in the ensuing centuries.

The public ideal of womanhood towards the end of the seventeenth century is given in a panegyric, preached as a sermon after the death of Queen Mary on 28 December 1694, and later printed.[16] Nothing is rarer than to find the heroic character in a woman, declared the panygyrist, the Rev. James Abbadie, minister at the French church in the Savoy, while going on happily to discover such heroism in the character of the deceased sovereign.

Only the heroism which distinguished her and which conjured forth his admiration was entirely based on modesty: it was modesty which had marked out Queen Mary from first to last, including modesty in abasing herself before her husband, William III; all kinds of modesty, ending with the notion that her own palace was 'a true temple of modesty'.

Yet this was an age which produced the quick-witted 'She-Champion and Midwife' Mrs Cellier as well as the modest Mary, born to rule, content to serve. Carving out a nursing career despite her dubious origins, holding her own against the officers of the law while on trial at the Old Bailey, indulging in *badinage* with Charles II on the same occasion, coolly storing the stones thrown at her in the pillory in her pocket and later ambitiously attempting to found a college of therapeutic midwifery, Mrs Cellier was also characteristic of a century when woman was widely held to be the weaker vessel.

To those that have come after, Mrs Cellier is a more engaging, and even perhaps a more admirable character than the submissive Queen – if not to her own society, which threw the stones.

References

Chapter 14: Worldly Goods

1 *Verney Memoirs*, II, p.480; *As You Like It*, Act III, scene V.
2 *Verney Memoirs*, II, pp.361, 365.
3 *Verney Memoirs*, II, pp.372, 215, 390; III, pp.213–15; II, p.383.
4 *Verney Memoirs*, IV, pp.33–7.
5 See Habakkuk, 'Marriage Settlements'; Stone, 'Social Mobility in England', p.52; Stone, *Crisis of the Aristocracy*, pp.637–45.
6 G.E.C., *Complete Peerage*, II, p.53.
7 cit. Coate, *Social Life*, p.25; cit. Habakkuk, 'Marriage Settlements', p.23; *Pepys Diary*, I, p.269; Hollingsworth, 'Demographic Study of the British ducal families', p.9, cites 6 per cent of ducal female offspring unmarried eventually, 1480–1679, compared to 17 per cent, 1680–1729 (at the age of twenty-five the relative figures were 19 per cent to 37 per cent).
8 King, *Natural and political observations*, p.39; Graunt, 'Natural Observations upon bills of Mortality', II, p.375.
9 *Marriage Promoted in a Discourse*, p.27.
10 cit. Appendix C, Berens, *Digger Movement*, p.252.
11 cit. Cartwright, *Madame*, p.153; Hamilton, *Gramont Memoirs*, p.108.
12 *Oglander Notebook*, p.95; *Killigrew Poems*, p.31.
13 Aphra Behn, *Feign'd Curtezans*, Act IV, scene II; Aphra Behn, *The Rover*, Part I, Act I, scene I; Charles Sedley, *Bellamira*, Act V, scene I.

14 Hamilton, *Gramont Memoirs*, p.232; Index, p.367.

15 *Verney Memoirs*, IV, pp.273–80.

16 *Verney Memoirs*, IV, pp.207, 452–4.

17 Newcastle, *Worlds Olio*, p.211.

18 HMC, Salisbury MSS, 1621–88, p.420.

19 Allestree, *Ladies Calling*, Part II, p.177; *Warwick Autobiography*, pp.35–6.

20 *Cust Family Records*, series II, p.74.

21 Woolley, *Gentlewomans Companion*, p.89.

22 See Finch MSS, I, pp.xxv, 461–4; III, p.139.

23 *Athenian Oracle*, II, p.155.

24 cit. Hiscock, *Evelyn and Mrs Godolphin*, p.166.

25 Although *Collins' Peerage*, V, p.516 gives 14 October 1679, I have followed Sidney, *Diary*, II, p.11, and Cartwright, *Sacharissa*, page 247, which make it clear the ceremony took place in March.

26 Cartwright, *Sacharissa*, p.247; Fraser, *King Charles II*, pp.348–9.

27 Cartwright, *Sacharissa*, p.247.

28 Cartwright, *Sacharissa*, p.215; Sidney, *Diary*, I, p.286.

29 Sidney, *Diary*, I, pp.238–9.

30 Sidney, *Diary*, I, pp.250–51.

31 Cartwright, *Sacharissa*, p.244.

32 Sidney, *Diary*, II, p.39; Cartwright, *Sacharissa*, p.247.

33 Cartwright, *Sacharissa*, pp.248–9.

34 Sidney, *Diary*, II, p.25; George Farquhar, *The Beaux' Stratagem*, Act II, scene I.

35 *Verney Memoirs*, IV, p.231; Newdegate, *Muniment Room*, p.178.

36 *Evelyn Diary*, II, p.160; *Pepys Diary*, VIII, p.139.

37 *Hatton Correspondence*, I, p.53.

38 Shannon, *Discourses and Essays*, Preface; cit. Jameson, *Beauties of Charles II's Court*, p.168.

39 See Jameson, *Beauties of Charles II's Court*, pp.169–70.

40 Sidney, *Diary*, I, p.302.

41 *Life of Lady Russell*, p.75.

42 *Hatton Correspondence*, I, p.236.

43 *Evelyn Diary*, II, p.160; *Life of Lady Russell*, p.75.

44 *House of Commons*, I, p.716.

45 Fea, *Some Beauties*, pp.40–50; *Hatton Correspondence*, II p.8; Newdegate, *Cavalier and Puritan*, p.154.

46 DNB (Thomas Thynne); *Evelyn Diary*, II, p.386.

47 Newdegate, *Cavalier and Puritan*, p.160.

48 cit. Fea, *Some Beauties*, p.69.
49 *Life of Lady Russell*, pp. xvi, xcviii.
50 Scott Thomson, *Russells in Bloomsbury*, pp.14, 17.
51 Scott Thomson, *Russells in Bloomsbury*, p.62.
52 *Lady Russell Letters*, I, p.36; *Life of Lady Russell*, p.36.
53 Fraser, *King Charles II*, p.429.
54 *Life of Lady Russell*, p.xxv; Pilkington, *Celebrated Female Characters*, p.311.
55 Burnet, *History*, II, p.380; *Life of Lady Russell*, p.xxvi.
56 See Strong, *When did you last see your father?*, p.21; Appendix, p.167.
57 *Life of Lady Russell*, pp.xxiv–xxxv.
58 *Life of Lady Russell*, p.xliii.
59 *Life of Lady Russell*, p.xcvi.
60 Mary Berry, anonymous editor, *Life of Lady Russell*, p.viii.
61 *Evelyn Diary*, II, p.173; *Life of Lady Russell*, p.lxxviii; G.E.C., *Complete Peerage*, II, p.81.
62 *Life of Lady Russell*, p.lxxix.
63 *Life of Lady Russell*, p.93.
64 *Life of Lady Russell*, p.223.

Chapter 15: Divorce from Bed and Board

1 Cripps, *Elizabeth of the Sealed Knot*, pp. 89–90.
2 Gardiner, *Oxinden and Peyton*, pp.219, 265, 344.
3 MacDonald, *Mystical Bedlam*, p.101.
4 Norsworthy, *Lady Hatton*, p.30.
5 *Osborne Letters*, p.169; *Waller Poems*, I, p.90; Aubrey, *Brief Lives*, ed. Powell, p.295.
6 Carte, *Ormonde*, IV, p.701; Burghclere, *Ormonde*, I, p.41.
7 Longleat NMR MS, 1847.
8 *Verney Memoirs*, III, p.435; Carte MSS, Vol. LXXVIII, fo. 412; *Giffard Correspondence*, p.4.
9 Fell Smith, *Warwick*, pp.284–90.
10 *Verney Memoirs*, III, pp.430–32; IV, p.199.
11 *Pepys Diary*, II, p.6 and note 6.
12 Hogrefe, *Tudor Women*, p.89.
13 Whateley's tracts, cit. Stenton, *English Woman*, pp.107–8; see Milton, *Doctrine and Discipline of Divorce*; Thompson, *Women in Stuart England*, pp.169–77.
14 *Ladies Dictionary*, p.165; HMC, Denbigh MSS, Part V, p.14.
15 Aphra Behn, *The Town-Fop*, Act V, scene IV; *Sir Patient Fancy*, Act V, scene I.

16 Houldsworth, *English Law*, I, p.623.

17 Robinson, *Dukes of Norfolk*, pp.145–7.

18 Thomas, 'Double Standard', p.201; *Athenian Oracle*, I, p.428.

19 Devereux, *Earls of Essex*, II, pp.304–6.

20 *Pepys Diary*, IV, p.254 and note 2.

21 G.E.C., *Complete Peerage*, XI, pp.262, 109–12.

22 *Clarendon Life*, III, p.17; G.E.C., *Complete Peerage*, XI, p.263; HMC, Rutland MSS, IV, p.519.

23 HMS, Rutland MSS, IV, p.540.

24 *Clarendon Life*, III, p.172.

25 *Clarendon Life*, III, p.172.

26 *Clarendon Life*, III, p.172.

27 *Clarendon Life*, III, p.173.

28 *Clarendon Life*, III, p.174.

29 *Dorchester's Letter to Lord Roos, with his Answer.*

30 *Dorchester's Letter to Lord Roos, with his Answer.*

31 *Clarendon Life*, III, p.175.

32 HMC, Salisbury MSS, XXII, p.441.

33 HMC, Salisbury MSS, XXII, p.442.

34 HMC, Rutland MSS, IV, p.547.

35 HMC, Salisbury MSS, XXII, p.442.

36 HMC, Salisbury MSS, XXII, p.444.

37 G.E.C., *Complete Peerage*, IV, p.406 and note A.

38 *Journal of the House of Lords*, XII, pp.17, 28.

39 *Journal of the House of Lords*, XII, pp.41–52.

40 *Journal of the House of Lords*, XII, p.95.

41 HMC, Rutland MSS, II, p.8.

42 G.E.C., *Complete Peerage*, XI, p.iii and note C.

43 *Journal of the House of Lords*, XII, p.324; Burnet, *History*, I, p.471, note 2.

44 HMC, 8th Report, Appendix, p.117.

45 Burnet, *History*, I, p.472; Matthew, 5, VS. 32; 19, VS. 9; Mark, 10, VS. 11–12; Luke, 16, VS. 18; *Case of my Lord Roos*.

46 *Journal of the House of Lords*, XII, p.323.

47 HMC, Rutland MSS, IV, p.647; *Journal of the House of Lords*, XII, p.350.

48 *Case of Divorce and Remarriage Discussed.*

49 i.e. Dorothy Lady Stanhope on behalf of her niece Lady Betty Livingstone, cit. Stone, *Family, Sex and Marriage*, p.184; HMC, Rutland MSS, IV, p.551.

50 G.E.C., *Complete Peerage*, IV, p.406; X, p.422; *Hatton Correspondence*, I, p.159.
51 HMC, 12th Report, Appendix, Part V, p.140.
52 *Life of Lady Russell*, p.lxxiv.
53 Nichols, *Leicestershire*, II, Part I, p.62.
54 HMC, 12th Report, Appendix, Part V, p.iv.

Chapter 16: Benefiting by Accomplishments

1 Woolley, *Queen-like Closet*, Part II, p.340.
2 Sidney, *Diary*, I, p.191 and note ii, p.22.
3 *Waller Poems*, I, p.56; Grant, *Margaret the First*, pp.195, 229: *Osborne Letters*, p.50; Stuart, *English Abigail*, p.51.
4 Evelyn, *Mrs Godolphin*, p.154.
5 Cripps, *Elizabeth of the Sealed Knot*, pp.10, 36, 59, 190.
6 Reid, *John and Sarah*, p.141.
7 Green, *Queen Anne*, p.99.
8 DNB (Abigail Masham).
9 *Pepys Diary*, I, p.288; II, p.232 and note 2, p.4.
10 *Pepys Diary*, II, p.139.
11 *Pepys Diary*, III, p.223.
12 *Pepys Diary*, II, pp.11, 204.
13 Her Christian name was probably Winifred; see *Pepys Diary*, III, p.256 and note 2; III, p.277; *Verney Memoirs*, IV, pp.20–21.
14 *Pepys Diary*, IV, pp.79, 280.
15 *Pepys Diary*, V, p.152; Lambley, *French Language*, pp.366–70; John Vanbrugh, *Provok'd Wife*, Act II, scene II; *Pepys Diary*, V, pp.265, 274.
16 *Pepys Diary*, VI, pp.252, 163–4; VII, p.138.
17 *Pepys Diary*, VIII, pp.471, 475; IX, p.210.
18 *Pepys Diary*, VII, p.311; VI, p.235; VIII, p.212.
19 *Pepys Diary*, IX, pp.337–8, 344, 367.
20 DNB (Woolley); see Woolley, *Gentlewomans Companion*, pp.15–17.
21 See Wallas, *Before the Bluestockings*, pp.17–54.
22 Woolley, *Gentlewomans Companion*, p.10.
23 Woolley, *Gentlewomans Companion*, p.288.
24 Woolley, *Gentlewomans Companion*, p.65.
25 Webster, *Great Instauration*, pp.219–20; Turnbull, *Hartlib*, pp. 120–21.
26 Reynolds, *Learned Lady*, pp.270–80; Lambley, *French Language*, p.381; Makin, *Essay on Education*, p.23.

27 cit. Green, *Queen Anne*, p.99; Lambley, *French Language*, p.392.

28 Hamilton, *William's Mary*, p.19.

29 *Winchilsea Poems*, p.5.

30 *Pepys Diary*, V, p.45; Ede, *Arts and Society*, pp.84–6; see Greer, *Obstacle Race*, pp.255–7; *Ladies Dictionary*, p.434.

31 Makin, *Essay on Education*, p.22.

32 Birch, *Anna van Schurman*, p.73; van Schurman, *Learned Maid*, p.5.

33 Stuart, *Girl through the Ages*, pp.196–7.

34 Fraser, *King Charles II*, p.194.

35 Makin, *Essay on Education*, Postscript.

36 Makin, *Essay on Education*, pp.3–7.

37 Bowle, *Evelyn*, p.213; Hiscock, *Evelyn and Mrs Godolphin*, p.167.

38 *Locke Correspondence*, III, p.105; II, p.485; DNB (John Locke); cit. Illick, 'Child-Rearing', p.30; Masham, *Occasional Thoughts*, p.197.

39 HMC, Hastings MSS, IV, p.348.

40 *Fox Journal*, pp.520, 748; see Cressy, *Literacy*, p.145.

41 BL Add MSS, 5858, fo. 213–21.

42 *Verney Memoirs*, IV, p.221.

43 'The New Letanie', Thomason Tract, 669. fo. 10/120; cit. Grant, *Margaret the First*, p.37.

44 Cressy, *Literacy*, p.37; Cressy, *Education*, p.114.

45 Makin, *Essay on Education*, p.33.

46 *Poems by Eminent Ladies*, I, p.215; Rochester, *Works*, p.18.

47 Halifax, *Complete Works*, p.289; Evelyn, *Mundus Muliebris*, p.8, Preface.

48 *Life of Lady Russell*, p.xcviii.

49 *Sedley Works*, II, p.112; cit. Utter and Needham, *Pamela's Daughters*, p.23.

50 *Verney Memoirs*, IV, pp.225–6.

51 Barksdale, *Letter touching a College of Maids or a Virgin Society*; see Florence Smith, *Mary Astell*, for this and other biographical details.

52 See Hartmann, *Vagabond Duchess*, for the life of Hortense Mancini.

53 Astell, *Reflections*, pp.4–5.

54 Burnet, *History*, 2 June 1708, cit. Smith, *Mary Astell*, p.22.

55 Astell, *Reflections*, Preface.

56 'The Saxon Nymph'.

57 Elstob, *English-Saxon Family*, Preface, p.ii.

58 'The Saxon Nymph'.

59 'The Saxon Nymph'; DNB (Elizabeth Elstob).

Chapter 17: Petticoat-Authors

1 Masham, *Occasional Thoughts*, p.199; *Winchilsea Poems*, p.5.

2 Aphra Behn, *Sir Patient Fancy*, Act I, scene I.

3 Thomas Wright, *The Female Vertuosos*, Act III, scene I; William Congreve, *The Double Dealer*, Act III, scene X.

4 Gildon, *Comparison Between Two Stages*, pp.26–7.

5 Needham, 'Mrs Manley', p.265.

6 Mary Manley, *The Lost Lover*, Prologue, cit. Needham, 'Mrs Manley', p.263; Duffy, *Passionate Shepherdess*, p.138.

7 There are two recent biographies of Aphra Behn: Maureen Duffy, *The Passionate Shepherdess* (1977) which casts fresh light on the mystery of her birth, and Angeline Goreau, *Reconstructing Aphra, A Social Biography* (1980).

8 *Life of Mr Joseph Alleine*, Printer's Note.

9 Barham, 'Discovery of the Authorship of the *Whole Duty of Man*'; *Winchilsea Poems*, p.xxxviii; Ballard, *Memoirs of Several Ladies*, p.363.

10 See her biography by P.M. Souars, *The Matchless Orinda* (1931).

11 cit. Souars, *Orinda*, p.189.

12 cit. Souars, *Orinda*, p.91; *Aubrey's Brief Lives*, ed. Lawson Dick, p.242.

13 cit Souars, *Orinda*, pp.91, 98.

14 Souars, *Orinda*, p.253.

15 cit. Souars, *Orinda*, pp.110, 43.

16 Taylor, 'Treasures of Friendship', pp.63–5.

17 Souars, *Orinda*, p.277.

18 *Killigrew Poems*, Publisher's Note; Dryden's 'Prefatory Ode'.

19 *Killigrew Poems*, p.85.

20 *Killigrew Poems*, p.79.

21 *Killigrew Poems*, p.32.

22 *Killigrew Poems*, p.51.

23 *Killigrew Poems*, ed. Morton, p.xi.

24 *Killigrew Poems*; Dryden's 'Prefatory Ode'.

25 *Killigrew Poems*, p.13.

26 See Greer, *Obstacle Race*, p.255, where it is pointed out that her Christian name was Joan, not Anne, as stated previously.

27 Greer, *Obstacle Race*, pp.255–7.

28 *Woodforde Papers*, p.5.

29 Sir Oliver Millar in a letter to the author; Millar, *Lely*; Blunt, *Botanical Illustrations*, pp.129–30.

30 See *Winchilsea Poems*, Introduction by Myra Reynolds, for biographical details.

31 *Winchilsea Poems*, p.21.

32 *Winchilsea Poems*, p.4.

33 *Winchilsea Poems*, pp.268–70, lxxvi.

34 i.e. by Dale Spender in *Man Made Language*, pp. 194–5, 230.

35 cit. *Winchilsea Poems*. p.lxii.

36 M.H. Nicholson in *Conway Letters*, p.xxv.

37 *Conway Letters*, p.47.

38 *Conway Letters*, p.57, note 7.

39 *Conway Letters*, p.152.

40 *Conway Letters*, p.53.

41 Sacks, *Migraine*, p.241.

42 See *Conway Letters*, esp. pp.113, 91 note I, 114, 79.

43 *Conway Letters*, p.106, 116.

44 *Conway Letters*, pp.248–9.

45 *Conway Letters*, p.282.

46 *Conway Letters*, p.168.

47 *Conway Letters*, p.337.

48 cit. *Conway Letters*, p.299–300.

49 *Conway Letters*, p.278.

50 *Conway Letters*, p.412.

51 *Conway Letters*, p.413.

52 By M.H. Nicolson, *Conway Letters*, p.378.

53 *Conway Letters*, p.433.

54 *Conway Letters*, p.436.

55 *Conway Letters*, pp.456, 481.

56 *Conway Letters*, pp.451, 457.

57 *Conway Letters*, p.159; *Principles of the most Ancient and Modern Philosophy*, Preface.

58 *Principles of the most Ancient and Modern Philosophy*, pp.3, 11, 14.

59 *Principles of the most Ancient and Modern Philosophy*, p.77.

60 *Conway Letters*, p.451; *Principles of the most Ancient and Modern Philosophy*, Preface; *Conway Letters*, p.456.

61 *Conway Letters*, p.457.

62 *Conway Letters*, pp.465–8.

Chapter 18: Helping in God's Vineyard

1 *Conway Letters*, pp.412, 433.

2 Brailsford, *Quaker Women*, p.70.

3 Brailsford, *Quaker Women*, p.324.

4 Ross, *Margaret Fell*, p.35; *Trapnel's Report and Plea*, p.24; see Brailsford, *Quaker Women*, pp.159–76, 213–16.

5 Nalson, *Countermine*, p.93.

6 cit. Brailsford, *Quaker Women*, p.15.

7 See Brailsford, *Quaker Women*, pp.16–41 for the story of Elizabeth Hooton.

8 *Fox Journal*, p.9.

9 Brailsford, *Quaker Women*, p.19.

10 Brailsford, *Quaker Women*, p.333.

11 cit. Manners, 'Elizabeth Hooton', pp.14–15.

12 See Brailsford, *Quaker Women*, pp.94–113.

13 See Scales, 'Quaker Women in Dover, New Hampshire'.

14 *Pepys Diary*, V, pp.12–13; Bryant, *Pepys. Years of Peril*, p.204 and note.

15 Roberts, *Monmouth*, II, p.205.

16 Scales, 'Quaker Women in Dover, New Hampshire'.

17 *Fox Journal*, II, pp.213, 436 and note.

18 See Braithwaite, *Beginnings of Quakerism*, pp.422–4; Brailsford, *Quaker Women*, pp.114–32 for Mary Fisher's expedition.

19 Braithwaite, *Beginnings of Quakerism*, p.423.

20 Marsh, *New Survey of Turkish Empire*, Part 2, p.33; Paul Ruycaut (later English Consul in Smyrna), *Ottoman empire*, p.120.

21 Taken from the account of Willem Sewel, in his *History of the Quakers*, first published (in Dutch) in 1717. According to M.R. Brailsford, *Quaker Women*, p.128, Sewel may have heard the details directly from Mary Fisher.

22 Thurloe Papers, VII, p.287; Brailsford, *Quaker Women*, p.116.

23 G.E.C., *Complete Peerage*, XII/2, p.778, note 1; *Collins' Peerage*, pp.384–5.

24 Ross, *Margaret Fell*, p.226; see this biography in general for details of her life.

25 Ross, *Margaret Fell*, p.24.

26 cit. Knox, *Enthusiasm*, p.161.

27 Ross, *Margaret Fell*, p.37.

28 Ross, *Margaret Fell*, p.170.

29 Ross, *Margaret Fell*, p.138.

30 Spufford, 'Portraits of Society', p.12; *Fox Journal*, p.421.

31 *Athenian Oracle*, I, p.33.

32 *Fox Journal*, p.554.

33 Ross, *Margaret Fell*, p.220.

34 Ross, *Margaret Fell*, pp.228 note 2, 226.

35 *Sarah Fell Account Book*, pp.xx, xix.

36 Thomas, *Women and Sects*, p.48.

37 Margaret Fell, *Womens Speaking*, pp.3 (sic: Joel 2, VS. 28 differs slightly), 4, 10.

38 Margaret Fell, *Womens Speaking*, p.5.

39 Margaret Fell, *Womens Speaking*, p.14.

40 Braithwaite, *Second Period of Quakerism*, pp.270–72, 286–8.

41 Letter of Isabel Yeamans, 8 August 1676, MSS, Religious Society of Friends, Nottingham Meeting.

42 *Fox Journal*, pp.629, 647, 666–8.

43 Ross, *Margaret Fell*, pp.313–14; Katz, *Readmission of the Jews*, p.238.

44 Ross, *Margaret Fell*, p.318.

45 Ross, *Margaret Fell*, p.370.

Chapter 19: The Delight of Business

1 Ede, *Arts and Society*, p.14; see Clark, *Working Life*, pp.32–3 for Joan Dant's story.

2 Brailsford, *Quaker Women*, p.15.

3 Ballard, *Memoirs of Several Ladies*, p.287; Anderson, *Friends and Relations*, p.68.

4 See *Sarah Fell Account Book*.

5 Scott Thomson, *Noble Household*, pp.189, 199.

6 Miranda Chaytor and Jane Lewis in Clark, *Working Life*, p.xxxi.

7 *Pepys Diary*, I, p.30; X. p.241.

8 i.e. see *The Diary of Roger Lowe*; its editor, William L. Sachse (p.7), describes the alehouse of this period, on the diary's evidence, as 'the unofficial club' of both poor man *and* poor woman.

9 cit. Bridenbaugh, *Vexed Englishmen*, p.195; cit. Pinto, *Sedley*, p.58; Gough, *Myddle*, pp.197–8.

10 Finch MSS, III, p.438.

11 *Pepys Diary*, V, p.62.

12 *Pepys Diary*, V, p.266.

13 The story of Mrs Pley and Colonel Reymes is told in Helen Andrews Kaufman's biography of the latter, *Conscientious Cavalier*.

14 Hutchins, *Dorset*, II, p.459.

15 Kaufman, *Conscientious Cavalier*, p.182.

16 Fraser, *King Charles II*, p.223.

17 Kaufman, *Conscientious Cavalier*, pp.182, 247 note 7.

18 *Pepys Diary*, VII, pp.199–200.

19 *Pepys Diary*, VII, p.200 note 2.

20 Balleine, *All for the King*, p.127.

21 CSP Domestic, 1664–5, pp.500–501.

22 CSP Domestic, 1664–5, p.525.

23 *Pepys Diary*, VI, p.187: *Carlingford papers*, II of III, Osborn Collection, Yale.

24 Defoe, *Journal of the Plague Year*, p.120.

25 CSP Domestic, 1665–6, p.108.

26 CSP Domestic, 1665–6, pp.219, 244; 1666–7, 66; 1665–6, pp.357, 272.

27 Kaufman, *Conscientious Cavalier*, p.237.

28 Kaufman, *Conscientious Cavalier*, p.184.

29 CSP Domestic, 1665–6, p.207.

30 'Of Persons one would wish to have seen', in *Hazlitt Selected Essays*, p.532.

31 See Howell, 'Image of Cromwell in Restoration Drama'.

32 Waylen, *House of Cromwell*, p.81.

33 Waylen, *House of Cromwell*, p.77.

34 Noble, *Cromwell Memoirs*, II, p.337.

35 Nall, *Yarmouth*, p.154; Ogg, *England of Charles II*, pp.72–3.

36 Collins, *Salt and Fishery*, p.61; Waylen, *House of Cromwell*, p.77.

37 Costello, *Eminent Englishwomen*, III, p.55.

38 Waylen, *House of Cromwell*, pp.82–3.

39 Waylen, *House of Cromwell*, pp.82–3.

40 Noble, *Cromwell Memoirs*, II, p.332.

41 Sloane MSS, 2069, fo. 96 B; Baxter, *Reliquiae Baxterianae*, p.57.

42 The Rev. Samuel Say's account is printed in full in Noble, *Cromwell Memoirs*, II, pp.329–33, first published in 1727; the Rev. James Waylen in *The House of Cromwell*, 1880, suggests the explanation for Say's hostility.

43 Dr Jeremy Brooke's account in full in Noble, *Cromwell Memoirs*, II, pp.333–8.

44 Hewling Luson's account in full in Noble, *Cromwell Memoirs*, II, pp.338–46.

45 Noble, *Cromwell Memoirs*, II, p.346.

Chapter 20: Wanton and Free

1 Aphra Behn, *The Feign'd Curtezans*, Act IV, scene I; Allestree, *Ladies Calling*, p.26.

2 Newcastle, *CCXI Letters*, p.76.

3 Allestree, *Ladies Calling*, p.157; OED; Barker, *Poetical Recreations*, Part I, pp.12–13; Fraser, *King Charles II*, p.285.

4 Evelyn, *Mundus Muliebris*, Preface; *Womens Complaint*; John Dryden, *Marriage-à-la-Mode*, Act I, scene I.

5 North, *Lives*, II, p.164; Needham, 'Mrs Manley', p.276.

6 Aphra Behn, *The Town-Fop*, Act IV, scene II.

7 See Sidney, *Diary*, I, pp.xxviii–xxxiv, for the sufferings of Mrs Worthley.

8 *Pepys Diary*, IV, pp.114, 270, 303.

9 *Pepys Diary*, IV, pp.281, 387–8.

10 *Pepys Diary*, V, pp.173–4.

11 *Pepys Diary*, V, p.184.

12 *Pepys Diary*, V, p.179.

13 *Pepys Diary*, IX, p.455.

14 Thomas Otway, *Venice Preserv'd*, Act III, scene I; Act II, scene I; Aphra Behn, *The Rover*, Part I, Act I, scene I.

15 HMC, 12th Report, Appendix, Part V, p.158.

16 cit. Pinto, *Sedley*, Appendix III, p.355.

17 Pinto, *Sedley*, pp. 120–25.

18 *Evelyn Diary*, II, p.84.

19 BL Add MSS, 30, 382.

20 cit. Pinto, *Sedley*, p.129; Wolseley, *Marlborough*, I, pp.188–9.

21 Dorset, *Works*, XI, p.16.

22 Dorset, *Works*, XI, p.209.

23 Wilson, *Court Wits*, p.113; Pinto, *Sedley*, p.137.

24 cit. Pinto, *Sedley*, p.140 note 2.

25 Burke's *Extinct Peerages*, p.492; Pinto, *Sedley*, p.140.

26 Turner, *James II*, p.142.

27 Pinto, *Sedley*, p.238.

28 Pinto, *Sedley*, p.158.

29 Pinto, *Sedley*, Appendix III, p.355.

30 Stanley, *Memorials of Westminster Abbey*, Appendix, p.507.

31 Miller, *James II* (1978), p.151; F.C. Turner in his biography *James II* (1948), p.294, also thought the evidence came from Sunderland and was therefore suspect.

32 *Evelyn Diary*, II, p.248.

33 cit. Turner, *James II*, p.300.

34 Pinto, *Sedley*, Appendix III, pp.355–60.

35 Pinto, *Sedley*, Appendix III, p.360.

36 Turner, *James II*, p.300.

37 Pinto, *Sedley*, Appendix III, pp.346–7.

38 Finch MSS, III, p.347; cit. Pinto, *Sedley*, p.174.

39 See Pinto, *Sedley*, pp.204–5 and note 2.

40 Finch MSS, III, p.34.

41 Finch MSS, III, pp.348, 351.

42 *Hatton Correspondence*, II, p.128 and note A; p.129.

43 *Case of the Countess of Dorchester relating to the Torrington Bill.*

44 Dorset, *Works*, XI, p.198; Pinto, *Sedley*, pp.218–19; DNB (Catherine Sedley).

45 See Myddelton, *Chirk Castle Accounts*.

46 *Pepys Diary*, VI, p.64 and note 2; *Evelyn Diary*, II, p.183.

47 *Ladies Dictionary*, pp.219, 63; *Pepys Diary*, VIII, p.46.

48 *Aeneid*, Book I, l.402 (trans. J. Middleton Murry); Hamilton, *Gramont Memoirs*, p.204.

49 *Cholmley Memoirs*, p.12; Gardiner, *Oxinden Letters*, p.164.

50 Hamilton, *Gramont Memoirs*, pp.109, 131; Newcastle, *CCXI Letters*, p.215; *Ladies Dictionary*, p.212.

51 *Pepys Diary*, VIII, pp.286, 251; Myddelton, *Chirk Castle Accounts*; cit. Jameson, *Beauties of Charles II's Court*, p.163.

52 Lecky, *History of European Morals*, II, pp.220–30; Mary Pix, *The Innocent Mistress*, cit. Morgan, *Female Wits*, p.266; Clark, *Working Life*, Introduction, p.xxxi.

53 Macfarlane, *Marital and Sexual Relationships*, p.104; Quaife, *Wanton Wenches*, p.150; cit. Stone, *Family, Sex and Marriage*, pp.561–3; *Wandering Whore*, No. 1, p.12.

54 Macfarlane, *Marital and Sexual Relationships*, p.105; May, *Social Control of Sex Expression*, p.110; Wilson, *Court Wits*, p.79.

55 Pierpont Morgan Library MSS, R. of E., box IX, Part 2, fo. 55, 57, 62, 64.

56 *Wandering Whore*, No. 1, p.10; No.2. pp.4–6; *Otway Works*, I, p.lxx; Wilson, *King's Ladies*, p.167.

57 See Hamilton, *Gramont Memoirs*, pp.131–220.

58 Gouge, *Domesticall Duties*, cit. Laslett, *World we have lost* (1968), p.131 and note p.267; see May, *Social Control of Sex Expression*, p.132.

59 *Verney Memoirs*, III, p.51; *Humble Remonstrance of the Batchelors*, p.481.

60 *Middlesex County Records*, III, p.13.

61 *Wandering Whore*, Prefatory Note, and No.2, p.9; Wilson, *King's Ladies*, p.18.

62 Stone, *Family, Sex and Marriage*, pp.616, 619; *Pepys Diary*, VIII, p.466, note I; Quaife, *Wanton Wenches*, p.150.

63 Hair, *Before the Bawdy Court*, p.136.

64 *Pepys Diary*, VII, pp.62, 142; IX, p.521.

65 *Pepys Diary*, IX, p.132; Thomas Otway, *Venice Preserv'd*, Prologue; *Whore's Rhetorick*, p.117.

66 *Wandering Whore*, Prefatory Note; DNB (Cresswell).

67 *Whore's Rhetorick*, pp.29, 24.

68 *Whore's Rhetorick*, pp.58, 117.

69 *Whore's Rhetorick*, pp.108, 148, 96, 62.

70 *Wandering Whore*, No.3, p.11.

71 Dorset, *Works*, XI, p.205; cit. Greene, *Rochester*, p.121.

Chapter 21: Actress as Honey-Pot

1 Evelyn, *Mrs Godolphin*, p.97 (still Blagge in fact); *Evelyn Diary*, I, p.332.

2 Having to appear in public still unmarried, see Hiscock, *Evelyn and Mrs Godolphin*, p.113.

3 Nicoll, *English Drama*, I, pp. 70–71; Roberts, *Social History*; Gregg, *Charles I*, p.275; *Pepys Diary*, II, p.5, note 2.

4 Marvell, *Poems*, I, pp.125, 331.

5 cit. Findlater, *Player Queens*, p.12; Nicoll, *English Drama*, I, p.70.

6 See Wilson, *King's Ladies*, pp.5–8 (although he does not totally dismiss the claim of Katherine Corey).

7 Gildon, *Betterton*, p.7; Hamilton, *William's Mary*, p.25; *Pepys Diary*, X, p.86.

8 See Wilson, *King's Ladies*, pp.17–19.

9 William Wycherley, *Country Wife*, Act II, scene I; Wilson, *King's Ladies*, p.14.

10 cit. Wilson, *Court Wits*, p.80.

11 cit. Wilson, *King's Ladies*, p.16.

12 Wilson, *King's Ladies*, pp.9–10; Hamilton, *Gramont Memoirs*, p.314.

13 Woolley, *Queen-like Closet*, p.134; *Pepys Diary*, IV, p.162; V, p.267; IX, p.268 and note 5; Wilson, *King's Ladies*, p.146.

14 *Pepys Diary*, VIII, p.503, note 1; Wilson, *King's Ladies*, pp.110–11, summarizes the various stories.

15 By J.H. Wilson in *King's Ladies*, p.73.

16 See Wilson, *King's Ladies*, pp.68–70 for details of the actresses' costumes.

17 Wilson, *Nell Gwynn*, p.288.

18 *Pepys Diary*, VII, p.463.

19 *Pepys Diary*, V, p.240 and note 3; Wilson, *King's Ladies*, p.34.

20 See Wilson, *King's Ladies*, Appendix I, pp.109–92, for a list of actresses, 1660–89, including biographical details.

21 Wilson, *King's Ladies*, p.127.

22 Wilson, *King's Ladies*, p.130; 'Commentary', C.H. Hartmann in Hamilton, *Gramont Memoirs*, p.338.

23 *Brown Works*, II, p.303.

24 Hamilton, *Gramont Memoirs*, pp.233–4.

25 'Commentary', C.H. Hartmann in Hamilton, *Gramont Memoirs*, pp.361, 233; Wilson, *King's Ladies*, pp.12–13.

26 Wilson, *King's Ladies*, p.14.

27 Hamilton, *Gramont Memoirs*, p.234.

28 For the correct dating of her career, see J.H. Wilson's article, 'Pepys and Peg Hughes'.

29 cit. Morrah, *Prince Rupert*, pp.400, 415.

30 cit. Morrah, *Prince Rupert*, p.415.

31 cit. Morrah, *Prince Rupert*, pp.416–17, 426.

32 *Brown Works*, II. p.241.

33 See J.H. Wilson's article, 'Marshall Sisters and Anne Quin', where their careers are disentangled.

34 *Pepys Diary*, V, p.34 and note 1.

35 John Dryden, *The Indian Emperor*, Act I, scene II.

36 John Dryden, *The Indian Emperor*, Act V, scene I.

37 CSP Domestic, 1665–6, p.157.

38 *Pepys Diary*, VIII, pp.91,235.

39 cit. Wilson, 'Marshall Sisters and Anne Quin', p.106.

40 *Pepys Diary*, IX, p.250.

41 *Pepys Diary*, IX, p.19 and note; see Wilson, *King's Ladies*, Appendix A, pp. 142–4.

42 CSP Domestic, 1664–5, pp.139–40.

43 Aston, 'Brief Supplement', in Cibber, *Apology*, II, p.302.

44 Gildon, *Comparison between Two Stages*, p.18.

45 van Lennep, *London Stage*, I, p.210; DNB (Elizabeth Barry); Cibber, *Apology*, I, p.159; Aston, 'Brief Supplement', in Cibber, *Apology*, II, p.303.

46 Aston, 'Brief Supplement', in Cibber, *Apology*, II, p.303.

47 Curll, *Betterton's History*, pp.14–16.

48 See van Lennep, *London Stage*, I, p.245; Treglown, *Rochester's Letters*, p.29 for the point that it is unlikely Rochester saw *Alcibiades* as he was in the country.

49 Thomas Otway, *Caius Marius*, Act I, scene II.

50 Thomas Southerne, *The Fatal Marriage*, Dedication, 1694.

51 Thomas Otway, *Venice Preserv'd*, Act I, scene I.

52 Gildon, *Comparison Between Two Stages*, p.18; Wilson, *King's Ladies*, pp.115–16, 61–2.

53 *Brown Works*, III, p.39; cit. *Otway Works*, I, p.lxiv

54 *Rochester Familiar Letters*, pp.90, 88.

55 *Rochester Familiar Letters*, p.82.

56 Rochester, *Works*, pp.11, 269, 277, 280. There is no direct evidence linking Rochester's poem 'The Mistress' with Mrs Barry, despite its title; none of Rochester's poems are dated by him and their dating from other evidence presents difficulties (Treglown, *Rochester's Letters*, p.25). Graham Greene in *Rochester*, p.132, suggests the connection with Mrs Barry.

57 cit. Pinto, *Rochester*, p.189.

58 Rochester, *Works*, p.274.

59 Rochester, *Works*, p.280.

60 DNB (Mrs Barry).

61 Cibber, *Apology*, I, p.160.

Chapter 22: The Modest Midwife

1 Rueff, *Expert Midwife*, Introduction.

2 *Midwives Just Petition: Midwives Just Complaint, 1646*, cit. Aveling, *English Midwives*, p.30.

3 Eccles, *Obstetrics in Stuart England*, p.121.

4 See 'Anonymous Business Diary of a Midwife', Rawlinson MSS, D.1141.

5 *Pepys Diary*, II, p.110; *Calverley Memorandum Book*, pp.62, 67.

6 Aveling, *English Midwives*, pp.31–4.

7 Hamilton, *Henrietta Maria*, p.95; Fraser, *King Charles II*, p.13.

8 Clark, *Working Life*, p.274.

9 See G.C.R. Morris, 'Which Molins treated Cromwell for stone?', p.431, and letter to the author concerning girls baptized Aurelia, 1618–39, in the registers of St Andrew, Holborn.

10 Eccles, *Obstetrics In Stuart England*, p.12.

11 Rueff, *Expert Midwife*, Introduction.

12 cit. Cutter and Viets, *Midwifery*, p.48; Sharp, *Midwives Book*, pp.2–3; Sharp, *Compleat Midwife*, Preface.

13 Exodus, I, VS. 15–21.

14 Sharp, *Midwives Book*, p.3.

15 Walker, *Holy Life*, p.86; *Hoby Diary*, p.63.

16 *Pepys Diary*, IX, p.260.

17 Rueff, *Expert Midwife*, Introduction.

18 See Willughby, *Country Midwife's Opusculum*, Sloane MSS, 529.

19 Willughby, *Country Midwife's Opusculum*, Sloane MSS, 529; *Thornton Autobiography*, p.96; see *Freke Diary*, pp.24–5.

20 Aveling, *English Midwives*, pp.55–6; Stenton, *English Woman*, p.228.

21 *Verney Memoirs*, IV, p.169; Ross, *Margaret Fell*, p.351.

22 Ross, *Margaret Fell*, p.292.

23 *Humble Remonstrance of the Batchelors*, p.479; Sermon, *Ladies Companion*, p.5; *Pepys Diary*, III, p.16.

24 i.e. *Wandering Whore*, No. 2, p.5; No. 5, p.13.

25 Gouch, *Myddle*, p.173; Willughby, *Country Midwife's Opusculum*, Sloane MSS, 529.

26 See Cutter and Viets, *Midwifery*, pp.44–7 for the early history of the Chamberlen family.

27 Cutter and Viets, *Midwifery*, p.50.

28 Aveling, *English Midwives*, p.8.

29 cit. Thomas, *Religion*, p.259.

30 cit. Aveling, *English Midwives*, pp.8–9.

31 Cutter and Viets, *Midwifery*, p.47.

32 Cutter and Viets, *Midwifery*, p.49.

33 See *Mrs Shaw's Innocency Restored*.

34 cit. Cutter and Viets, *Midwifery*, p.49.

35 cit. Illick, *Child-Rearing*, pp.306, 333, 13.

36 Sharp, *Midwives Book*, p.3.

37 Clark, *Working Life*, p.263.

38 Shorter, *Women's Bodies*, pp.141–3, 123–38; Eccles, *Obstetrics in Stuart England*, pp.123–4.

39 Donnison, *Midwives and Medical Men*, p.190.

40 By J.H. Aveling (founder of *The Obstetrical Journal of Great Britain and Ireland*) in *English Midwives*, 1872, p.39.

41 Sharp, *Midwives Book*, pp.6, 13, 38; Sermon, *Ladies Companion*, p.94.

42 Sermon, *Ladies Companion*, p.94; *Conway Letters*, p.153.

43 Sermon, *Ladies Companion*, p.94.

44 Aveling, *English Midwives*, p.39; Sharp, *Midwives Book*, p.184; Sermon, *Ladies Companion*, p.5.

45 Shorter, *Women's Bodies*, pp.125–6.

46 Aveling, *English Midwives*, p.112.

47 Cellier, 'Scheme for the Foundation of a Royal Hospital', p.136.

48 Kenyon, *Popish Plot*, pp.189–90; Cellier, *Malice Defeated*, Preface.

49 But see J.H. Kenyon, *Popish Plot*, for the clearest summary of the various facts and suppositions.
50 Cellier, *Malice Defeated*, p.10.
51 Warner, *English Persecution of Catholics*, I, p.314.
52 Caulfield, *Portraits*, I, pp.25–6.
53 Dangerfield, *Grand Impostor*, p.4; Cellier, *Malice Defeated*, p.19.
54 Cellier, *Malice Defeated*, p.38.
55 cit. Aveling, *English Midwives*, p.64.
56 Cellier, *Malice Defeated*, p.28.
57 Cellier, *Malice Defeated*, p.42.
58 *Hatton Correspondence*, I, p.236.
59 Cellier, *Malice Defeated*, p.32,
60 *Life of Lady Russell*, p.44.
61 *Midwife Unmask'd*, p.134.
62 See Aveling, *English Midwives*, pp.76–7.
63 Cellier, 'Scheme for the Foundation of a Royal Hospital', p.137.
64 See Cellier, *To Dr–, An Answer*, pp.1–2.
65 Cellier, *To Dr–, An Answer*, p.7.
66 Cellier, *To Dr–, An Answer*, p.8.
67 Strickland, *English Queens*, V, pp.214–26.
68 Dr Chamberlen's Letter, Sloane MSS, 4107, p.150.

Epilogue: How Strong?

1 *Mercurius Militaris*, 22 April 1649.
2 cit. Green, *Queen Anne*, p.111.
3 Makin, *Essay on Education*, p.11; Notestein, 'English Woman', p.83.
4 Astell, *Reflections*, p.85.
5 Agrippa, *Female Pre-eminence*, pp.1–2.
6 Sprint, *Bride-Woman Counseller*.
7 *Lawes Resolutions*, p.144; *Essay in Defense of the Female Sex*, p.38. (Probably written by Mrs Judith Drake, see Reynolds, *Learned Lady*, p.297.)
8 Hieron, *Helpe unto Devotion*, p.386.
9 Chambers, *Mary Ward*, II, p.33.
10 HMC, 12th Report, Appendix, Part V, p.158.
11 Seaver, *Seventeenth-Century England*, p.9.
12 *Cust Family Records*, series II, p.120.
13 Cartwright, *Sacharissa*, p.74.
14 'The Female Warrior', *Douce Ballads*, I (79).
15 Taylor, 'Treasures of Friendship', p.53.

16 Abbadie, *Panégyrique de Marie, Reine d'Angleterre*, see esp. pp.2, 7, 8, 13, 31; it was also printed in English.

Reference Books

This is not a complete list of all works consulted (which would be impossible for reasons of space) but a list of those books to which allusion is made under short titles in the References.

The place of publication is London unless otherwise stated.

Abbadie, J., Docteur-en-Théologie, Ministre de la Savoye, *Panégyrique de Marie, Reine d'Angleterre, d'Ecosse, de France et d'Irlande, de glorieuse et immortelle mémoire, Décédée à Kensington le 28 décembre 1694.*

Adair, John, *Roundhead General, A Military Biography of Sir William Waller,* 1969.

Agrippa, Henry Cornelius, *Female Pre-eminence or the Dignity and Excellency of that Sex, above the Male,* Done into English with Additional Advantages, H.C. (Henry Care), 1670.

The Life and Death of that Excellent Minister of Christ, Mr Joseph Alleine, 1672.

Allestree, Richard, *The Ladies Calling. In Two Parts. By the author of the Whole Duty of Man etc.,* 5th impression, Oxford, 1677.

Ambrose, Isaac, *Works, including Prima, Media & Ultima,* 1674.

Anderson, Verily, *Friends and Relations. Three Centuries of Quaker Families,* 1980.

'Anonymous Business Diary of a Midwife', Rawlinson MS, D. 1141, Bodleian Library, Oxford.

'Anonymous Folio Volume' (of Anna Trapnel's verse), S.1.42. Th., Bodleian Library, Oxford.

Artamenes or The Grand Cyrus. An Excellent new Romance. Written by that famous Wit of France, Monsieur de Scudéry ... and now Englished by F.C., Gent, 2 Vols, 1653.

Ashley, Maurice, *James II*, 1977.

Ashley, Maurice, *Life in Stuart England*, 1964.

Ashley, Maurice, *The Stuarts in Love*, 1963.

Astell, Mary, *Reflections upon Marriage*, 3rd edition. To which is Added a Preface, in Answer to some Objections, 1706.

Athenae Oxonienses, ed. P. Bliss, 1813.

The Athenian Oracle, Being an Entire collection of all the Valuable Questions and Answers in the Old Athenian Mercuries, 1703.

Aubrey, John, *Aubrey's Brief Lives*, ed. and with a life of John Aubrey, Oliver Lawson Dick, 1968.

Aubrey, John, *Brief Lives and Other Selected Writings*, ed. and with an Introduction, Anthony Powell, 1949.

Austin, William, *Haec Homo. Wherein the Excellency of the Creation of Woman is described. By way of an essay*, 1637.

Aveling, J.H., MD, *English Midwives. Their History and Prospects*, 1872.

Ballard, George, *Memoirs of Several Ladies of Great Britain Who have been celebrated for their Writings or skill in the learned languages, arts, and sciences*, Oxford, 1752.

Balleine, G.R., *All for the King. The Life Story of Sir George Carteret (1609–1680)*, Channel Islands, La Société Jersiaise, 1976.

Bankes, Viola, *A Dorset Heritage, The Story of Kingston Lacey*, 1953.

Barham, Francis, 'Discovery of the Authorship of the *Whole Duty of Man*', *The Journal of Sacred Literature*, Vol. 5, 4th series, July 1864.

Barker, Jane, *Poetical Recreations Consisting of Original Poems, Odes, etc*, 2 parts, 1688.

Barksdale, Clement, *Letter touching a College of Maids or a Virgin Society*, 1675.

Batchiler, John, *The Virgin's Pattern; in the Exemplary Life and lamented Death of Mrs Susanna Perwick*, 1661.

Reliquiae Baxterianae, or Mr Richard Baxter's Narrative of the Most Memorable Passages of his Life and Times, 1696.

Bayley, A.R., BA, *The Great Civil War in Dorset, 1642–1660*, Taunton, 1910.

Beard, Charles A. and Mary R., *The Rise of American Civilization*, Vol. 1, New York, 1929.

Reference Books

Behn, Aphra, *The Works*, 6 Vols, 1904.

Berens, Lewis H., *The Digger Movement in the Days of the Commonwealth*, 1906.

Birch, Una, *Anna van Schurman. Artist, Scholar, Saint*, 1909.

Black, W. George, *Folk-Medicine*, 1883.

Blundell, William, of Crosby, Lancashire, Esquire, *A Cavalier's Notebook, Being Notes, Anecdotes and Observations*, ed. with introductory chapters, Rev. T. Ellison Gibson, 1880.

Blunt, Wilfrid, *The Art of Botanical Illustrations*, 1950.

Bowden, James, *The History of the Society of Friends in America*, 2 Vols, 1850.

Bowle, John, *John Evelyn and his World*, 1981.

The Works of Anne Bradstreet in Prose and Verse, ed. John H. Ellis, Charlestown, 1867.

Brailsford, M.R., *Quaker Women, 1650–1690*, 1915.

Braithwaite, W.C., *The Beginnings of Quakerism*, 1912.

Braithwaite, W.C., *The Second Period of Quakerism*, 1919.

Brathwaite, Richard, *The English Gentlewoman, Drawne out to the full Body: Expressing what Habilliments doe best attire her, what Ornaments doe best adorne her, what Complements doe best accomplish her*, 3rd edition, 1641.

Bridenbaugh, Carl, *Vexed and Troubled Englishmen 1590–1642* (pbk), Oxford, 1976.

Brodrick, James, SJ, *Mary Ward 1585–1645*, Society of St Paul, Langley, Bucks, 1945.

Works of Mr Thomas Brown, 5 Vols, 1719.

Bryant, Arthur, *Samuel Pepys, The Years of Peril* (pbk), 1961.

Budgell, E., Esq., *Memoirs of the Lives and Characters of the Illustrious Family of the Boyles*, 3rd edition, 1737.

Burghall, Edward 'Providence Improved', A Manuscript by the Puritanical Vicar of Acton, 1628–1663', in T. W. Barlow, *Cheshire: Its Historical and Literary Associations*, 1855.

Burghclere, Lady, *The Life of James, First Duke of Ormonde 1610–1688*, 2 Vols, 1912.

Burke, Sir Bernard, *A Genealogical History of the Dormant, Abeyant, Forfeited and Extinct Peerages of the British Empire*, 1883.

Burnet, Gilbert, *History of my own Time*, ed. Osmund Airy, 2 Vols, with supplement, Oxford, 1897.

Burrage, Champlin, 'Anna Trapnel's Prophecies', *English Historical Review*, Vol. 26, 1911.

Burstein, Sona Rosa, MA, 'Aspects of the Psychopathology of Old

Age. Revealed in Witchcraft Cases of the Sixteenth and Seventeenth Centuries', *British Medical Bulletin*, Vol. 6, Nos. 1–2, 1949.

Burton, Robert, *The Anatomy of Melancholy*, ed. Holbrook Jackson, 1936.

Butler, Samuel, *Hudibras*, ed. John Wilders, Oxford, 1967.

(CSP Domestic) Calendars of State Papers, Domestic.

(CSP Venetian) Calendars of State Papers, Venetian.

Memorandum Book of Sir Walter Calverley Bart, Surtees Society, LXXVII, 1883.

Camden, Caroll, *The Elizabethan Woman*, 1952.

Capp, Bernard, *Astrology and the Popular Press, English Almanacs 1500–1800*, 1979.

Capp, B.S., *The Fifth Monarchy Men – A Study in Seventeenth-Century English Millenarianism*, 1972.

Carlingford Papers, Osborn Collection, Yale University.

Carlyle, Thomas, *Critical and Miscellaneous Essays*, 4 Vols, 1847.

Carte MSS, Bodleian Library, Oxford.

Carte, Thomas, *A Collection of Original Letters and Papers ... Found among the Duke of Ormonde's Papers*, 2 Vols, 1739.

Cartwright, Julia, *Madame. A life of Henrietta, daughter of Charles I and Duchess of Orleans*, 1891.

Cartwright, Julia, *Sacharissa – Some Account of Dorothy Sidney, Countess of Sunderland, her Family and Friends 1617–1684*, 1937.

Cary, Mary, *The Resurrection of the Witnesses*, 1648.

The Case of Divorce and Remarriage thereupon Discussed by a Reverend Prelate of the Church of England and a private Gentleman Occasioned by the late Act of Parliament for the Divorce of the Lord Rosse, 1673.

The Case of the Right Honourable Katherine Countess of Dorchester relating to the Bill lately brought in for the confirming the Grant made to the Right Honourable Arthur Earl of Torrington, by his present Majesty King William, and the late Queen Mary.

The Case of my Lord Roos. Printed with an Act touching the Lord Marquess of Northampton and the Lady Elizabeth his wife, Anno V, Ed. VI, Thomason Tract, 669, fo. 24/34.

Caulfield, James, *Portraits, Memoirs and Characters of Remarkable Persons, from the Reign of Edward the Third, to the Revolution*, 2 Vols, 1794.

Cellier, Mrs Elizabeth, *To Dr–, An Answer to his Queries, Concerning the Colledg of Midwives*, 16 January 1688.

Cellier, Mrs Elizabeth, *Malice Defeated. Or a Brief Relation of the Accusation and Deliverance of Elizabeth Cellier etc.*, 1680.

Cellier, Mrs Elizabeth, 'A Scheme for the Foundation of a Royal Hospital, and Raising a Revenue of Five or Six-thousand Pounds a year, by, and for the Maintenance of a Corporation of skilful Midwives, and such Foundlings or exposed Children, as shall be admitted therein, etc.', 1687, Harleian Miscellany, IV, 1745.

'Certaine Informations', E. 65 (8), British Library.

Dr Hugh Chamberlen to the Princess Sophia, 4 October 1713, Sloane MSS, 4107, British Library.

The Letters of John Chamberlain, ed. N.E. McClure, 2 Vols, Philadelphia, 1939.

Chambers, M.C.E., *The Life of Mary Ward, 1585–1645*, 2 vols, 1885.

Chapman, A. Beatrice Wallis, and Chapman, Mary Wallis, *The Status of Women under the English Law*, 1909.

The Letters of King Charles II, ed. Sir Arthur Bryant, 1968.

Chidley, Katherine, *Good Counsell to the Petitioners for Presbyterian Government that they may declare their faith before they build their Church*, 1645, Thomason Tract, 699, fo. 10/39.

Chidley, Katherine, *The Justification of the Independent Churches of Christ. Being an Answer to Mr Edwards his Booke etc.*, 1641.

Chidley, Katherine, *A New Yeares Gift, or a Briefe Exhortation to Mr Thomas Edwards*, 1645, E. 23 (13), British Library.

The Memoirs of Sir Hugh Cholmley, Knt and Bart, 1870.

'Sir Hugh Cholmley's Narrative of the Siege of Scarborough, 1644–5', ed. C.H. Firth, *English Historical Review*, Vol. 32, 1917.

Christie, W.D., *A Life of Anthony Ashley Cooper First Earl of Shaftesbury, 1621–1683*, 2 Vols, 1871.

Cibber, Colley, *Apology*, ed. R.W. Lowe, 2 vols, 1887.

Clarendon, Edward Earl of, *The History of the Rebellion and Civil Wars in England*, 6 Vols, Oxford, reissued 1969.

The Life of Edward of Clarendon in which is included A Continuation of His History of the Grand Rebellion, 3 Vols, Oxford, 1827.

Clarendon MSS, Bodleian Library, Oxford.

State Papers collected by Edward Earl of Clarendon, commencing 1621, ed. R. Scrope and T. Monkhouse, 3 Vols, Oxford, 1767–86.

Clark, Alice, *Working Life of Women in the Seventeenth Century*, ed. Miranda Chaytor and Jane Lewis, reissued 1982.

Clark(e), Samuel, *The Lives of Sundry Eminent Persons in this Later Age, in Two Parts*, 1683.

The Clarke Papers, ed. C.H. Firth, 4 Vols, 1891–1901.

Clyde, William M., *The Struggle for the Freedom of the Press. From Caxton to Cromwell*, Oxford, 1934.

Coate, Mary, *Social Life in Stuart England*, 2nd edition, 1925.

Cocke, Thomas, 'Classical or Gothic? Lady Anne Clifford Reconsidered', *Country Life*, 31 January 1980.

Coke, Sir Edward, *Institutes of the lawes of England*, 4 Vols, 1628–44.

Cole, Susan, 'A Flower of Purpose – A Memoir of Princess Elizabeth Stuart (1635–1650)', *Royal Stuart Papers* VIII, The Royal Stuart Society, 1975.

Collins, John, *Salt and Fishery. A Discourse thereof*, 1682.

Collins' Peerage of England, ed. Sir Egerton Brydges, 9 Vols, 1812.

A Complete History of Magick, Sorcery and Witchcraft, 2 Vols, 1715.

Conway Letters. The Correspondence of Anne Viscountess Conway, Henry More and their Friends 1642–1684, ed. M.H. Nicolson, 1930.

Costello, Louisa Stuart, *Memoirs of Eminent Englishwomen*, 4 Vols, 1844.

The Poems, English, Latin and Greek, of Richard Crashaw, ed. L.E. Martin, Oxford, 1957.

Cressy, David, *Education in Tudor and Stuart England*, Documents of Modern History series, 1975.

Cressy, David, *Literacy and the Social Order – Reading and Writing in Tudor and Stuart England*, Cambridge, 1980.

Cripps, Doreen, *Elizabeth of the Sealed Knot*, Kineton, 1975.

'Oliver Cromwell's Cousin's Diary', transcribed by Rev. William Cole, Additional MS, 5858, fo. 213–21, British Library.

Writings and Speeches of Oliver Cromwell, with an Introduction, notes and sketch of his life, W.C. Abbott, 4 Vols, Cambridge, Massachusetts, 1937–47.

Cromwelliana, A Chronological detail of events in which Oliver Cromwell was engaged from the year 1642 to his death, 1810.

Curll, Edmund, *Betterton's History of the English Stage*, 1741.

Records of the Cust Family, series II, *The Brownlows of Belton, 1550–1779*, compiled by Lady Elizabeth Cust, 1909.

Cutter, S., and Viets, Henry R., *A Short History of Midwifery*, 1964.

Dangerfield, Thomas, *The Grand Impostor Defeated*, 1682.

The Life and Adventures of Mrs Christian Davies, commonly call'd Mother Ross ... Taken from her own mouth when a Pensioner of Chelsea Hospital, 1740.

'The humble petition of the Lady Eleanor (Davies)', 21 March 1644, Thomason Tract, 669, fo. 10/2.

Defoe, Daniel, *Conjugal Lewdness; or, Matrimonial Whoredom*, 1727.

Defoe, Daniel, *A Journal of the Plague Year*, London, 1950.

Denbigh, Cecilia Countess of, *Royalist Father and Roundhead Son – Being the memoirs of the First and Second Earls of Denbigh 1600–1675*, 1915.

Derby, James Earl of, 'The History and Antiquities of the Isle of Man', in *Desiderata Curiosa*, Francis Peck, Vol. II, 1770.

Devereux, Walter B., *Lives and Letters of the Devereux, Earls of Essex*, 2 Vols, 1853.

(DNB) *Dictionary of National Biography*.

Dobell, Bertram, 'A Unique Book: Anna Trapnel', *Notes and Queries*, 21 March 1914.

Donnison, Jean, *Midwives and Medical Men: A History of Inter-professional Rivalries and Women's Rights*, New York, 1977.

The Lord Marquesse of Dorchester's Letter to the Lord Roos With the Lord Roos's Answer thereunto. Whereunto is Added the Reasons why the Lord Marquess of Dorchester published his letter of the 25 of Feb. 1659. Dated the 13 of the same moneth. With his Answer to the Lord Roos his Letter, 1660.

Dorset, Charles Sackville, Earl of, 'Poems', in *Works of the English Poets*, ed. Samuel Johnson, Vol. XI, 1779.

Douce Ballads, Bodleian Library, Oxford.

'Dougle Fooleries' (S.G.W.), *Bodleian Quarterly Record*, VIII, 1932.

Duffy, Maureen, *The Passionate Shepherdess; Aphra Behn 1640–1689*, 1977.

Duffy, Maureen, *Inherit the Earth*, 1980.

Duncon, John, *A Letter containing Many Remarkable passages in the most Holy Life and Death of the Late Lady, Letice, Vi-Countess Falkland. Written to the Lady Morison at Gt Tew in Oxfordshire*, 2nd edition, 1649.

Duncon, John, *The Returns of Spiritual Comfort and Grief in a Devout Soul. Represented (by entercourse of Letters) to the Right Honourable the Ladie Letice, Vi-Countess Falkland in her life time etc.*, 2nd edition, enlarged, 1649.

'The Life and Letters of Sir Lewis Dyve', ed. H.G. Tibbutt, *Bedfordshire Historical Record Society*, Vol. XXVII, Luton, 1946.

Eccles, Audrey, *Obstetrics and Gynaecology in Tudor and Stuart England*, 1982.

Ede, Mary, *Arts and Society in England under William and Mary*, 1979.

Edwards, Thomas, *Gangraena*, 1646.

Elstob, Elizabeth, *An English-Saxon Homily on the Birth-Day of St Gregory*, trans. with Notes, 1709.

An Essay in Defense of the Female Sex, 1696.

Essays and Literature by the Members of the English Association, XIX, Oxford, 1934.

Diary and Correspondence of John Evelyn FRS, ed. William Bray, 4 Vols, 1850.

Evelyn, John, *The Life of Mrs Godolphin. Now first published and ed. Samuel Lord Bishop of Oxford*, 1848.

Evelyn, Mary, *Mundus Muliebris: Or, The Ladies Dressing-Room Unlock'd and her Toilette spread In Burlesque etc.*, 1690.

Everitt, Alan, *The Community of Kent and the Great Rebellion, 1640–1660*, Leicester, 1966.

Ewen, C. L'Estrange, 'A Noted Case of Witchcraft at North Moreton, Berks, in the early 17th century', *Berkshire Archaeological Journal*, Vol. 40, No. 2, 1936.

Ewen, C. L'Estrange, *Witchcraft and Demonianism, A Concise account derived from sworn depositions and confessions obtained in the courts of England and Wales*, 1933.

Ewan, C. L'Estrange (ed. with an Introduction), *Witch Hunting and Witch Trials. The Indictments for Witchcraft from the Records of 1373 Assizes held for the Home Circuit, A.D. 1559–1736*, 1929.

Eyre, Adam, *A Dyurnall, or Catalogue of all my Accions and Expences, from the 1st of January 1646–7, Surtees Society*, LXV, 1877.

Fanshawe, Sir Richard, Bt, *Shorter Poems and Translations*, ed. N.W. Bawcutt, Liverpool, 1964.

'Martha Farthing's affidavit', *Notes and Queries*, V, 11th series, 1912.

Fea, Allan, *Some Beauties of the Seventeenth Century*, 1906.

Fell, Margaret, *Womens Speaking, Justified, Proved and Allowed of by the Scriptures, All such as speak by the Spirit and Power of the Lord Jesus*, 1666.

The Household Account Book of Sarah Fell of Swarthmoor Hall, ed. Norman Penney, FSA, Cambridge, 1920.

Fell Smith, Charlotte, *Mary Rich, Countess of Warwick 1625–1678, Her Family and Friends*, 1901.

Fieldhouse, R.T., 'Parliamentary Representation in the Borough of Richmond', *Yorkshire Archaeological Journal*, XLIV, 1972.

The Journeys of Celia Fiennes, ed. and with an Introduction, Christopher Morris, 1649.

Fildes, Valerie, 'Infant Feeding Practices in the Sixteenth and Seventeenth Centuries', seminar, University College, London, 14 January 1981.

Report on the Manuscripts of Allan George Finch Esq., HMC, 3 Vols, 1913–61.

Findlater, Richard, *The Player Queens*, 1976.

Firth, C.H., *Cromwell's Army, A History of The English Soldier during the Civil Wars, the Commonwealth and the Protectorate*, 1912.

Life and Death of Mistress Mary Firth, 1662.

Foster, Michael, 'Major-General Sir John Digby "Peerlesse Champion and Mirrour of Perfect Chivalrie"', *Royal Stuart Papers* XX, The Royal Stuart Society, 1982.

The Journal of George Fox, revised by John L. Nickalls, with an epilogue by Henry J. Cadbury, and an introduction by Geoffrey F. Nuttall, Cambridge, 1952.

Frank, Joseph, *The Beginnings of the English Newspaper, 1620–1660*, Cambridge, Massachusetts, 1961.

Fraser, Antonia, *Cromwell: Our Chief of Men*, 1973.

Fraser, Antonia, *King Charles II*, 1979.

Mrs Elizabeth Freke. Her Diary. 1671 to 1714, ed. Mary Carbery, Cork, 1913.

Fuller, Thomas, *History of the Worthies of England*, ed. J. Nichols, 2 Vols, 1811.

Fussell, G.E. and K.R., *The English Countrywoman, A Farmhouse Social History*, 1953.

Gardiner, Dorothy, *English Girlhood at School. A Study of Women's Education through Twelve Centuries*, 1929.

Gardiner, Dorothy, ed., *The Oxinden Letters, 1607–1642*, 1933.

Gardiner, Dorothy, ed., *The Oxinden and Peyton Letters, 1642–1678*, 1937.

Gardiner, S.R., *History of England From the Accession of James I to the Outbreak of the Civil War 1603–1642*, 10 Vols, 1883–4.

Gardiner, S.R., *History of the Great Civil War, 1642–9*, 3 Vols, 1886–91.

Gataker, Thomas, 'A Good Wife Gods Gift', in *Two Marriage Sermons*, 1624.

G.E.C. (Cokayne), *The Complete Peerage*, 6 Vols, Gloucester, reprinted 1982.

George, Margaret, 'From "Goodwife" to "Mistress": the Transformation of the Female in Bourgeois Culture', *Science and Society*, 37, 1973.

Gibb, M.A., *John Lilburne the Leveller, A Christian Democrat*, 1947.

Gibb, M.A., *The Lord General. A Life of Thomas Fairfax*, 1938.

Martha Lady Giffard. Her Life and Correspondence, 1664–1722, ed. Julia G. Longe, 1911.

Gildon, Charles, *A Comparison Between the Two Stages, with an Examen of the Generous Conqueror; in Dialogue*, 1702.

Gildon, Charles, *The Life of Mr Thomas Betterton*, 1710.

Godwin, Rev. G.N., *The Civil War in Hampshire (1642–45) and the Story of Basing House*, Southampton, 1904.

Goreau, Angeline, *Reconstructing Aphra – A Social Biography of Aphra Behn*, Oxford, 1980.

Gouge, William, *Of Domesticall Duties, Eight Treatises*, 3rd edition, 1634.

Gough, Richard, *The History of Myddle* (pbk), 1981.

Grant, Douglas, *Margaret the First. A Biography of Margaret Cavendish, Duchess of Newcastle 1623–1673*, 1957.

Graunt, John, 'Natural and Political Observations mentioned in a following index and made upon the bills of mortality', 1662, in *Economic Writings of Sir William Petty*, ed. C.H. Hull, New York, 1964.

Green, David, *Queen Anne*, 1970.

Greene, Graham, *Lord Rochester's Monkey, Being the Life of John Wilmot, Second Earl of Rochester*, 1974.

Greer, Germaine, *The Obstacle Race – The fortunes of women painters and their work*, 1979.

Gregg, Edward, *Queen Anne*, 1980.

Gregg, Pauline, *Free-Born John. A Biography of John Lilburne*, 1961.

Gregg, Pauline, *King Charles I*, 1981.

Grisar, Joseph, SJ, 'Mary Ward 1585–1645', *The Month*, 1945.

Habakkuk, H.J., 'Marriage Settlements in the Eighteenth Century', *Transactions of the Royal Historical Society*, XX, 1949.

Hair, Paul, (ed.) *Before the Bawdy Court, Selections from church court and other records relating to the correction of moral offences in England, Scotland and New England, 1300–1800*, 1972.

Halifax, George Savile, Marquis of, *Complete Works*, ed. and with an introduction by J.P. Kenyon (pbk), 1969.

The Memoirs of Anne, Lady Halkett and Ann, Lady Fanshawe, ed. John Loftis, Oxford, 1979.

Hamilton, Anthony, *Memoirs of the Comte de Gramont*, translated by Peter Quennell, 1930.

Hamilton, Elizabeth, *Henrietta Maria*, 1976.

Hamilton, Elizabeth, *William's Mary: A Biography of Mary II*, 1972.

The Harcourt Papers, ed. E.W. Harcourt, Vol. I, Oxford, 1880.

Harleian MSS, British Library.

Letters of Lady Brilliana Harley, with an Introduction and Notes, Thomas Taylor Lewis, MA, Camden Society, 1854.

Hartmann, C.H., *The King's Friend, A Life of Charles Berkeley, Viscount Fitzhardinge Earl of Falmouth, 1630–1665*, 1951.

Hartmann, C.H., *The Vagabond Duchess*, 1926.

Correspondence of the Family of Hatton, 1601–1704, ed. E.M. Thompson, Camden Society, 2 Vols, 1878.

Selected Essays of William Hazlitt 1778–1830, ed. Geoffrey Keynes, FRCS, 1970.

The Remains of Thomas Hearne. Reliquiae Hearnianae. Being extracts from his MS Diaries, compiled by Dr Bliss, now newly revised by John Buchanan-Brown, 1966.

Henry, Louis, 'Anciennes Familles Genevoises', Étude démographique: *XVIe-XXe siècle, Travaux et Documents*, cahier no. 26, Presses Universitaires de France, 1956.

The Autobiography of Edward, Lord Herbert of Cherbury, ed. Sidney Lee, 1886.

Works of George Herbert, ed. F.E. Hutchinson, 2nd edition, 1945.

Herbert, William, *History of the Twelve Great Livery Companies of London*, 1836.

The Poems of Robert Herrick, ed. L.C. Martin, 1965.

The Rev. Oliver Heywood B.A., 1630–1702; His Autobiography, Diaries, Anecdote and Event Books, 3 vols, ed. J. Horsfall Turner, Brighouse, 1882.

Hic Mulier: Or, The Man-Woman and Haec-Vir; Or, The Womanish-Man, 1620, reprinted Exeter, The Rota, 1973.

Hieron, Samuel, *A Helpe unto Devotion; Containing Certain Moulds or Forms of Prayer, fitted to several occasions; and penned for the furtherance of those, who have more desire than skill, to poure out their soules by petition unto God*, 4th edition, 1613.

Higgins, P.M., 'Women in the English Civil War', MA thesis (unpublished), Manchester, 1965.

Hill, Christopher, *Antichrist in Seventeenth-Century England*, 1971.

Hill, Christopher, 'Clarissa Harlowe and her Times', *Essays in Criticism*, IV, 1955.

Hill, Christopher, *Some Intellectual Consequences of the English Revolution*, 1980.

Hillier, George, *A Narrative of the Attempted Escapes of Charles the First from Carisbrook Castle ... Including the letters of the King to Colonel Titus now first deciphered and printed from the originals*, 1852.

Himes, Norman E., *Medical History of Contraception*, 1936.

Hirst, Derek, *The Representative of the People? Voters and Voting in England under the Early Stuarts*, 1975.

Hiscock, W.G., *John Evelyn and Mrs Godolphin*, 1951.

HMC (Historical Manuscripts Commission), Bath MSS, Vol. I, 1904.

HMC (Historical Manuscripts Commission), Denbigh MSS, 7th Report, Part V, 1911.

HMC (Historical Manuscripts Commission), 8th Report, Appendix, 1881.

HMC (Historical Manuscripts Commission), R.R. Hastings MSS, 4 Vols, 1928–47.

HMC (Historical Manuscripts Commission), Leyborne-Popham MSS, Norwich, 1899.

HMC (Historical Manuscripts Commission), Rutland MSS, 12th Report, IV–V, 1888–91.

HMC (Historical Manuscripts Commission), Salisbury MSS, Vol. XXII, 1612–68, 1971.

Diary of Lady Margaret Hoby, 1599–1605, ed. Dorothy M. Meads, 1930.

Hogrefe, Pearl, *Tudor Women – Commoners and Queens*, Iowa, 1975.

Hollingsworth, T.H., 'A Demographic Study of the British Ducal Families' in *Population in History*, ed. D.V. Glass and D.E.C. Eversley, 1965.

Hookes, Nicholas, *Amanda, A Sacrifice to an Unknown Goddesse, Or, a Free-will offering of a loving Heart to a Sweet-Heart*, 1653.

Houblon, Lady Alice Archer, *The Houblon Family, Its Story and Times*, 2 Vols. 1907.

Houldsworth, W., *A History of English Law*, 3rd edition, 5 Vols, 1942.

The House of Commons 1660–1690, ed. Basil Duke Henning, *The History of Parliament* series, 3 Vols, 1983.

Howell, James, *Ho-Elianae or Familiar Letters*, ed. J. Jacobs, 2 Vols, 1892.

Howell, Roger, '"The Devil cannot match him": the Image of Cromwell in Restoration Drama', *Cromwelliana*, Cromwell Association, 1982–3.

'A humble Remonstrance of the Batchelors, in and about London, to the honourable House, in Answer to a late Paper, intitled, A Petition of Ladies for Husbands', Harleian Miscellany, IV, 1747.

Hunter, Joseph, *The History and Topography of Ketteringham*, Norwich, 1851.

Hunter, Rev. Joseph, FSA, *The Life of Oliver Heywood 1630–1702*, 1842.

Hutchins, John, MA, *The History and Antiquities of the County of Dorset*, 3rd edition, 4 Vols, 1861.

Hutchinson, Lucy, *Memoirs of the Life of Colonel Hutchinson*, ed. James Sutherland, reprinted 1973.

Illick, Joseph E., 'Child-Rearing in Seventeenth Century England and America', in *The History of Childhood*, ed. Lloyd deMause, 1976.

Memoirs of James II, 2 Vols, Colchester, 1821.

Jameson, A., *The Beauties of the Court of King Charles the Second*, 1833.

Johnson, G.W., *The Evolution of Woman. From subjection to comradeship*, 1926.

Jonson, Ben, *The Gypsies Metamorphosed*, ed. from original and unexpurgated sources by George Watson Cole, New York, 1931.

Josceline, E., 'The Mothers Legacy to her Unborn Child', Additional MSS, 27, 467, British Library.

Journals of the House of Lords.

Katz, David S., *Philo-Semitism and the Readmission of the Jews to England, 1603–1655*, Oxford, 1982.

Kaufman, Helen Andrews, *Conscientious Cavalier, Colonel Bullen Reymes, MP, FRS, 1613–1672*, 1962.

Kenny, C.S., *The History of the Law of England as to the Effects of Marriage on Property and on The Wife's Legal Capacity*, 1879.

Kent, Countess of, *A Choice Manuall of Rare and Select Secrets in Physics and Chyrurgery*, 2nd edition, 1653.

Kenyon John, *The Popish Plot*, 1972.

Kerridge, Eric, 'The Revolts in Wiltshire against Charles I', *The Wiltshire Archaeological and Natural History Magazine*, Vol. 57, 1958–60.

Poems by Mrs Anne Killigrew, 1686.

Poems (1686) by Mrs Anne Killigrew, facsimile reproduction with an Introduction, Richard Morton, Gainesville, Florida, Scholars' Facsimiles and Reprints, 1967.

King, Gegory, *Natural and political observations and conclusions upon the state and condition of England. To which is prefixed a life of the Author by George Chalmers*, 1810.

Kingdomes Weekly Intelligencer, British Library.

K(irkman), F., *The Unlucky Citizen*, 1673.

Knevet, Ralph, *Funerall Elegies; Consecrated to the Immortall memory of the Right Honourable the Lady Katherine Paston, late wife to the truly noble and heroicke, William Paston of Oxned Esquire*, 1637.

Knox, R.A., *Enthusiasm. A Chapter in the History of Religion*, Oxford, 1950.

Knyvett Letters, 1620–1644, ed. Bertram Schofield, Norfolk Record Society, 1949.

Lacy, John, *The Old Troop, or Monsieur Raggou*, 1672, in *Dramatists of the Restoration: John Lacy*, Edinburgh, 1875.

The Ladies Dictionary being a General Entertainment for the Fair-Sex. A Work never attempted before in English. Printed for John Dunton, 1694.

Lambley, Kathleen, MA, *The Teaching and Cultivation of the French Language in England during Tudor and Stuart times*, Manchester, 1920.

Lang, R.G., 'The Greater Merchants of London in the Early Seventeenth Century', D. Phil. thesis (unpublished), Oxford, 1963.

Larking, Rev. Lambert B. (ed.), *Proceedings, Principally in the County of Kent. In Connection with the Parliaments called in 1640*, Camden Society, 1862.

Larner, Christina, *Enemies of God – The Witch-hunt in Scotland*, 1981.

Laslett, Peter (ed.), with Oosterveen, Karla, and Smith, Richard M., *Bastardy and its Comparative History*, 1980.

Laslett, Peter, *Family Life and Illicit Love in Earlier Generations*, 1977.

Laslett, Peter, *The World we have lost* (pbk), 1968.

Laslett, Peter, *The World we have lost – further explored*, 3rd edition, 1983.

'A Briefe Journall of the Siege against Lathom', see under Ormerod, *Tracts Relating to Military Proceedings in Lancashire during the Great Civil War*.

The Lawes Resolutions of Woman's Rights, or the Lawes Provision for Women, 1632.

Lecky, William, *History of European Morals*, 2 Vols, 1869.

Leigh, Mrs Dorothy, *The Mothers Blessing*, 7th edition, 1621.

Lennep, W. van, *The London Stage*, Vol. I, Illinois, 1960.

Lewenhak, Sheila, *Women and Work* (pbk), Glasgow, 1980.

Lilburne, John, *The Freemans Freedome Vindicated*, 1646.

Lilburne, John, *Jonah's Cry out of the Whale's Belly*, 1647.

William Lilly's History of his Life and Times. Reprinted for Charles Baldwin, 1822.

'The Countess of Lincoln's Nursery', Oxford, 1622, Harleian Miscellany, IV, 1747.

The Lismore Papers, First Series, Viz. Autobiographical Notes etc., of Richard Boyle, First and 'Great' Earl of Cork, ed. A.B. Grosart, Vol. V, 1886.

Littlehales, Margarey Mary, IBVM, *Mary Ward (1585–1645)*, Catholic Truth Society, 1974.

Lloyd, David, *Memoires of the Lives, Actions, Sufferings and Deaths of those Noble, Reverend and Excellent Personages that Suffered ... for the Protestant Religion etc.*, 1668.

The Correspondence of John Locke, ed. E.S. de Beer, 4 Vols, Oxford, 1976–9.

Lockyer, Roger, *The Life and Political Career of George Villiers, First Duke of Buckingham 1592–1628*, 1981.

Longleat MSS, Longleat, Wilts.

The Poems of Richard Lovelace, ed. C.H. Wilkinson, Oxford, 1930.

The Diary of Roger Lowe, of Ashton-in-Makerfield, Lancashire, 1663–1674, ed. William L. Sachse, Foreword by Professor Wallace Notestein, Yale University Press, New Haven, 1938.

The Letter Books 1644–45 of Sir Samuel Luke, ed. H.G. Tibbutt, FSA, HMC, HMSO, 1963.

Lupton, Donald, *London and the Countrey Carbonaded and quartred into severall Characters*, 1632.

McArthur, Ellen A., 'Women Petitioners and the Long Parliament', *English Historical Review*, XXIV, 1909.

Macdonald, Isabel, *Elizabeth Alkin*, 1934.

MacDonald, Michael, *Mystical Bedlam. Madness, anxiety and healing in seventeenth century England*, Cambridge, 1981.

McElwee, William, *The Murder of Sir Thomas Overbury*, 1952.

Macfarlane, Alan, *The Family Life of Ralph Josselin. A Seventeenth Century Clergyman. An Essay in Historical Anthropology*, Cambridge, 1970.

Macfarlane, A.D.J., 'The Regulation of Marital and Sexual Relationships in Seventeenth Century England, with special reference to the county of Essex', M. Phil. thesis (unpublished), London, 1968.

Macfarlane, Alan, *Witchcraft in Tudor and Stuart England – A Regional and Comparative Study*, 1970.

McLaren, Dorothy, 'Nature's Contraceptive. Wet-Nursing and Prolonged Lactation: The Case of Chesham, Buckinghamshire, 1578–1601', *Medical History*, 23, 1979.

Makin, Basua, *An Essay to Revive the Antient Education of Gentlewomen. In Religion, Manners, Arts and Tongues. With an Answer to the Objections against this Way of Education*, 1673.

Manners, Emily, 'Elizabeth Hooton, first Quaker Woman preacher, 1600–1672', *Journal of the Friends Historical Society*, Supplement No. 12, 1914.

Markham, Gervase, *The English Huswife: containing the inward and outward vertues which ought to be in a complete Woman* (Book 2 of *Countrey Contentments*), 1615.

Marriage Promoted in a Discourse of its Ancient and Modern Practice etc., By a Person of Quality, 1690.

Marsh, Henry, *New Survey of the Turkish Empire*, 1663.

The Life of Adam Martindale. Written by himself, ed. Rev. Richard Parkson, Chetham Society, 1845.

The Poems and Letters of Andrew Marvell, ed. H.M. Margoliouth, 2 Vols, Oxford, 1971.

Masham, Damaris, *Occasional Thoughts in reference to a Vertuous or Christian Life*, 1705.

Masson, David, *The life of John Milton*, 7 Vols, 1859–94.

Matthew, Sir Tobie, *The Life of Lady Lucy Knatchbull*, Introduction by Dom David Knowles, 1931.

May, Geoffrey, *Social Control of Sex Expression*, 1930.

Mercurius Militaris.

Mercurius Pragmaticus.

Middlesex County Records, ed. J.C. Jeaffreson, Vol. III, 1888.

The Midwife Unmask'd; or The Popish Design of Mrs Cellier's Meal-Tub plainly made known: being a Second Answer to her Scandalous Libel, in short Remarques upon the same etc., 1680.

The Midwives Just Petition: or, A complaint of divers good Gentlewomen of that faculty; Shewing to the whole Christian world their just cause of their sufferings in these distracted Times, for their want of Trading, 25 January 1643.

Millar, Oliver, *The Age of Charles I: Painting in England 1620–1649*, Tate Gallery, 1972.

Millar, Oliver, *Sir Peter Lely, 1618–1680*, National Portrait Gallery Exhibition Catalogue, 1978.

Miller, John, *James II – A Study in Kingship*, 1978.

M(ilton), J., *The Doctrine and Discipline of Divorce, Restor'd to the good of both Sexes, etc.*, 1645.

'Minute Book of a Puritan Congregation, 1654', Rawlinson MSS, D. 828, Bodleian Library, Oxford.

Mitchell, R.J., and Leys, M.D.R., *A History of London Life*, 1958.

The Private Diarie of Elizabeth Viscountess Mordaunt, Duncairn, 1856.

Morgan, Fidelis, *The Female Wits – Women Playwrights of the Restoration*, 1981.

Morrah, Patrick, *Prince Rupert of the Rhine*, 1976.

Morris, G.C.R., 'Which Molins treated Cromwell for Stone – and did not prescribe for Pepys?', *Medical History*, 26, 1982.

Myddelton, W.M., *Chirk Castle Accounts 1666–1753*, privately printed, Horncastle, 1931.

Nall, J.G., *Great Yarmouth and Lowestoft*, 1867.

Nalson, John, *The Countermine*, 3rd edition, 1678.

Nash, Thomas, *History and Antiquities of Worcestershire*, 3 Vols, 1781.

Needham, Gwendolyn B., 'Mrs Manley: An Eighteenth Century Wife of Bath', *Huntingdon Library Quarterly*, No. 3, April, 1938.

Neville, Henry, *The Ladies Parliament*, 1647.

(Neville, Henry), *The Ladies, a Second Time, Assembled in Parliament. A Continuation of the Parliament of Ladies*, 2 August 1647.

Nevil(l)e, Henry, *Newes from the New Exchange, or the Commonwealth of Ladies, Drawn to the Life, in their severall Characters and Concernment*, 1650.

'A New Bill, drawn up by the Committee of Grievances, in Reply, to the Ladies and Batchelors Petition and Remonstrance, etc.', 1693, Harleian Miscellany, IV, 1745.

Letters and Poems In Honour of the Incomparable Princess Margaret, Dutchess of Newcastle, 1676.

Philosophical and Physical Opinions Written by the Thrice Noble, Illustrious and Excellent Princess, the Lady Marchioness of Newcastle, 1663.

CCXI Sociable Letters written by the Thrice Noble, Illustrious and Excellent Princess The Marchioness of Newcastle, 1664.

A true relation of the Birth, Breeding, and Life, of Margaret Cavendish, Duchess of Newcastle, written by herself, with a Critical Preface, etc. by Sir Egerton Brydges, MP, Kent, privately printed, 1814.

The Worlds Olio. Written by the Right Honourable the Lady Margaret Newcastle, 1655.

'The New Letanie', 15 March 1647, Thomason Tract, 669, fo. 10/120.

Newdigate-Newdegate, Lady, *Cavalier and Puritan in the Days of the Stuarts, Compiled from the Private Papers and Diary of Sir Richard Newdigate, second Baronet, etc.*, 1901.

Newdigate-Newdegate, Lady, *Gossip From a Muniment Room – Being Passages in the Lives of Anne and Mary Fytton 1574–1618*, 1897.

Nichols, John, FSA, *The History and Antiquities of the County of Leicester*, 2 Vols, 1795.

Nichols, John, *The Progresses, Processions and Magnificent Festivities, of King James the First*, 4 Vols, 1828.

Nicoll, Allardyce, *A History of English Drama, 1660–1900*, Vol. I, *Restoration Drama*, Cambridge, 1952.

Noble, Mark, *Memoirs of the Protectoral-House of Cromwell*, 3rd edition, 2 vols, with improvements, 1787.

Norsworthy, Laura, *The Lady of Bleeding Heart Yard. Lady Elizabeth Hatton 1578–1646*, 1935.

North, Roger, *The Lives of Francis North, Baron Guilford ... Sir Dudley North; and Rev. Dr John North etc*; ed. A. Jessopp, 3 Vols, 1890.

Notestein, Wallace, 'The English Woman, 1580–1650', in *Studies in Social History*, ed. J.H. Plumb, 1955.

Notestein, Wallace, *Four Worthies*, 1956.

Notestein, Wallace, *A History of Witchcraft in England from 1558 to 1718*, 1911.

Ogg, David, *England in the Reign of Charles II* (pbk), 3rd edition, Oxford, 1963.

A Royalist's Notebook. The Commonplace Book of Sir John Oglander Kt. of Nunwell, ed. Francis Bamford, 1936.

Oman, Carola, *Elizabeth of Bohemia*, 1964.

Ormerod, George (ed.), *Tracts Relating to Military Proceedings in Lancashire during the Great Civil War*, Chetham Society, Manchester, 1844.

Letters from Dorothy Osborne to Sir William Temple (1652–54), ed. E.A. Parry, 1914.

The Complete Works of Thomas Otway, ed. Montague Summers, 3 Vols, 1926.

Miscellaneous Works in prose and verse of Sir Thomas Overbury, with a memoir of his life, 1756.

'The Appeal and Petition of Mary Overton', 24 March 1647, E. 381/10, British Library.

Owen, Dorothy M., 'Lincolnshire Women in History', *The Lincolnshire Historian*, Vol. 2, No. 6, 1959.

'Family of Oxinden Correspondence', Vol. V, 1652–7, Additional MSS, 28, 003, British Library.

Parker, M. Pauline, IBVM, *The Spirit of Mary Ward*, Bristol, 1963.

Pearl, Valerie, 'Social Policy in Early Modern London', in *History and Imagination. Essays in honour of H.R. Trevor-Roper*, ed. Hugh Lloyd Jones, Valerie Pearl and Blair Worden, 1981.

The Diary of Samuel Pepys, ed. with Companion and Index, Robert Latham and William Matthews, 11 Vols, 1970–83.

Perkins, William, *Discourse of the Damned Art of Witchcraft; so far forth as it is revealed in the Scriptures and Manifest by True Experience*, 1608.

The Humble Petition of divers well-affected Women inhabiting the City of

London, Westminster, the Borough of Southwark, Hamblets and places adjacent, 1649, E. 551 (14), British Library.

Pierpont Morgan Library MSS, New York.

Pilkington, Mrs, *Memoirs of Celebrated Female Characters etc.*, 1804.

Pinto, V. de Sola, *Rochester. Portrait of a Restoration Poet*, 1935.

Pinto, V. de Sola, *Sir Charles Sedley, 1639–1701*, 1927.

Poems by Eminent Ladies, 2 Vols, 1755.

Pope, Mary, *A Treatise of Magistracy, shewing The Magistrate hath been, and for ever is to be the cheife Officer in the Church etc.*, 1647.

Powell, C.L., *English Domestic Relations, 1487–1653*, New York, 1917.

Powicke, F.M., 'Notes on Hastings Manuscripts', *Huntingdon Library Quarterly*, No. 3, April 1938.

Price, F. Hilton, FSA, *A Handbook of London Bankers*, 1890–91.

Price, F. Hilton, *The Marygold at Temple Bar*, 1902.

The Principles of the most Ancient and Modern Philosophy. A little Treatise published since the Author's death, translated out of the English into Latin ... and now again made English by J.C. Medicinae Professor, printed in Latin, Amsterdam, 1690, reprinted, London, 1692.

'Puritan Congregation Minute Book', 1654, Rawlinson MSS, D. 828 fo. 30/32.

Quaife, G.R., *Wanton Wenches and Wayward Wives*, 1979.

The Queen's Closet Opened. Incomparable secrets in Physick, Chirurgery, Preserving, Candying and Cookery. As they were presented to the Queen. Never before published. Transcribed from the true Copies of her Majesties own recipe books, by W.M., one of her late Servants, 1655.

Rawlinson MSS, Bodleian Library, Oxford.

Reid, Stuart, *John and Sarah*, 1913.

Reynolds, Myra, *The Learned Lady in England 1650–1760*, New York, 1920.

Roberts, George, *The Life, Progresses, and Rebellion of James Duke of Monmouth*, 2 Vols, 1844.

Roberts, George, *The Social History of the People of the Southern Counties of England*, 1856.

Robinson, John Martin, *The Dukes of Norfolk – A Quincentennial History*, Oxford, 1982.

Familiar Letters Written by the Right Honourable John late Earl of Rochester. And several other Persons of Honour and Quality. With Letters written by the most Ingenious Mr Thomas Otway and Mrs K. Philips, etc, 1697.

Rochester, John Wilmot, Earl of, *Collected Works*, ed. John Hayward, 1926.

Rogers, Daniel, *Matrimoniall Honour*, 1642.

Ross, Isabel, *Margaret Fell. Mother of Quakerism*, 1949.

Rowse, A.L. (ed. and with an Introduction by), *The Poems of Shakespeare's Dark Lady*, 1978.

Roxburghe Ballads, 9 Vols, Ballad Society, Hertford, 1871–99.

Rueff, Jacob, *The Expert Midwife, or An Excellent and most necessary Treatise of the generation and birth of Man, etc*, 1637.

Rushworth, John, *Historical collections of private passages of state etc.*, 7 Vols, 1659–1701.

The Letters of Lady Russell, ed. Lord John Russell, 1853.

The Life of Rachael Wriothesley, Lady Russell; followed by a series of letters to her husband 1672–1682. With eleven letters from the Countess of Sunderland to the Marquis of Hallifax, ed. anonymously by Mary Berry, 1819.

Ruycaut, Paul, *Present state of the Ottoman empire*, 1668.

Sacks, Oliver, *Migraine. Evolution of a common disorder. A practical guide to treatment and relief*, revised edition, 1981.

Sackville-West, V. (ed.), *The Diary of Lady Anne Clifford*, with an Introductory Note, 1923.

Salmon, W., *Aristotle's Masterpiece*, in Two Parts, 1697.

'The Saxon Nymph' (Elizabeth Elstob), *Times Literary Supplement*, 28 September 1933.

Scales, John, 'The Quaker Women who were whipped in Dover (Noted women of Old Dover, New Hampshire)', Dover Public Library MSS, New Hampshire, USA.

Schnucker, R.V., 'Elizabethan Birth Control and Puritan Attitudes', *Journal of Interdisciplinary History*, V, 4, 1975.

Schnucker, R.V., 'The English Puritans and Pregnancy, Delivery and Breast Feeding', *History of Childhood Quarterly*, I, 1973–4.

Schücking, Levin L., *The Puritan Family. A Social Study from the Literary Sources*, 1969.

Schurman, Anna van, *The Learned Maid; or whether a Maid may be a Scholar?*, 1659.

Scot, Reginald, *Discoverie of Witchcraft, 1584*, ed. Brinsley Nicolson, 1886.

Scott Thomson, Gladys, *Life in a Noble Household 1641–1700* (pbk), 1965.

Scott Thomson, Gladys, *The Russells in Bloomsbury, 1669–1771*, 1940.

'The Scourge of Civil War and the Blessing of Peace, 1645', Thomason Tract, 669, fo. 10/27.

Seaver, Paul S. (ed.), *Seventeenth-Century England, Society in an Age of Revolution*, New York, 1976.

The Poetical and Dramatic Works of Sir Charles Sedley, collected and ed. by V. de Sola Pinto, 2 Vols, 1928.

'The Arms of Katherine Sedley', Additional MSS, 30, 382, British Library.

Sensabaugh, G.F., 'Love Ethics in Platonic Court Drama, 1625–1642', *Huntingdon Library Quarterly*, No. 3, April 1938.

Sermon, William, *The Ladies Companion, or The English Midwife*, 1671.

Shannon, Francis Boyle, Viscount, *Discourses and Essays, Useful for the Vain Modish Ladies and their Gallants*, 2nd edition, with new additions, 1696.

Sharp, Mrs Jane, *The Compleat Midwife's Companion etc.*, 4th edition, 1725.

Sharp, Mrs Jane, *The Midwives Book. Or the whole art of Midwifery Discovered etc.*, 1671.

Mrs Shaws Innocency restored, and Mr Clendons Calumny retorted. Notwithstanding his late Triumphing, 1653.

Shirley, John, *The Illustrious History of Women*, 1686.

Shorter, Edward, *A History of Women's Bodies*, 1983.

Sidney, Henry, *Diary of the Times of Charles the Second*, 2 Vols, ed. and with notes by R.W. Blencowe, 1843.

Sloane MSS, British Library.

Smith, Florence, *Mary Astell*, New York, 1916.

Smith, Steven R., 'Growing Old in Early Stuart England', *Albion*, Vol. 8, 1976.

Souars, P.M., *The Matchless Orinda*, Cambridge, Massachusetts, 1931.

Spencer, Theodore, 'The History of an Unfortunate Lady', *Harvard Studies and Notes in Philology and Literature*, XX, 1938.

Spender, Dale, *Man Made Language* (pbk), 1980.

Sprint, John, *The Bride-Woman Counseller, Being a Sermon Preach'd at a Wedding, May the 11th, 1699 at Sherbourn in Dorsetshire*.

Spufford, Margaret, 'Portraits of Society, Popular fiction in 17th-century England', *History Today*, February 1982.

Stafford, Anthony, Gent., *The Femall Glory or The Life and Death of our Blessed Lady, the holy Virgin Mary, Gods owne immaculate Mother*, 1635.

Staffordshire and the Great Rebellion, Staffordshire County Council, 1964.

Stanley, Dean, *Memorials of Westminster Abbey*, 1867.

Stearne, John, *A Confirmation and Discovery of Witchcraft*, 1648, reprinted Exeter, The Rota, 1973.

Stenton, D.M., *The English Woman in History*, 1957.

Stone, Lawrence, *Crisis of the Aristocracy 1558–1641*, Oxford, 1965.

Stone, Lawrence, *Family and Fortune. Studies in aristocratic finance in the sixteenth and seventeenth centuries*, 1973.

Stone, Lawrence, *The Family, Sex and Marriage in England 1500–1800*, 1977.

Stone, Lawrence, 'Social Mobility in England 1500–1700', *Past and Present*, No. 33, April 1966.

Autobiography of William Stout of Lancaster, 1665–1752, ed. J. Harland, 1851.

Strange and Wonderful News from Whitehall, proceeding from Mistris Anna Trapnel . . . With her Declarations concerning the State Affairs of Great Britain etc., 1654.

Strickland, Agnes, *Lives of the Queens of England*, facsimile edition, 8 vols, 1972.

Strong, James, Batchelour, *Joanereidos: or, Feminine Valour Eminently discovered in Westerne Women, etc.*, 1645.

Strong, James, *Joanereidos: or, Feminine Valour Eminently discovered in Westerne Women, at the Siege of Lyme etc.*, reprinted 1674 ('with additions for the Satisfaction of his Friends').

Strong, Roy, *And when did you last see your father? The Victorian Painter and British History*, 1978.

Stuart, D.M., *The English Abigail*, 1946.

Stuart, D.M., *The Girl through the ages*, 1933.

Swetnam, Joseph, *The Arraignment of Lewd, Idle, Froward, and Unconstant Women: Or, the vanitie of them, chuse you whether*, 1634.

Tannahill, Reay, *Sex in History*, New York, 1980.

Tanner, John, 'Lucius Cary, Viscount Falkland – Cavalier and Catalyst', *Royal Stuart Papers* V, The Royal Stuart Society', 1974.

Taylor, G. Rattray, *Sex in History*, new edition, 1959.

Taylor, Jeremy, 'The Treasures of Friendship', in Bp Taylor's *Opuscula*, 1678.

Thomas, Keith, 'The Double Standard', *Journal of the History of Ideas*, XX, 1959.

Thomas, Keith, *Religion and the Decline of Magic. Studies in Popular Beliefs in Sixteenth and Seventeenth Century England*, 1971.

Thomas, Keith, 'Women and the Civil War Sects', *Past and Present*, 13, 1958.

Thomason Tracts, British Library.

Thompson, Roger, *Women in Stuart England and America*, 1974.

The Autobiography of Mrs Alice Thornton of East Newton, Co. York, Surtees Society, Vol. LXII, Durham, 1873.

'Thurloe Papers', XXI, 1654, Rawlinson MSS, A. 21, Bodleian Library, Oxford.

Timbs, John, *Curiosities of London*, 1869.

To the House of Commons for Lockier and other Leveller prisoners from women of London and parts adjacent, 5 May 1649, 669, fo. 14/27, British Library.

To the Parliament of the Commonwealth … petition of afflicted women in behalf of Mr J. Lilburn, 24 June 1653, 669, fo. 17/24, British Library.

Trapnel, Anna, *Cry of a Stone, or a Relation of Something spoken in Whitehall by Anna Trapnel*, 1654.

Trapnel, Anna, *A Legacy for Saints; being several Experiences of the dealings of God with Anna Trapnel, In, and after her Conversion … together with some letters of a later date*, 1654.

Anna Trapnel's Report and Plea, Or, a Narrative of her Journey from London into Cornwall … Whereto is annexed a Defiance against all the reproachful, vile, horrid, abusive and scandalous reports raised out of the bottomless pit against her etc., 1654.

'Anna Trapnel's verse', anonymous folio volume, S.I. 42, Th., Bodleian Library, Oxford.

Treglown, Jeremy (ed. with an Introduction), *The Letters of John Wilmot, Earl of Rochester*, 1980.

Turnbull, G.H., *Hartlib, Dury and Comenius. Gleanings from Hartlib's Papers*, 1947.

Turner, F.C., *James II*, 1948.

'The Diary of Isabella, wife of Sir Roger Twysden, Baronet, of Royden Hall, East Peckham 1645–1651', Rev. F.W. Bennet, MA, *Archaeologica Cantiana, Transactions of the Kent Archaeological Society*, Vol. LI, 1939.

The Family of Twysden and Twisden. Their History of Archives from an original by Sir John Ramskill Twysden, 12th Bt, completed by C.H. Dudley Ward, DSO, MC, 1939.

'Sir Roger Twysden's Notebooks', 2 Vols, Additional MSS, 34, 163, British Library.

Unto every individual member of Parliament, the Humble Representation of afflicted Women Petitioners on behalf of Mr John Lilburne, 26 July 1653, 669, fo. 17/37, British Library.

Upham, A.H., 'English *Femmes Savantes* at the end of the seventeenth century', *Journal of English and Germanic Philology,* Vol. XII, 1913.

Utter, R.P., and Needham, G.B., *Pamela's Daughters,* 1937.

The Narrative of General Venables, ed. and with an introduction by C.H. Firth, 1900.

Verney, Frances Parthenope, *Memoirs of the Verney Family During the Civil War,* 4 Vols, 1892.

Letters and Papers of the Verney Family, down to the end of the year 1639, ed. John Bruce Esq., Camden Society, 1853.

Vicars, John, *The Burning-Bush not Consumed Or the Fourth and Last Part of the Parliamentary Chronicle,* 1646.

Vicars, John, *Gods Arke Overtopping the Worlds Waves, or The Third Part of the Parliamentary Chronicle etc.,* 1646.

Vicars, John, *The Schismatick Sifted: Or, a picture of Independents freshly and fairly washt over again,* 1646.

Walker, Anthony, DD, *The Holy Life of Mrs Elizabeth Walker,* new edition, abridged and revised by the Rev. J. W. Brooks, 1823.

Wallas, Ada, *Before the Bluestockings,* 1929.

The Poems of Edmund Waller, ed. G. Thorn Dury, 1905.

The Wandering Whore,-numbers 1–5, 1660–1661, reprinted Exeter, The Rota, 1977.

Warner, John, *History of English Persecution of Catholics and the Presbyterian Plot,* 2 Vols, *Catholic Record Society,* Vol. 48, 1953.

Warner, Marina, *Alone of All Her Sex, The Myth and the Cult of the Virgin Mary,* 1976.

Warren, Elizabeth, *The Old and Good Way vindicated in a Treatise etc.,* 1645.

Warren, Elizabeth, *Spiritual Thrift, Meditations, wherein humble Christians (as in a mirror) may view the Verity of their saving Graces etc.,* 1647.

Autobiography of Mary Countess of Warwick, ed. and with an Introduction, T.C. Croker, Percy Society, 1848.

Memoir of Lady Warwick: also Her Diary from AD 1666 to 1672, now first published, to which are added Extracts from her other Writings, The Religious Tract Society, 1847.

'Some Specialities in the life of M. Warwicke' (autobiography of Mary Lady Warwick), Additional MSS, 27, 357, British Library.

Washbourn, John (ed.), *Biblioteca Gloucestrensis,* Gloucester, 1825.

Waylen, Rev. James, *The House of Cromwell and the Story of Dunkirk,* 1880.

Webster, C., *The Great Instauration,* 1975.

Wedgwood, C.V., *The Trial of Charles I,* 1964.

Weigall, David, 'Women Militants in the English Civil War', *History Today,* June 1972.

Wetter, Immolata, IBVM, 'Mary Ward Apostolic Vocation', *The Way,* Supplement 17, Autumn 1972.

Whitaker, T.D., *The history and antiquities of the deanery of Craven,* 3rd edition, by A.W. Morant, 1878.

Whitelocke, Bulstrode, *Memorials from the Beginning of the Reign of Charles I to the Restoration,* 4 Vols, Oxford, 1853.

The Whore's Rhetorick, 1683, reprinted 1960.

Wilkinson, Rev. Robert, 'The Merchant-Royal or Woman a Ship', 1607, in *Conjugal Duty: Set forth in a Collection of Ingenious and Delightful Wedding-Sermons,* 1732.

Williams, E.M., 'Women Preachers in the Civil War', *Journal of Modern History,* Vol. I, Chicago, 1929.

Willson, David Harris, *King James VI and I,* 1956.

Willughby, Dr (Percival), *De Puerperio Tractatus, Country Midwife's Opusculum,* Sloane MSS, 529, British Library.

The Life of Mr Arthur Wilson the Historian, Written by Himself, in *Desiderata Curiosa,* a collection by Francis Peck, Vol. II, 1779.

Wilson, J.H., *All the King's Ladies, Actresses of the Restoration,* Chicago, 1958.

Wilson, J.H., *The Court Wits of the Restoration,* Princeton, 1948.

Wilson, J.H., 'The Marshall Sisters and Anne Quin', *Notes and Queries,* March 1957.

Wilson, J.H., *Nell Gwynn: Royal Mistress,* 1952.

Wilson, J.H., 'Pepys and Peg Hughes', *Notes and Queries,* October 1956.

The Poems of Anne Countess of Winchilsea, ed. Myra Reynolds, Decennial Publications, Vol. V, second series, Chicago, 1903.

Wolseley, Sir Garnet, *Life of John Churchill, Duke of Marlborough,* 2 Vols, 1894.

The Womens Complaint Against their Bad Husbands, Or the good Fellows Anatomized by their Wives, 1676.

The Womens Sharpe Revenge, 1640.

Woodforde Papers and Diaries, ed. and with an Introduction, Dorothy Heighes Woodforde, 1932.

Woolley, Hannah, *The Gentlewomans Companion, or a Guide to the Female Sex... With Letters and Discourses upon all occasions, Whereunto is added, a Guide for Cook-maids, Dairy-maids, Chamber-maids, and all others that go to service,* 1675.

Woolley, Hannah, *The Queen-like Closet or, Rich Cabinet... To which is added a supplement presented to all Ingenious Ladies and Gentlewomen,* 5th edition, 1684.

Wrigley, E.A., 'Family Limitation in Pre-Industrial England', *Economic History Review,* 2nd series, Vol. XIX, 1966.

Letter of Isabel Yeamans, 8 August 1676, MS, Religious Society of Friends, Nottingham Meeting, 35 Clarendon Street, Nottingham.

Young, Peter, *Edgehill 1642 – The Campaign and the Battle,* Kineton, 1967.

Young, Peter, *Marston Moor 1644 – The Campaign and the Battle,* Kineton, 1970.

Index